ENVIRONMENT, SECURITY AND TOURISM DEVELOPMENT IN SOUTH ASIA

ENVIRONMENT, SECURITY AND TOURISM DEVELOPMENT IN SOUTH ASIA

(In 3 Volumes)

Environment Development in South Asia

(Volume-1)

Editor

V.C. Pandey

ISHA BOOKS

DELHI-110 033

Environment, Security and Tourism Development in South Asia

Rs.2700 (Set)
Rs. 900 (each volume)

ISBN: 81-8205-136-3 (Set)
ISBN: 81-8205-137-1 (Vol. 1)

Published in 2004 in India by
Isha Books, D-43, Prithviraj Road,
Adarsh Nagar, Delhi-110 033

Laser Typesetting at : Shree Vaishnavi Creations, Delhi
Printed at : Chawla Offset Press, Delhi

Contents

Preface

The South Asian region comprising the seven countries—Bangladesh, Bhutan, India, the Maldives, Nepal, Pakistan and Sri Lanka—is a home to more than one-fifth of the world's people. Its population growth rate exceeds the developing world's average and places strains on key natural resources such as water, air, land and sea. Competition over increasingly scarce natural resources represents a very real threat to regional security.

South Asia's environmental problems are enormous. They include resource depletion and ecological degradation, indoor and urban air pollution, lack of access to clean water supplies and sanitation, toxic and hazardous agroindustrial waste generation and disposal, and vulnerability to natural disasters. Causes of this pity condition include lack of incentives for resource conservation and protection, lack of institutional frameworks for the integrated management of natural resources, inadequate legal and policy frameworks, weak governance, low institutional capacity, subsidies and policy distortions, lack of public awareness of the value of healthy and sustainable ecosystems, and limited data on resources and environmental quality. All these together threaten or cause losses of life and livelihoods of millions of people.

The need for protecting environment and sustainable development has been much more recognised and visible today. The high level of public concern about environmental issues will provide a political foundation for generating additional financing for the environment and sustainable development. Governments, international finance institutions, and the private sector all have critical and mutually reinforcing roles to play.

This book comprehensively describes the issues of environment development in South Asia. It will serve as a highly valuable reference tool for policy makers, researchers, scholars and environmentalists.

Editor

1

Introduction

The South Asian region comprising the seven countries—Bangladesh, Bhutan, India, the Maldives, Nepal, Pakistan and Sri Lanka—is a home to more than one-fifth of the world's people. Its population growth rate exceeds the developing world's average and places strains on key natural resources such as water, air, land and sea. Competition over increasingly scarce natural resources represents a very real threat to regional security.

South Asia is also confronting both the positive and negative economic and cultural dimensions of globalization while coping with gross inequities in the distribution of development's benefits within society. This poses severe challenges to the region's established, though still maturing, democratic institutions, which continue to evolve as models observed by the rest of the developing world.

Foremost among the challenges is the region's rapidly increasing level of greenhouse gas emissions that result from an enormous population base that uses fossil fuels—especially coal—as the principal source of energy for a burgeoning power sector. If significant mitigation measures are not undertaken soon, emissions are expected to surpass those of the United States during the early part of the 21st century.

Environmental Issues

While the region is already heavily populated, settlement patterns are not uniform. Where land is arable, especially where irrigated, population density is high. Population is particularly crowded into the sharp band that runs east from the Pakistani Punjab across northern India and Nepal and into Bangladesh. This region closely follows the upper Indus Basin and Ganges-Brahmaputra River Basin. Additional striking concentrations of population—although geographically smaller—are visible in the southern areas of the sub-continent and in coastal zones.

The region consist of nearly continuous cropland, freckled with urban and built-up areas. It has been said that a river basin is a good metaphor for a macro economy, with upstream and downstream linkages. If this is true, then the region is a series of interdependent sub-economies.

The largest and most important basins—the Brahmaputra, the Ganges, and the Indus—are indifferent to political boundaries and have long formed the basis for the region's main civilizations. They cross current national borders and play a vital role in regional political and economic stability. It also is worth noting that these and other basins cross state borders within countries. Further, they transect what has been the traditional frontier of the now blurring rural-urban divide—at a time when urban-rural competition for water is becoming acute.

Rainfall variability is highest almost in precisely the regions where precipitation is lowest. South Asia is currently facing one of its most severe droughts on record—with effects stretching from Central Asia through Southwestern China, Afghanistan, and Pakistan and into northern India.

Climatic events such as these respect no political borders. In times of great stress, neither will environmental refugees, creating political, economic, and environmental consequences. As population density grows, competition for water will increase, and soil and water resources will continue to be degraded because of pressures on their use. The potential implications of water-related climatic events, causing floods and droughts, are clear and constitute an important area for policy and program response at national and regional levels.

Surface water availability varies greatly and roughly follows the pattern of mean annual precipitation. A consideration of water supply in physical volume provides only a partial picture of water availability relative to needs. The areas of "water stress," "water scarcity" and "absolute water scarcity" will be at tremendous risk in the future. The "water riots" that occurred recently in Hyderabad, competition over this vital resource can be expected to intensify over the next decades—potentially to the point of outright conflict. Yet, this analysis of water availability is incomplete without consideration of the amount of water that is usable, based on its quality.

Water pollution from urban settlements and industry already presents major problems in the most densely populated parts of the region. Five of the subcontinent's eight major watersheds already suffer either "significant" or "major" degradation of water quality, based on 1995 data. Only the blue-colored basins—representing average concentrations of less than 1000 mg per liter—are considered acceptable. The Brahmaputra's favorable condition is largely due to the "dilution solution" derived from the vast amounts of water flowing through the system during the rainy season. Water quality will have at least as important an impact on its effective availability in the future.

The conservation of natural forests and associated biodiversity is another issue of importance both within the region and from a global standpoint. Most of South Asia is already used for settlements or is characterized by rural landscapes heavily influenced by human activity. Forests remain an important part of the landscape and rural economy, but, in an environment that has already been fundamentally altered by human settlement, "forestry" is not synonymous with "natural forests". Significant forested areas in the region outside of natural forests hold resources that clearly provide a range of environmental and economic services to the human population of South Asia.

A striking band of forested area running from northern Pakistan and India through southern Nepal and into Bhutan and northeast India and juxtaposed just to the north of the densely populated zone already identified. This holds implications for the legal and illegal trade in forest products and regional thinking about this issue. There is already a thriving cross-border market for timber and forest products from the Nepali terai to meet market demand in India.

The region's soils are being heavily affected by degradation derived from a range of causes and forces. The extent to which degradation has taken place in the sensitive coastal areas of the sub-continent. Except in the forested areas of India's western coast and the coastal desert of Pakistan, the coastal landscape is largely altered, indicating a decline in the integrity of coastal ecosystems.

Energy Issues

Demographic and economic trends in the region also are driving some significant shifts in energy-use patterns that already have had profound environmental consequences. These will be even more important to South Asia and the planet's atmosphere in the future. There has been no growth in per capita renewable energy consumption, while non-renewable energy consumption shows substantial expansion. This is particularly striking in India and Bangladesh.

Economic history tells us that the region is at an income level and development stage where energy demand will rise much faster than population. In economic terms, there is a high "income elasticity of demand" for modern energy sources (primarily electric power produced with fossil fuels). The reasons are straightforward:

— Renewable fuels are becoming increasingly scarce.

— Urbanization and rising incomes are leading to more energy-intensive lifestyles.

The region is at a stage in its development in which large numbers of people will switch from using traditional (wood, dung, etc.) fuels to modern fuels. We are entering a period of accelerating and potentially explosive demand for modern energy in the region. For Asia as a whole, the World Bank has estimated that $1 trillion of investment will be needed over the next 20 years to meet this burgeoning demand for electricity. The extent of power consumption already apparent in the regio. It is fairly easy to locate the region's capitals and other major cities and to discern areas of high energy use. Energy demand is likely to rise much faster than income over the next 25 years.

Nepal and Bhutan are in a position to produce hydropower for their own demands and India's, as well. In addition, Bangladesh could ceitainly export gas or gas-derived electricity to India if the political situation would allow. Such issues will become even more important and may well shape major aspects of the regional political dialogue over the next 25 years. As energy use rises, it will be increasingly difficult to simply "export" pollution from the cities to the suburbs, as has been done around Delhi and elsewhere. Transboundary air pollution already is becoming a potentially contentious issue in the region, with implications for agricultural productivity, as well. As the "continuous canvas of cropland" gives way to one of urban, peri-urban, and suburban settlements, crops will receive less light and hundreds of millions of inhabitants will breathe more polluted air.

Future Trends

The region is comprises huge number of urban areas and their trade zones, having between 500 thousand and 1 million people and the largest with more than 5 million.

There are hundreds of smaller urban areas—many in the 250,000 to 500,000 range. Most projections—including the rigorous "2047" study done by the Tata Energy Research Institute (TERI)—show that the region's urban population will likely grow from today's 25 to 30 percent of the total population to around 50 percent of the total by the middle of the century, even as overall population rises.

Thus, within the next two generations, virtually all of the region's more populated zones will lie within the market influence of a small, medium, or large city. As populations come under increasing market influence, the economics of rural production are likely to change, the impact of urban pollution is likely to spread, and the urban-rural competition for resources may intensify–including pressure on water, forests, trees, and soils.

As the region's population turns the corner past the 1.5 billion mark and moves toward 2 billion, South Asia's environment must be understood and managed in fundamentally new ways. Whether the "green," "blue," or "brown" environment is under consideration, it must be managed as an essentially man-made space in South Asia. This is true even when considering the fate of such resources as biodiversity—the "greenest" and "purest" of natural resources. Natural resource management cannot be separated from the trajectory of industry, urban and rural incomes, productivity, trade, technology, and governance.

Environmental Governance

The lack of effective environmental governance institutions is a key crosscutting constraint to action in response to pressing environmental and natural resource management challenges. Government environmental institutions in all branches—executive, legislative, and judicial—are generally weak and uncommitted to devising policies and programs to respond to environmental problems.

Information on environmental conditions and trends is poorly collected and, even where it exists, it is often withheld to serve narrower bureaucratic interests. The costs of inattention to the environmental consequences of development remain poorly understood by governments and the public. The institutions of civil society hold the key to a future of transparency and broad-based response to environmental challenges in the region, but they currently lack maturity.

Cabinet-level environmental agencies are now established in all South Asian countries, but they remain generally weak and without clear direction. Their principal regulatory vehicle has been the application of environmental impact assessments to review large development projects, but this process has been poorly implemented and even subject to considerable corruption in several countries.

Efforts to control industrial pollution through rigid permitting schemes—tied often to unrealistic emissions and discharge standards—have also had disappointing results. The over-emphasis of donors in supporting these fragile government environmental bodies has been to the detriment of other potentially more influential institutions.

Line ministries of central governments deserve much greater attention. Outside of the executive branch, legislative bodies are of growing importance as sources of innovation and action to address environmental issues of social concern, but they have received very little support with respect to their dealings with environmental matters.

Likewise, as illustrated by the activist high court of India, the judicial branch can play a significant role in shaping environmental policy. However, it, too, has received relatively little assistance in building its understanding of environmental issues and exploring options for positive action.

At the same time, there is a strong trend toward decentralization and devolution within the region. This means that an entirely new group of government agencies--at state, city, and local levels—will require environmental management skills. The task ahead in this area is indeed daunting, but it also offers opportunities for innovation and the leapfrogging of technologies and tools-such as the application of advanced urban planning and geographic information system techniques. It also holds the promise of empowering those who stand to benefit more directly from environmental improvements.

Existing economic policies at the central and regional government levels are replete with subsidies and other distortions that under price natural resources and a clean environment. Policy formulation also is weak, with limited policy expertise within government and only a handful of university centers or think tanks available to carry out the necessary analysis and evaluate policy options.

In part because of poor policy design—but also due to ineffective institutions and faltering political will—policy implementation remains extremely weak across the region. Policy approaches need to be devised that are sensitive to limited enforcement capacities and take full advantage of both economic incentives and public pressures.

As encountered by UNEP/SACEP in their current efforts to prepare State of the Environment 2001 reports for each of the SAARC-member countries, there are severe shortages of reliable data on environmental and natural resources trends and conditions. This further hinders effective policy formulation, as do significant constraints on the release of what little information is available to the public or even to other government agencies or industries.

The adage "information is power" remains apt for this sector in the region, though the realities of Internet-based information exchange and the ready access to remote sensing data are rapidly breaking this down. An environmental NGO in Sri Lanka is preparing to introduce public right-to-know legislation, and the region would benefit greatly from further testing of disclosure-based policy incentives that rely on public pressure to encourage altered behavior among industries and individuals. Improved mechanisms-beyond the scoping exercises of environmental impact assessment-also are needed in better organizing and incorporating public consultation on and participation into decision-making on environmental policies and programs.

Notwithstanding considerable legislative progress in recent years within the region, the development of laws to provide basic democratic rights of discourse, assembly, and information access, the institutions of civil society still remain weak. NGOs continue to grow in their capacity and influence, and they deserve further encouragement. The media is maturing in its coverage of environmental news, and a regional network of environmental journalists—with a secretariat in Sri Lanka—has been established and is functioning.

Professional associations in environmental fields also are beginning to develop and play more important roles in setting standards for credentials and behavior as well as shaping society's thinking on key environmental topics. Examples include associations of environmental impact assessment practitioners in Sri Lanka and urban planners in India. As these institutions mature, the region will likely see a more robust set of approaches to its environmental problems, and direct assistance to this process seems strongly warranted.

The current USAID programs that attempt to address environmental governance issues as an explicit target. Instead, such efforts are woven into the more sector-oriented programs of the missions, such as those dealing with water management in Bangladesh, hydropower in Nepal, and both urban and industrial issues in India. While some aspects of US-AEP's assistance activities to the region address issues of environmental governance—especially by encouraging attention to environmental issues by professional and industry associations—this appears to be a secondary goal.

At a more basic strategic level, the region has no systematic environmental policy support programs (since completion of the USAID NAREP Project in Sri Lanka), even though severe policy and institutional shortcomings constrain progress.

Environmental governance topics deserving much stronger attention include the failure of key institutions at the regional, national, and local levels; widespread corruption hindering the implementation of existing environmental policies; and unrealistic policy frameworks, often based on Western standards and taking little account of either enforcement or compliance costs. Adjustments to or introduction of new systems of governance interventions in these areas would be cost-effective—and potentially able to reach tens of millions of beneficiaries. They also can strongly reinforce democratic reforms.

Explicit regard be given to adding further emphasis on environmental governance in USAID's assistance programs to the region—either as a part of environmental assistance or building environmental dimensions into democracy and economic growth programs. Attention also should be given to the analysis and development of improved environmental and natural resources policies as a complement to all other environment-related assistance and, to the extent possible, integrated into broader economic and trade assistance.

Water Resource Mismanagement

A widening body of literature makes the economic and environmental case for increased attention to water management problems in the region, primarily based on the effects of poor water quality on human health and of water misallocation and use inefficiency on the productivity of agriculture and industry. Despite increasing competition between expanding urban and industrial water users and those in the agricultural and rural sectors, good economic and institutional approaches are limited for dealing with matters of efficient water use and allocation.

The prospect of national and regional conflict over water resource repeatedly was raised as an issue of growing concern. The pattern of inefficient and unsustainable water resource exploitation must be altered if severe development constraints and human suffering are to be avoided.

Rapidly increasing competition among users includes agricultural, rural, municipal, industrial, hydropower, transport, and in-stream flow. At the same time, supplies are being constrained by pollution, which reduces effective surface and groundwater availabilities. Especially on the sub-continent, unsustainable deep aquifer exploitation is widespread and deserves immediate attention.

In general, the region's water suffers from inefficient allocation and use—with higher-valued urban and industrial users often unable to use market or other mechanisms to bid away scarce water resources from those who derive lower marginal benefits from irrigation water use.

Although regional cooperation on transboundary water allocation and water quality issues remains problematic in South Asia, there is encouraging progress in response to the common threat of flooding and other hydrological disasters. A meeting of the heads of meteorological departments of all South Asian countries was held in May 2001 with USG support and in cooperation with the World Meteorological Organization and the Kathmandu-based International Center for Integrated Mountain Development. A joint action plan was agreed at the meeting that will lead to greatly improved information exchange and collective efforts on flood forecasting.

Water management issues in the region already receive considerable attention, and there are plans to expand this further. In Bangladesh the MACH Project deals with inland fisheries management increasingly in a sub-catchment context. USAID/Nepal focuses a significant portion of its resources on environmentally and socially sound hydropower development.

In India, progress has been made in developing successful models for financing urban water infrastructure, and the mission is moving ahead with plans for a new program to address the "water-energy" nexus. The recently developed regional action plan for flood information exchange represents an important-if modest-step forward to encourage greater cooperation across South Asia on addressing hydrological risks as well as related issues.

There are opportunities for improved coordination of mission-level, water-related activities across the region, especially where the possibility of cross-border bilateral cooperation exists. The potential for expanding regional cooperation in response to the common threat of hydrological disasters—based on the recent successful dialogue on this subject—also should be further supported.

Drinking Water : South Asia is urbanizing very rapidly, and the provision of water supply to burgeoning cities is a top priority for municipal authorities. Water-borne diseases are a major contributor to high infant mortality where access to clean drinking water is limited. In the arid regions especially of Western India, Southern Pakistan and Afghanistan, water supply shortages become acute whenever there is a drought—as is currently occurring. Optimism of the past few years regarding the ability of the private sector to invest in water infrastructure is fading, though this must continue to be an important part of the financing and water supply management.

Irrigation : Agriculture remains by far the largest water consumer in the region. The efficiency of irrigation remains generally low, and many perverse incentives constrain efforts to improve the situation. Prices paid for water (or its delivery) are very low relative to the marginal cost of water provision and marginal value of water to production.

In India, subsidized energy in agricultural areas compounds the problem by encouraging highly wasteful pump irrigation practices. Transfer of authority over the management of local irrigation systems is moving ahead only slowly. There are opportunities for market-oriented and other policy changes that would have far reaching effects on the efficiency of water allocation and use both within the agricultural sector and between agriculture and other, often higher-valued, users.

Aquatic Ecosystems and In-Stream Water Flows : There is almost categorical under-appreciation of the important biophysical—and sometimes directly economic, such as transportation-services provided by maintaining minimum in—stream flows of waterways and both natural and manmade drainage systems. Only in Bangladesh has there been any recent attention to the importance-in this case to inland fisheries and associated aquatic ecosystems—of maintaining appropriate drainage patterns and minimum flows. Elsewhere, inattention to this issue is contributing to problems of waterlogging and/or salinization associated with irrigation systems. Deltaic ecosystems are at the greatest risk from the consequence of low-and often highly polluted-river and drainage system flows and saltwater intrusion into coastal aquifers.

Unsustainable Groundwater Extraction : The rate of groundwater extraction for agricultural and other uses in many arid and semi-arid parts of South Asia is clearly greater than the natural recharge rates of these aquifers. This is particularly troubling because of the highly dense and poor populations that have come to rely on these unsustainable water sources. This situation is further complicated in southern Nepal, West Bengal, and Bangladesh by the discovery of toxic levels of arsenic in many wells—effectively rendering them unusable. Sound scientific analysis of groundwater management problems and programs to address these issues are urgently needed.

Maintaining Urban Environmental Quality

The phenomenon of urbanization is so pervasive a force within the region that it is difficult to separate it from the other identified topics, and, in many key respects, it should be considered a sign of progress. However, it creates tremendous environmental management challenges associated with the reengineering of natural systems and the sheer numbers of people crowded onto a finite natural resource base.

A loose consensus among the South Asian mayors attending the recent "Mayors' Asia-Pacific Environmental Summit" emerged that air pollution is fast becoming their top environmental priority. While new research on the high health costs from respiratory illness partially explains this concern, there is also a growing realization that outdoor air pollution spreads its ills without respect to economic or social class. The two most important targets for air pollution reduction appear to be transport (for outdoor pollution) and cooking stoves (for indoor pollution).

Water management concerns also rank as an important consideration, with urban water supply systems remaining under funded and inefficient. Likewise, sewage and sanitation systems have poor geographic coverage within cities, and daunting investment requirements hang over the heads of urban planners throughout the region.

Municipal waste remains the largest source of organic pollution in surface waters-contributing greatly to the spread of water-borne disease and associated human suffering. Solid waste management also presents enormous challenges, along with a wider range of urban planning and "green space" considerations of importance to urban residents.

At the mission level, through RUDO/SA and with inputs from US-AEP, USAID is already dealing with several important environmental dimensions of the region's urbanization process. More than any other of the region's environmental activities, urban programs address environmental governance issues, such as those dealing with city managers' associations, government capacity building, and the establishment of healthy urban financial institutions. Structural issues within USAID remain—mostly to do with the relationships between the RUDO office and bilateral mission programs—that also need to be addressed in planning appropriate responses.

Given the importance placed on both urbanization and environmental governance issues by the assessment, it would seem prudent for USAID's urban programs to build on the foundations of existing assistance and look to its expansion with respect to environmental dimensions. Target areas might include issues such as urban property rights as they affect incentives for sound urban landscape planning, as well as support to decentralization and devolution processes that will influence the efficient provision of environmental services.

Managing Energy-related Environmental Issues

South Asia is rapidly making the transition to use of a modern electricity grid. This can reduce the burning of traditional fuels with associated air pollution reductions, but, with coal as the principal power source, some of these gains will simply be offset by other problems. The energy-environment connection is also regional or even global in nature, from issues of transboundary air pollution to interstate cooperation for natural gas or hydropower trade.

Greater efforts need to be made to see that energy and environmental management go hand-in-hand in the region if synergy among these closely interrelated concerns is to be achieved. This is true at all scales of analysis: regional, national, and local. The regional linkages between upstream hydropower and downstream consumers have been noted, as have potential relationships between Bangladesh and its neighbors as natural gas supplies are exploited.

At the national levels, power-sector restructuring will improve efficiencies in energy production and distribution, and decisions regarding especially India's coal-based electricity sector will have significant environmental implications with national, regional, and global dimensions. At the more localized level, USAID/ India seems intent on exploring an integrated strategy to improve simultaneously the efficiency of municipal water supply and rural energy services. Likewise, USAID/ Nepal's efforts to help develop that country's vast hydropower resources must be centered on ensuring that the full social and environmental costs of investments are incorporated into planning and decision-making.

It is important that environmental considerations not be taken as an afterthought in energy planning and investment, and, likewise, environmental planners ignore energy issues at the peril of their efforts to improve environmental quality and the sustainability of natural resource systems. Fortunately, much of the energy-related assistance provided to the region already has explicit environmental dimensions, though there does not seem to be any systematic attention to measuring these benefits. Support for power sector restructuring is an area of assistance that must be mindful of local, national, regional, and global environmental implications of alternative patterns of reform.

2

Environmental Problems of South Asia

South Asia's environmental problems are enormous. They include resource depletion and ecological degradation, indoor and urban air pollution, lack of access to clean water supplies and sanitation, toxic and hazardous agroindustrial waste generation and disposal, and vulnerability to natural disasters. These problems, magnified by the inadequacy of governance structures in every country of the region and at all levels, threaten or cause losses of life and livelihoods of millions of people. Estimates suggest that premature deaths and illness linked to major environmental health risks account for one fifth of the total burden of disease in the region. This is comparable to malnutrition (15 percent) and is larger than the toll from any other preventable risk factor. In India, inadequate water supply and sanitation are estimated to account for 9 percent and indoor air pollution for 6 percent of the environmental health burden. It is estimated that air pollution causes 168,000 premature deaths annually in Pakistan and 132,000 premature deaths in Bangladesh.

Significant natural resource concerns in South Asia include water quality degradation and local and regional water scarcity; dwindling forests, coastal wetlands, freshwater bodies, and fisheries; soil degradation resulting from nutrient depletion and salinization; and poorly managed water resources. Many of these issues are particularly important for the rural poor and disadvantaged groups, who depend heavily on renewable natural resources.

Enviornmental Problems of India

Biodiversity

Approximately 5.3% of the total geographical area of country has been earmarked for extensive in situ conservation of habitats and ecosystems through a protection area network of 80 National Parks and 44 Wildlife Sanctuaries. This network has played a significant role in restoring viable populations of large mammals such as the tiger, lion, rhinoceros, crocodiles, elephants, etc. Attention has been paid to ex situ conservation measures as they complement and are important to situ conservation.

The Central and State Governments together run and manage 33 Botanical Gardens. In addition, universities have their own Botanical Gardens. There are 275 centres of ex situ wildlife preservation in the form of zoos, deer parks, safari parks, aquaria, etc. The Government of India has set up a Central Zoo Authority to oversee, monitor, and coordinate the management and the development of zoos in the country. Surveys of the floral and faunal resources in the country are carried out by the Botanical Survey of India established in 1890 and the Zoological Survey of India established in 1916. The National Institute of Oceanography and several other specialized institutions and universities further strengthen the taxonomic data base.

Participatory Forest Management as an effective means of regenerating degraded forests has been increasingly gaining ground in India. In 1990, the Government issued guidelines to State Governments highlighting the need and the procedure for the involvement of village communities and voluntary agencies in the protection and development of degraded forests. In response to these guidelines, 22 out of 25 States have issued orders for creating resolutions enabling mechanisms for public participation in the management of degraded forests. The participatory forest management approach promotes active participation and involvement of the people in forest conservation and development, including the development of micro-level plans and their implementation. At present, approximately 10 million ha of forest area is being maintained through more than 36,000 Village Forest Protection Committees. Although many States have accepted the initiative in principle, effective implementation of the new approach at the field level has taken root only in a few States. One of the important elements of the Participatory Forest Management System relates to the use of indigenous capacity and local knowledge regarding various aspects of conservation, development, and use of forests.

The rural people, particularly women, have an intimate knowledge about various species, growth characteristics, utility, and medicinal value. They are also well informed about the species to be planted in a given locality to satisfy the specific requirements of fuel, fodder, timber, and other non-wood forest products. In participatory forest management, planning and implementation of most of the activities related to regeneration and protection are completed with the active involvement of rural people. There is a symbiotic relationship between tribal people and forests.

In 1991, various issues related to forest-tribal interface were examined and detailed guidelines issued by the Government of India to the State Governments in order to ameliorate the socioeconomic conditions of tribal people. These guidelines cover a number of subjects including addressing old encroachments of forest lands, disputed claims over forest land, elimination of intermediaries to stop exploitation, conversion of forest villages to revenue villages, and payment of compensation for loss of life and property due to depredation by wild animals. A review of social forestry programme launched during the 1980s resulted in a consolidation of gains and a strengthening of the weaker links. The conservation of the existing natural forests with emphasis on natural regeneration is given increasing focus. The current approach towards afforestation and forest conservation is to integrate the activities and expertise of different sectors so that various pressures responsible for forest degradation are adequately addressed. Introduction of the Eco-Development Programme has been one of the recent developments in the field of wildlife management. The objective is economic development for the people residing in and around sanctuaries and National parks, in order to reduce their dependence on forest products and improve the ecological health of the protected areas.

The scheme aims to increase land and forest resource productivity so that alternative avenue of employment and income are made available in the immediate neighborhood of people. The Eco-Development

Programme proposes a package of activities including developing agriculture, improving land productivity and developing minor irrigation, raising fodder and fuel plantations, providing livestock care and improvement, introducing fuel saving devices, providing medical care including family planning, and creating environmental awareness. It is increasingly thought that the eco-development concept should not be limited to protected areas. It is believed that the scope and content of such schemes should be extended to cover other villages lying in the immediate vicinity of forests. The comprehensive State Forestry Projects, which have been recently launched by a number of States, incorporate elements of eco-development as a means of ensuring sustained development of forests. The cross-sectoral issues like rural employment, water and soil conservation, fodder production, firewood production to meet energy requirements of 80% of the rural population, etc. has been taken care of in the National Forestry Action Programme.

The forestry management in the country is being practiced on the basis of sustainable management for more than a century. However efforts are being made to ensure that the management plans of the forest areas are prepared taking advantage of the important latest technology like GIS, etc. and so as to reduce the period of preparation as well as the period of management plans in the country. Accordingly a comprehensive working plan code is being prepared for the whole country. The assessment of forest cover in the first three cycles was based only on visual interpretation of satellite imagery, while the fourth cycle has been subjected to computer analysis. As a result, it has been possible to systematically interpret a part of the area more objectively. As per the latest 1997 assessment forest cover of the country is at

6,33,397 sq. kms. Thus in the comparison of forest cover figures of 1995 and 1997 assessments, there is a slight decrease of forest cover from 6,38,879 sq. kms in 1995 assessment.

India has been participating in all the IPF/IFF meetings and India agrees with the overall action relating to National Forest Programme, Forest assessment, criteria and indicators, traditional forest related causes and underline causes of deforestation. However, India has taken a view that there has to be an instrument to coordinate the efforts of various international instruments and institutions. Accordingly, India has moved for creation of a permanent forum like Global Forest Facility on the lines of the Global Environmental Facility (GEF), to further carry out the dialogue and discussions on the contentious and unresolved issues. India has also taken a view that financial resources/funding is one of the major problem areas and therefore, it is necessary to assign this exclusive function to one of the International Arrangements and Mechanisms (IAMs).In consonance with the recommendation of IPF, India has prepared the National Forest Action Programme in the year 1999 in consultation with FAO which incorporates the agreed commitments by India.

India's economic and trade policies which have a bearing on forest and forest products are being progressively fine-tuned to facilitate the conservation and sustainable use of forests. This is reflected in liberal imports of forest products to relieve pressures on forests, nationalization of trade of certain forest products, incentives for wood substitution, subsidies for the use of fuel-saving devices and alternative sources of energy supply such as biogas and solar energy, and financial incentives to supply seedlings free of cost or at subsidized rates. India has actively participated in the deliberations of the Intergovernmental Panel on Forests, established by the Commission on Sustainable Development.

Ecosystems

As a major ecosystem representing the complex and interrelated ecology of our planet, mountain environments are essential to the survival of the global ecosystem. Mountains are, however, vulnerable to human and natural ecological imbalance. The Himalayas represent one of the most fragile mountain ecosystems and, furthermore, sustain a large human population. This sets them apart from Alpine or other ranges, where human habitation is not so high. Mountains and their people deserve consideration and attention, so that local knowledge can be used, and sustained and accelerated development becomes a reality in the context of the promotion and protection of the ecosystem as a whole.

The Himalaya system is vast and diverse, and represents the youngest mountain system in the world. It occupies 18% of the geographical area of India and regulates climate of the entire Indian subcontinent. The existence of valuable flora, fauna, and minerals exclusive to the region is unique. The Himalayas feed the major river systems of the Indian sub-continent. Mountains are an important sources of water, energy, minerals, forests, and agricultural products; and serve as areas of recreation. They are store houses of biological diversity, home to endangered species, and an essential part of the global ecosystem. Therefore, the development of mountains has to be viewed in a holistic manner, encompassing economic development, technological improvement, environmental protection, and human resource development. All these activities are interrelated and gains in one will produce benefits in others. In India, a number of important priority activities have been augmented and strengthened as a follow up of Agenda 21. While a large number of existing institutions in the region have continued their efforts, the Government has established the GB Pant Institute for Himalayan Environment and Development with the specific mandate for generating and strengthening knowledge about the ecology and sustainable development of the Indian Himalayas. The Institute is also involved in integrating and collecting traditional knowledge for sustainable and integrated development of watersheds.

Fisheries play an important role in the Indian economy and supports about 6.0 million full time or occasional fishermen. It continues to be a thrust area of India's development programmes due to its vital contributions to employment generation, food security and foreign exchange earnings. Fish production in India reached a level of about 5.40 million tonnes in 1998 and the country is now sixth largest producer of fish in the world. Out of this, 2.90 million tonnes is from the marine sector. The earnings from export of fish and fishery products crossed US$1.30 billion in 1998. While fish production form 0-50 m. zone has been harvested to maximum sustainable yield levels, the zone beyond 50-200 m and 200-500 m has been harvested up to about 50% levels.The oceanic resources are harvested up to 10% of the potential. In the Indian Ocean context, the over-exploitation and destruction of eco-system and habitat is not alarming as in some other parts of the World.

The recent review of the state of World fishery resources by FAO has revealed that while the Atlantic Ocean and in different parts of the Pacific Ocean the fishery resources are largely over-exploited, in the Indian Ocean fish production is on the increase with relative stability and healthy state of fish stocks. Various measures are being undertaken to optimise and rationalise the fishing fleet as well as the fishing effort by area-wise deployment of different categories of fishing vessels, regulation of fishing, gear and mesh size, uniform closed fishing season, development of deep sea fishing including diversified fishing, replenishment of fish stocks by undertaking projects on sea ranching, setting up of artificial reef, etc.

Wastes Materials

At present, solid wastes are utilized to the extent possible by the following processes: conversion of garbage into energy pellets; anaerobic digestion/biogas generation from garbage; and composting by vermiculture and other means. A pilot plant has been set up in Bombay for the conversion of garbage into energy pellets. It is proposed to set up ten more such plants for which external assistance is likely to be sought. The process of anaerobic digestion/biogas generation from garbage is being applied at medium and small scale levels at several places in India, and is being encouraged at other places. The conversion of garbage into compost by vermiculture and other processes is also being promoted. All these processes not only help in waste utilization but also in producing energy or useful products. Apart from organic wastes, several other urban wastes such as wastepaper, plastics, glass, rubber, textiles, metals, coconut shells, etc.

are extensively recycled. This is encouraged by the Government. Some of the industrial wastes such as fly ash, blast furnace slag, lime sludge, phosphogypsum, red-mud, etc. are generated in large quantities and are sources of environmental pollution. Reuse and recycling of these wastes is being encouraged. Fiscal incentives in the form of excise duty exemption have been provided on the production of building materials using fly ash or phosphogypsum. An exemption of custom duty is also applied on imports of equipment and machinery for the conversion of these wastes to useful purposes.

The collection and disposal of solid wastes is another area of concern for city management in India. No city collects and disposes of its solid wastes in a safe manner and the coverage is often inadequate. An ORG study of 24 cities in 1989 revealed that, while daily solid waste generation was about 15,000 tonnes, only 11,500 tonnes was collected, leaving almost one-fourth to degenerate within the city environment. Even when the collection rate is high, say 90%, the collection frequency is not satisfactory. There is no relationship between solid waste collection and city size. Furthermore, collection does not necessarily suggest regular service and the frequency varies from twice a week in the mega cities to fortnightly collection in the intermediate towns. This relates to domestic wastes as collection of industrial and commercial wastes is more regular. The disposal of wastes is another issue of concern to city managers. The method seems to improve with the level of urbanization, from open-dumps in the small and intermediate towns to sanitary landfills in the mega cities.

The major environmental concerns in an urbanizing India relate to high levels of water pollution due to poor waste disposal, inadequate sewerage and drainage, and improper disposal of industrial effluents. The dumping of solid waste in low-lying areas contributes to land and groundwater pollution. All these developments have contributed to the deterioration of the urban environment, a critical concern that requires specific interventions to achieve sustainability of human settlements. In order to improve the management of urban solid wastes and sewage related issues, there is need for capacity building, awareness and training, improved technologies, and the creation of infrastructure facilities. The lack of adequate financial resources, especially at the municipal and local levels remains a constraint. In India, a National Waste Management Council (NWMC) has been constituted by the Ministry of Environment and Forests to provide advice on various matters related to waste management including the incentives/disincentives required to facilitate waste utilization. Representatives of concerned Central and State Government departments, municipal corporations, industry associations, experts, NGOs, and media people meet from time to time under the Chairmanship of the Minister for Environment and Forests.

There are three Centrally sponsored schemes for pollution abatement of rivers presently under implementation by the Ministry. These are the Ganga Action Plan (GAP) Phase I, Ganga Action Plan Phase II, and National River Conservation Plan. The main objective of the Ganga Action Plan is to improve the water quality of the Ganga to acceptable standards by preventing the pollution load reaching the river. The Action Plan primarily addresses itself to the interception, diversion, and treatment of 873 million litres per day of municipal sewage out of the estimated 1,340 million litres per day from 25 towns, 6 in Uttar Pradesh, 4 in Bihar, and 15 in West Bengal. Under the GAP, emphasis has been given to the improvement of sewage treatment technologies. As a result, the programme has led to the development of some appropriate technologies like the Upflow Anaerobic Sludge Blanket (UASB), improved oxidation ponds, sewage treatment through plantation, etc.

These technologies are cost effective in terms of operation and maintenance and, thus, will reduce the burden on the State Government. These developments will make the Ganga Action Plan and future programmes sustainable. The programme also emphasizes resource recovery from sewage treatment to improve its sustainability. These aspects include utilization of biogas for co-generation of power, and sale of treated sewage and sludge (a bio-fertilizer and nutrient rich treated effluents for agriculture). Pisciculture is proposed in most of the stabilization ponds constructed under GAP. The Plan serves as a model for other river systems. Thus, action plans for the rivers Yamuna, Gomti, and Damodar are being developed. For proper management of urban solid wastes, it is essential to know the quantity and nature of wastes being generated and utilized.

The Ministry of Environment and Forests has initiated a scheme to survey the solid wastes generated, utilized, and disposed off in important towns of the country. A scheme to develop pilot projects, conduct surveys, and fund promotional activities in the following areas have been initiated to emphasize waste reduction, recycling, and reuse in industries, and better management of municipal solid wastes:

a) survey of urban municipal wastes in important cities and the setting up of pilot plants on the utilization of municipal solid wastes;

b) establishing pilot plants to utilize industrial wastes; and

c) development and other promotional activities for municipal and industrial wastes.

With rapid growth of population and industrialization during the last two decades, there has been a tremendous increase in the generation of domestic, urban, and industrial wastes. Although a major part of the wastes generated are non-hazardous, substantial quantities are hazardous wastes. In spite of the several steps taken for the management of wastes generated by various sources, only a small proportion of solid wastes are properly utilized and disposed of, with the result that some wastes cause environmental degradation and health risks. The Hazardous Wastes Rules, under the authority of the Environment Act, 1986, were announced by the Ministry of Environment and Forests in July, 1989. These Rules regulate the generation, collection, storage, transport, treatment, disposal, and import of hazardous wastes. The Rules apply to 18 categories of hazardous wastes which have been identified and listed in the Schedule annexed to the Rules. One of the important stipulations under the Rules is that the importation of hazardous wastes from any other country to India is not permitted for dumping or disposal. However, importation is allowed for processing or reuse as raw material, after examination of the merits of each case by the competent authorities.

Under Rule 11 of the Hazardous Wastes Rules, 1989, the exporting country or exporter is required to communicate details about the proposed transboundary movement of hazardous wastes to the Central Government. The importer is also required to provide details regarding the wastes to the relevant State

Pollution Control Boards. After examining the details provided by the importer/exporter, suitable instructions are issued by the concerned authorities. The Port Authorities are also advised. The wastes from other countries are exported in large quantities and are received in bulk shipments. Such shipments enter through India's ports and the Ports and Customs Authorities have a major role in checking and granting permission for entry of these shipments.

The hazardous wastes are included in the restricted lists of imports requiring a license, which is granted subject to the recommendation under the Hazardous Wastes Rules. Intimations are required to be given by the exporter/importer concerning the proposed transboundary movement of the hazardous wastes. Under the Hazardous Wastes Rules, complete information on the exporter, importer, source of generation, type of waste and its constituents, method of disposal, safety data sheet, etc., is required on Form 6 of these Rules. According to the Basel Convention, the exporter should seek prior consent in writing from the importing country's Competent Authority (Ministry of Environment and Forests) before the commencement of the shipment. A movement document should accompany the consignment. Due to indiscriminate exports, including those from non-signatories to the Basel Convention, huge quantities of hazardous wastes may reach Indian ports.

In order to arrest this phenomena, cyanide waste (waste category No. 1), and mercury and arsenic bearing wastes under the Hazardous Wastes Rules have been prohibited for export and import from December 26, 1996. The Basel Convention on the Control of Transboundary Movements of Hazardous Wastes and their Disposal was signed by India in 1992. The Ministry of Environment and Forests has been designated as the Competent Authority for the Convention. The Convention seeks to promote the reduction in the generation of waste and calls for international cooperation in development of cleaner technologies. In addition, such movements of wastes destined for recycling and recovery were to be phased out by December 31, 1997. This ban would only be applicable to those wastes that are characterized as being hazardous under the Convention. The task of hazard waste classification has been entrusted to the Technical Working Group of the Basel Convention. Developing countries have become major recipients of hazardous wastes generated in the industrially advanced countries. Due to stringent legislation and regulations, and the prohibitive costs of treatment and disposal of such wastes in the developed countries, producers of such wastes and their agents find it cheaper to ship hazardous wastes to developing countries.

The Ministry of Environment and Forests has been receiving communications seeking permission to import hazardous wastes. These include metal- containing wastes (ferrous and non-ferrous), waste oil, oil sludge, etc. These are processed in accordance with the requirements of the Hazardous Wastes (Management and Handling) Rules and the Basel Convention. A Committee has been constituted for this purpose. There is a legal framework in India for the management of radioactive wastes and an independent regulatory body with responsibilities to carrying out statutory control with regard to health, safety, and environmental protection. India is concerned with the environmentally sound management of radioactive wastes.

The need for the establishment of a nuclear waste management system in the country was recognized at an early stage of India's nuclear programme. The system takes care of all radioactive waste generated from nuclear facilities as well as nuclear materials from industry, research, and medicine. Documentation and dissemination of information regarding waste generation storage and disposal is also undertaken though there is scope for increased interaction and exchange of information, especially among the developing countries.

Toxic Chemicals

Chemicals occupy an important place in India's effort to meet the social and economic goals of the community. However, many chemicals are toxic, highly reactive, explosive or flammable, or have a combination of these characteristics, and represent a potential risk to human, animal and plant life, and the environment in general. Extreme care is necessary in handling such chemicals at all stages of manufacture, processing, transportation, and use. The risk of poisoning from exposure to dangerous chemicals is acute and casualties occur each year. The adverse effects of pesticide poisoning are well known. In 1982, it was estimated that while developing countries accounted for only 50% of the use of pesticides worldwide, over 50% of pesticide poisonings occurred in these countries. A global survey undertaken in 1984-86 indicated that while most developed countries had well-established capabilities for poison control, very few developing countries had such facilities. To reduce the risk, the long-term objective of Government is to eliminate the use of chemicals. However, the technological information on viable alternatives is generally not available. Consequently, the immediate and complete elimination of toxic chemicals seems difficult.

Purification techniques and other end-of-pipe measures are capital and energy intensive and, taken alone, have not yielded the desired success in reducing the discharges of hazardous substances. Considerable research expertise exists in India on issues related to the manufacture, use, and handling of toxic and hazardous materials. However, the difficulty lies in the inadequate exchange of information and the training of persons actually involved in such processes. It is recognized that capacity building is essential in industry especially at the factory and plant levels. In India, the Environment (Protection) Act, 1986 lays down procedures and safeguards to regulate the handling of hazardous and toxic chemicals and preventing accidents.

For prevention and control of major chemical hazards, legal safeguards have been framed under the Hazardous Chemicals Rules. Specific requirements have been prescribed for the safe transportation of hazardous chemicals. Exposure limits for chemicals and toxic chemicals have also been established. Recently, environmental audits have been made mandatory, one of the aims being to reduce environmental risk. Government is also encouraging the use of Cleaner Production Technologies by providing fiscal benefits. The award of the Ecomark on environment friendly consumer products also encourages the use of safer chemicals and technologies. To limit the discharge of pollutants into water and into the air, standards have been laid down under the relevant Acts. The "Polluter Pays Principle" has also been adopted. Environmental impact assessment has been made mandatory for specified projects. Where feasible, such assessment is also recommended for less toxic chemicals, prior to the sanction of environmental clearance.

Several work programmes for the promotion of safety in the handling of hazardous substances have been planned and implemented. Risk assessment of chemicals is time and resource intensive. At the National level, the following efforts are underway:

a) a centrally sponsored scheme to create infrastructure in certain regulatory organizations;

b) hazard analysis and off-site emergency plans in sensitive industrial pockets;

c) the establishment of emergency response centres;

d) the establishment of poison control centres at select places with some available infrastructure; and

e) the promotion of epidemiological studies in areas of high risk involving the collection of data from hazardous installations and relating this to the pollution status.

To complement the legislation listed above, there is a need in view of the anticipated rise in the number of cases of chemical poisoning for institutions with qualified staff that would treat poison cases, using the latest information and detection methods. The Ministry of Environment and Forests, and the Ministry of Health and Family Welfare have felt the need for setting up a National Poison Control Centre with a network of Regional Centres. A Poison Control Centre has been set up at the All India Institute of Medical Sciences (AIIMS), New Delhi to provide a full range of clinical, analytical, toxicological and information services to provide quick response against the effects of chemicals on human health. The Ministry of Environment and Forests has set up a Central Crisis Group Alert System with a Central Control Room for the management of emergencies due to hazardous chemicals.

The Ministry has also established the National Register for Potentially Toxic Chemicals (NRPTC) for the collection, collation, analysis, and dissemination of existing National and international information on the lines of the International Register of Potentially Toxic Chemicals (IRPTC). However, the Centre requires a widespread network throughout the country to facilitate coordination with other organizations. An effort in this direction has been made with the establishment of Regional Registers in three regions. There is increasing concern over the movements of products across the boundaries of developing countries completed in contravention of internationally adopted guidelines and principles. This is especially true of developing countries which do not have the adequate infrastructure to determine the risks associated with such products or to adequately monitor their ingress and egress.

India participates regularly in the meetings of the London Guidelines for the Exchange of Information on Chemicals in International Trade. Modalities for strengthening the legal basis of these guidelines are being considered. A voluntary code of ethics on international trade in chemicals has also been finalized in consultation with representatives of the chemical industry. India is a member of International Programme on Chemical Safety (IPCS) and the IRPTC.

Pollution Control

In India, the National Committee of Environmental Planning and Co-ordination (NCEPC) was set up in 1972 under the Department of Science and Technology. A separate Empowered Committee was set up in 1980 for reviewing the existing legislative measures and administrative machinery for ensuring environmental protection and for recommending ways to strengthen them. On the recommendations of this Empowered Committee, a separate Department of Environment was set up in 1980 which was subsequently upgraded to a full-fledged Ministry of Environment and Forests in 1985 to serve as the focal point in the administrative structure of the Government of India for the planning, promotion and co-ordination of environmental and forestry programmes. Other Government partners in carrying out environmental protection activities include:

— The State departments of environment;

— Central and State Pollution Control Boards;

— the Botanical and Zoological Survey of India;

— the Forest Survey of India;

— the National River Conservation Authority;

— the National Afforestation and Eco-development Board;

— the Indian Council for Forestry Research and Education; and

— the Wildlife Institute of India and the National Museum for Natural History.

The Government of India has entrusted the work relating to Ozone layer Protection and phase out of the Ozone depleting substances programme under the Montreal Protocol to the Ministry of Environment and Forests. There are several inter ministerial committees and working groups to coordinate issues relating to policy and legislation. In case of implementation of the Montreal Protocol the Empowered Steering Committee consists of members from the Ministry of Science and Technology and other line Ministries. The Ministry cf Environment and Forests has set up an Ozone Cell as a national unit to implement the Protocol and the Ozone Depleting Substances phase out programme in India. The decisions related to Ozone Depleting Substances phase-out and protection of Ozone Layer are being taken at the Central Government level. The Government of India frequently consults NGO's research organizations and regional expertise as and when needed. India's approach towards implementation of the UNFCC and associated environmental parameters is covered within policy declarations:

— the National Conservation Strategy and policy statement on Environment and development and the policy statement on abatement of pollution for regulating various environmental parameters.

— In addition various other enactments such as Air pollution (prevention and control) Act 1981 amended in 1987 and Motor Vehicles Act 1939, amended in 1988.

— the Forest Conservation Act amended in 1988 contribute significantly towards minimizing the causes of climate change.

— The Environmental Protection Act 1986 is an umbrella legislation and it also empowers the government to formulate statutory rules for fulfilling various requirements.

— Further EIA has been made statutory for various developmental activities and the Coastal Resource Zones notification provides guidelines for protection and management of coastal zones.

India has taken a series of fiscal and regulatory measures to facilitate Ozone Deleting Substances (ODS) phase out in the country. Trade in ODS with non-Parties to the Montreal Protocol has been banned. Harmonized classifications of commodity codes consistent with the international system have been introduced. Controlled substances under the Protocol have been brought under the ambit of licenses for the purpose of export and import. The Ozone Depleting Substances (Regulation and Control) Rules, 2000 under the Environment Protection Act 1986 have been notified to Control and phase out production and consumption of Ozone Depleting Substances in order to comply with the Montreal Protocol.

The Government decided in 1995 to fully exempt payment of Customs and Excise Duties on capital goods required to implement ODS phase out projects funded by the multi lateral funding (MLF). This benefit was later extended for all MLF eligible projects whether or not MLF assistance was requested/available at the time of implementation of ODS phase out project. The Reserve Bank of India advised all commercial banks in September 1997 not to finance/refinance new investments with ODS technologies. In 1992, India adopted the policy statement on Abatement of Pollution, which provides instruments in the form of legislation and regulation, fiscal incentives, voluntary agreements, educational programmes and information campaigns to prevent and control pollution of water, air and land.

Since the adoption of the policy statement, the focus of activities has been on issues such as promotion of clean and low waste technologies, waste water minimization, reuse/recycling, improvement of water quality, environment audit, natural resource accounting, development of mass-based standards as well as institutional and human resource development. The issue of pollution prevention and control entails a combination of command and control methods; voluntary regulatory and fiscal measures; promotion of awareness and involvement of public. To facilitate industries in preparing environmental statements, sector-specific environmental audit manuals have been prepared.

Training programmes are also being organized for officials of Central Pollution Control Boards (CPCB) to enable them to use the software. An "Eco-mark" label has been introduced to label consumer products that are environment-friendly. Nineteen products have been identified for labelling and 18 notifications have been issued so far on different products criteria. The Bureau of India Standards (BIS)/Directorate of Marketing and Inspection (DMI) is the implementing agency for this scheme. So far one license has been granted by the BIS to a product under the soaps category. Under the scheme for adoption of clean technology in small-scale industries and for extending necessary technical support, training and awareness programmes for personnel in Small Industry Development Organization and for entrepreneurs are being organized. 'From Waste to Profits', a manual giving guidelines for waste minimization, has been prepared. Sector-specific manuals on waste minimization in the areas of pulp and paper, pesticides formulations and textiles, dyeing and printing and electroplating, have also been prepared.

Waste Minimization Circles (WMCs) are being established to promote group efforts in increasing productivity and improving the environmental conditions in small and medium-scale industries through adoption of waste minimization techniques. Fifteen Waste Minimisation Circles have been established so far in different industrial clusters across the country. An Indian

Centre for the Promotion of Cleaner Technologies (ICPC) with a network of institutions including industries, academic institutions and other user agencies is being set up for which the World Bank has provided $2 million as grant-in-aid. The Centre will provide evaluated and ranked technology options to entrepreneurs.

The Central Pollution Control Board (CPCB) is the national apex body for assessment, monitoring and control of water and air pollution. The executive responsibilities for enforcement of the Acts for Prevention and Control of Pollution of Water (1974) and Air (1981) and also of the Water (Cess) Act, 1977 are carried out through the Board. The CPCB advises the Central Government in all matters concerning the prevention and control of air, water and noise pollution and provides technical services to the Ministry of Environment and forests for implementing the provisions of the Environment (Protection) Act, 1986. Under this Act, effluent and emission standards in respect of 61 categories of industries have been notified.

Seventeen categories of heavily polluting industries have been identified. They are: cement, thermal power plant, distilleries, sugar, fertilizer, integrated iron and steel, oil refineries, pulp and paper, petrochemicals, pesticides, tanneries, basic drugs and pharmaceuticals, dye and dye intermediates, caustic soda, zinc smelter, copper smelter and aluminum smelter. Out of a total of 1,551 units identified under these 17 categories, 1,266 units have installed adequate facilities for pollution control and 130 units have been closed down. The Central Pollution Control Board, in consultation with State Pollution Control Boards, has identified critically polluted areas in the country which need special attention for control of pollution.

The CPCB in collaboration with the SPCBs monitors the quality of fresh water resources of the country through a network of 480 monitoring stations located all over the country. Based on such monitoring, 13 heavily polluted and 26 medium-polluted river stretches have been identified. Under the National Ambient Air Quality Monitoring programme, 290 stations covering over 90 towns/cities monitor the ambient air quality of the country. The Central and State Pollution Control Boards regularly conduct surveys in different cities of the country pertaining to vehicular and noise pollution, sanitation status, status of solid waste, etc.

A survey on the status of solid waste conducted in 299 Class I cities of the country indicates that 62 per cent of the total solid waste generated in the country comes from the 23 metro cities of the country. The average per capita generation of solid waste for Class I cities is about 376 gms per person per day. A total of 1,532 grossly polluting industries in 24 States/Union Territories have been identified under the National River Action Plan. Comprehensive River Basin Documents for the rivers Ulhas, Brahmaputra, Pennar, Indus Part II, Rishkulya and Chaliyar are being prepared by the Board. The Central Pollution Control Board has a NGO Cell for interacting with NGOs.

Simple water-testing kits are distributed free of cost to selected NGOs and financial assistance provided to them for conducting mass awareness programmes relating to prevention and control of pollution.

The White Paper on status of pollution in Delhi with an Action Plan for its control prepared earlier is being implemented. The Action Plan contains specific measures for control of pollution relating to vehicular pollution, water pollution, industrial air pollution, solid waste, hospital wastes, industrial hazardous wastes, noise pollution and people's participation in making Delhi a cleaner city. Directions have been issued by the National Capital Territory of Delhi for imposing restrictions on all commercial vehicles in Delhi in a time-bound programme beginning from April 1998. Based on the recommendations of a National Level Committee on Noise Pollution, directions have been issued to the State governments to check noise pollution from bursting of crackers. There is also a plan to introduce higher parking fees, to augment parking spaces in the city of Delhi and to introduce no traffic zones. A detailed India Country Programme for phase out of Ozone Depicting Substances (ODS) was prepared in 1993 to ensure the phase out of ODS according to the national industrial development strategy, without undue burden to the consumers and the industry and for accessing the Protocol's financial mechanism in accordance with the requirements stipulated in the Montreal Protocol. At present, an exercise is underway in consultation with CII to update the country programme.

The main objectives of the Country Programme has been to minimize economic dislocation as a result of conversion to non-ODS technology, maximize indigenous production, give preference to one-time replacement, emphasize decentralized management and minimize obsolescence.

Impact assessment is a pointer to the environmental compatibility of the projects in terms of their location, suitability of technology, efficiency in resource utilization, recycling and so on. A notification issued in January 1994 makes Environmental Impact Assessment statutory for 29 categories of developmental projects under various sectors such as industrial, mining, irrigation, power, transport, tourism, communication, etc. The Environmental Impact Assessment (EIA) Notification was amended in 1997 to provide for public hearing as well as for empowering State governments for according environmental clearance in respect of certain Thermal Power Projects. As per the provisions of the EIA Notification 1994, mining projects are subject to environmental clearance. However, it has been now decided to exempt prospecting through aerial survey and/ or test drilling in smaller areas from mandatory clearances.

Applications complete in every material aspect are normally examined and decision conveyed to the applicants within 30 days in cases of site clearance and 120 days in cases of environmental clearance of projects. Once an application has been submitted by the project authority, the preliminary scrutiny of the project is done by the respective technical divisions and the overall appraisal of the projects is undertaken by specially constituted environmental appraisal committees of experts. In addition, special groups/committees and task forces are constituted as and when needed for expert inputs on major projects. After detailed scrutiny and assessment, the appraisal committee makes its recommendations for approval or rejection of the project. Depending on the nature of the project, certain safeguards are recommended. For monitoring and timely implementation of safeguards suggested, six regional offices of the Ministry have been set up at Shillong, Bhubaneswar, Chandigarh, Bangalore, Lucknow and Bhopal.

Environmental Education

Priority is accorded by the Ministry of Environment and Forests to promote environmental education, create environmental awareness among various age-groups and to disseminate information through Environmental Information System (ENVIS) network to all concerned. A major initiative to include environment education as a separate and compulsory subject in the educational curricula has been taken by the Ministry at all levels of formal education, i.e., secondary, senior secondary and tertiary levels.

A discussion paper prepared on strengthening environment education was presented by the Minister for Environment and Forests at the State Education Ministers' Conference held from 22 to 24 October 1998. The paper was adopted by the Conference. The Chief Ministers were urged to introduce environment education in the school curricula from the 1999-2000 academic session. Maharashtra is the first State to introduce the subject in the school curriculum.

Paryavaran Vahinis (environment launch-vehicle) are proposed to be constituted in 194 selected districts all over the country which have a high incidence of pollution and density of tribal and forest population. The Vahinis also play a watch-dog role by reporting instances of environmental pollution, deforestation and poaching. They function under the charge of District Collectors, with the active cooperation of the State/Union Territory governments. This scheme is entirely financed by the Ministry of Environment and Forests. Seven Centres of Excellence have been set up by the Ministry to strengthen awareness, research and training in priority areas of Environmental Science and Management. These are:

Centre for Ecological Sciences, Bangalore; Centre for Mining Environment, Dhanbad; Centre for Environmental Education, Ahmedabad; CPR Environmental Education Centre, Chennai; Salim Ali Centre for Ornithology and Natural History, Coimbatore; the Centre for Environmental Management of Degraded Ecosystems, Delhi, and the Tropical Botanical Garden and Research Institute, Thiruvananthapuram, Kerala.

The National Museum of Natural History (NMNH) set up in New Delhi in 1978,is concerned with the promotion of non-formal education in the area of environment and conservation. Besides permanent exhibit galleries on various aspects of environment, the museum also conducts temporary exhibitions and a large number of educational programmes and activities for school children, college youth and the general public. Three Regional Museums of Natural History have been established at Mysore, Bhopal and Bhubaneswar. The Indian Council for Forestry Research and Education is the focal point for forestry education and extension development in the country. The Indira Gandhi National Forest Academy, Dehra Dun, imparts in-service professional training to Indian Forest Service (IFS) professionals. State forest service colleges provide training to the officers of the State Forest Service (SFS).

The Indian Plywood Industries Research and Training Institute, Bangalore, organizes short-term courses in the area of wood science. The Indian Institute of Forest Management, Bhopal, also provides training in forest management and allied subjects to persons from the Indian Forest Service, forest development corporations, and forest-related industries to develop forestry programmes. The Wildlife Institute of India, Dehradun, provides in-service training to forest officers, wildlife ecologists and other professionals for conseivation and management of the wildlife resources of the country.

Information dissemination package for school teachers and NGOs prepared by Centre for Environment Education was launched on 16th September, 1998 and distributed in four workshops organized in Calcutta, Delhi, Pune and Chennai in November-December, 1998. This kit has been developed in consultation with the UNEP-DTIE office in Paris. Painting Competitions are being organized by the Ozone Cell. An Indian entry won the prize in the international competition organized by UNEP in 1999. A National Painting Competition has been organized on the occasion of Sixty International Ozone Day, 16th September, 2000. Ozone-friendly equipment and products are being exhibited during 16-18th September every year.

A similar exhibition is being held on the occasion of the International Ozone Day, 2000. An information kit on Ozone Science and Ozone layer has been prepared by Centre for Environment Education, Ahmedabad. Chapters on pollution and environmental issues are part of the curriculum. Several training programmes are being organized on a regular basis. India is a member of WMO and is participating in various international research programmes on systematic observation atmosphere and ocean through IMD/ DST New Delhi. The Indian Meteorological Department (IMD) is the principal government agency in all matters relating to meteorology, seismology and allied subjects.

The Department has units all over the country engaged in collecting meteorological and seismological data besides providing various meteorological services.

Its main objective is to provide meteorological information for weather sensitive activities like aviation, shipping, agriculture, irrigation, off-shore oil exploration and industries. The Department also issues warnings against severe weather phenomena like cyclones, dust-storms, heavy rains, cold and heat waves that cause destruction of life and property. Besides, it also provides climatological information, records earthquakes and promotes research in meteorology. The Department maintains an extensive network of modern observatories and communication links all over the country. Observations received through high power radars and weather satellites are extensively used these days for analysis and prediction of weather.

A satellite based wide area network (WAN) using Very Small Aperture Terminals (VSATs) is being established for speedy dissemination of forecast products to various user agencies, particularly to AAS units. The plan is being implemented by installing VSATs in 127 locations out of which 47 have been installed. Scientific campaigns such as GAME-India (Global Energy Water Cycle Asian Monsoon Experiment), I-STEP (Indian Solar Terrestrial Energy Programme), OCEANSAT (IRS P4), Indo-US Agreement on Satellite Data Utilization, and INDOEX are being carried out. The Ozone measurement is being carried out at 5 stations by Indian Meteorological Department. These stations are at Srinagar, New Delhi, Varanasi, Pune and Kodaikenal. The total Ozone data and Umkehr data (vertical profile of Ozone) are being regularly sent in WMO format to the World Ozone Data Centre, Canada and are being regularly published by the Centre. India developed ozonesonde in 1963.

Since 1970, vertical Ozone distributions are being measured at 5 stations at New Delhi, Pune,

Thiruvananthapuram, Dakshni Gangtri and Maitri. Scientific data and information on the protection of atmosphere and ozone Layer are made available to potential users at national level via internet and other modes of information dissemination. Information on Ozone Science and non-ODS technology has been provided by UNEP DTIE Ozone Action Programme through its clearing housing mechanism and they send information directly to users. There are several programmes for awareness and information dissemination and websites exist for access to information. The Indian Government is making several efforts for developing new environmental friendly technologies for example, Dobson and Brewer Spectrophotometers are used to monitor total ozone measurement. It is disappointed by the non implementation of commitments made by the developed countries on providing new and additional financial resources as well as technology for promoting ecologically sustainable development. In order to implement measures to protect the atmosphere, India need the following new technologies:

— IGCC and other advanced clean coal technologies;

— state of art power generation technologies;

— Solar photovoltaic (advanced systems);

— Mass rapid transport system for urban transport; New non-ODS technology for refrigeration, aerosol, foam fire extinguisher and solvent sector; and

— Technology for manufacturing ODS substitutes.

Producers of CFCs, and the Government of India jointly supported research programmes to develop technology to produce HFC 134a at the Indian Institute of Chemical

Technology, Hyderabad. The pilot plant has been set up. Commercial production of HFC-134a is envisaged. Both Government and voluntary organizations are involved in climate change research in India with the former supporting a wide variety of projects in the area of global change research. The India Meteorological Department (IMD) monitors climate to detect change, predict climate change, determine the effects of climate change, and contribute to global observational efforts. Since 1983, IMD has maintained a meteorological observatory at the Indian permanent station in Antarctica. The Department has actively participated in various international and National observational efforts. A National Climate Centre (NCC) has been established at IMD's research wing in Pune to undertakes climate research, applications, data collection and management, and impact awareness studies. Data collected from the extensive network of observations are archived at the Department's National Data Centre in Pune. The Centre holds over 60 million records in its archives. About 2.5 million records are currently being added to the archives.

Through the Department of Science and Technology (DST) the Government has undertaken several projects to promote technologies that will reduce pollution of the atmosphere. Technologies that use compressed natural gas (CNG) as fuel in internal combustion engines have been developed for generating electricity in remote hilly areas. To help promote waste reduction, the production of fuel pellets from waste has been successfully demonstrated to industrial users in Mumbai. DST supports R&D efforts to promote environmental conservation conducted by several autonomous institutions and service organizations. Considerable research work has been completed on climate modeling, air pollution, and atmospheric ozone at the Institute of Tropical Meteorology, Pune, which has climate change as one of its major thrust areas. Activities concerning protection of Atmosphere cut across several government departments and the main source is public funding. Despite lack of external funding India has made big strides in protecting the atmosphere.

Climate change/ protection of atmosphere considerations have been in built into the five year plan process in the country and an adequate thrust has been accorded to it by GOI Ozone regulations and Market forces are driving the industries to invest money in non-ODS technologies. The Ministry of Environment and Forests functions as a nodal agency for United Nations Environment Programme (UNEP), South Asia Co-operation Environment Programme (SACEP), and International Centre for Integrated Mountain and Development (ICIMOD), International Union for Conservation of Nature and Natural Resources (IUCN) and various international agencies, regional bodies and multilateral institutions. India is signatory to the following important international treaties/ agreements in the field of environment:

i) International Convention for the regulation of Whaling;

ii) International Plant Protection Convention;

iii) The Antarctic Treaty;

iv) Convention on Wetlands of international importance;

v) Convention on International trade in Endangered Species of Wild Flora and Fauna;

vi) Protocol of 1978 relating to the international convention for the prevention of pollution from ships;

vii) Vienna Convention for the protection of the Ozone Layer;

viii) Convention on Migratory Species;

ix) Basel Convention on Trans-boundary movement of hazardous substances;

x) Framework Convention on Climate Change;

xi) Convention on conservation of bio-diversity;

xii) Montreal Protocol on the substances that deplete the ozone layer; and

xiii) International Convention for Combating Desertification.

The Ministry and its agencies cooperate with various countries such as Sweden, Netherlands, Norway, Denmark, Australia, U.K., U.S.A., Canada, Japan, FRG, etc., on bilateral basis and with several UN and other multilateral agencies such as UNDP, World Bank, Asian Development Bank, OECF (Japan) and ODA (U.K.) for various environmental and forestry projects.

India is a party to GEF and has following UNDP/ GEF projects:

i) GHG stabilization in India

ii) Enabling activities for preparation of an initial national communication

The Government of India is disappointed at the non implementation of two important / seminal commitments by the developed countries at UNCED 1992 relating to New and additional financial resources Transfer of EST's. It is a matter of regret there is no progress on transfer of EST's to developing countries. Technology for development of ODS substitute chemical is need to be transferred in fair and favorable terms.

The policies adopted by the Executive Committee of the Montreal Protocol do not address the special needs of small and medium enterprises. It is, therefore, special funding wind with differentiated cost effectiveness for all sectors in SMEs is need to be established.

Enviornmental Problems of Pakistan

Pakistan is an agricultural country, and more than 50% of its population is employed in the agricultural sector. Less than 20% of Pakistan's land can be intensively farmed, nearly all of which is cultivated. In 1990, 209,400 km^2 were in use as farmland. In general, farmers lack knowledge of operating characteristics and full capabilities of technologies within the agricultural sector. The decision for intensification of farm lands in Pakistan stems from demographic reality. In rough terms, one hectare of cultivated land supported an average 5 people in 1993; by the year 2010, it is estimated that the same land must support nearly 10. Pakistan has developed strategies to ensure food security by 1998, which also includes the agricultural sector. Local communities and NGOs are taken into consideration to review international trade relations and agricultural production.

Women, youth, indigenous people, and local communities are also involved through workshops in developing and strengthening institutional capacity for plant genetic resources. In 1981-82, a programme called "Matching Grants Programme" (MGP) focuses on the development of infrastructure in rural areas, and is based on community participation. To date, about 22,000 schemes have been implemented in 26.500 villages. Pakistan is faced with some common problems in both irrigated and rainfed areas used for agriculture. These problems can be summarized as erosion of soil, underuse of organic fertilizers and overuse of synthetic chemicals.

A National Rural Support Programme was established to promote education and health, based on community participation. In 1993, this programme was supported by the Government with Rs.1,000,000. MGP is structured so that the local councillor is normally the leader of the Project Committee which approves the projects. The councillor is responsible for collecting community finance. The Pakistan Environment Protection Council (PEPC) has jurisdiction in this area, and it has established National Environmental Quality Standards (NEQS). Protection of the atmosphere is one of the fourteen core issues in the National Conservation Strategy of Pakistan. PEPC has established a Committee on Clean Fuels, which has the mandate to make recommendations for the alleviation of atmospheric pollution.

An incentive reduction scheme has been recommended in relation to the emissions from Compressed Natural Gas and Liquid Petroleum Gas powered buses, trucks, and urban public services, and a mandatory introduction of catalytic converters in two-stroke engines by July 1997 has been suggested. The Energy Conservation Centre (ENERCON) has put together some programmes to reduce the output of greenhouse gases. These programmes involve:

— setting up tuning demonstration centres in nine cities;

— training 1,000 mechanics and workshop owners;

— providing funding for 100 tuning centres;

— conducting surveys that will lead to new policies and projects.

The diesel and furnace oil being marketed in Pakistan have a high sulphur (SO_2) content. Pakistan is also facing numerous problems from the lack of efficient fuel burning, abnormal exhaust emissions from automobiles, inadequate tuning of engines, and improper repairs and maintenance. These problems mainly affect the larger cities where breathing difficulties can occur during peak-hours. Air quality clashing with the WHO standards is costing Pakistan about Rs. 25 billion a year from adverse health and other effects. The number of vehicles in the country increased from 0.85 million in 1982 to 2.8 million in 1995, showing an overall increase of 229%. It is envisaged that, with the present rate of growth, the number of vehicles will increase to 4.5 million by the year 2000, thereby adding to quantum green house gases. Pakistan has developed a system of inventory of all green gases not controlled by the Montreal Protocol, which is periodically updated.

The United Nations Framework Convention on Climate Change was ratified on 1 June 1994 and entered into force on 30 August, 1994. The United Nations has extended major support to this project through UNDP. Support for phasing out Ozone Depletion Substances is provided through cooperation with UNDP, the World Bank and UNIDO. The Ministry of Environment, Local Government and Rural Development is responsible for the implementation of this sector. The Ministry is involved in national decision-making. Pakistan has initiated preparation of a Biodiversity Action Plan (BAP) which should be completed in its first phase by the time that CSDV is convened. Pakistan has 15 National Parks,

86 Wildlife Sanctuaries and an equal number of Game Reserves. Management Plans have been prepared for 3 National Parks.

The implementation of the management plans of these National Parks and preparation of the management plans for the remaining National Parks is required immediately. Similarly, many species are endangered and plans for their recovery are to be made immediately. The Provincial Wildlife Departments need to have permanent resource persons to make inventories in the protected areas, since the inventories that are made for PAs are not sufficient for policy formulation. The protected areas need well-equipped staff for checking the poaching of wildlife. Pakistan has many wetlands of international importance, but so far, few could be identified for listing in the Wetlands Conventions. This Convention also does not have an effective funding mechanism.

The Monitoring procedure of the Wetlands Convention could not assist Pakistan in developing its Wetlands and Coastal Areas, and there is a great need for such a mechanism to be strengthened. Pakistan has many sites which could qualify for designation as sites for the World Heritage Convention. The search for an outstanding site which may qualify needs special attention. Forest Officers are posted in the National Parks as Park Managers, but they can be transferred wherever needed to other forest areas without the consideration of the needs of the specific National Park or Protected Area. The reason for this is because of financial constraints, as the Provincial Forests Departments cannot afford to place separate Wildlife Managers. There is a great need for capacity-building in all of the relevant institutions in Pakistan in all of the components of biodiversity. For example, the conservation of species and protected areas management requires the capacity of the provincial wildlife departments.

Pakistan has been successful in implementing the above-mentioned Conventions and this has resulted in a new lease on life for wild animals and the conservation of protected areas, including wetlands, and coastal areas. There is a great need to develop a mechanism for the implementation of all the Conventions. CITES, can only be made effective if the Management and Scientific Authorities in the developing countries under CITES are made strong by increasing their capacity both in terms of finance, technology and staffing. Their research capabilities need to be extended. Rescue centres, which are required to be designated by the Parties, do not have the capacity to host confiscated species, and therefore specific funding for this is required, particularly for Authorities and Custom Officers.

Training of Customs Officers as well as Enforcement Officers is needed and which also requires funding in developing countries. Through the funding of US$ 313,000 being provided through the Global Environment Fund, Pakistan initiated the preparation of a Biodiversity Action Plan (BAP), to be completed by the first quarter of 1997. However, this is a continuous activity and the BAP is likely to require further funding for its second phase. An investment proposal is also being prepared for the management and development of three selected Protected Areas of Pakistan through possible funding by the GEF. A project entitled "Maintaining Biodiversity in Pakistan with Rural Community Development" is being funded by the GEF through UNDP at a cost of US$2.5 million. Upon the successful completion of the project, it is likely that

Pakistan may receive another 3.5 million US$ from GEF through UNDP. Only the Convention on Biological Diversity has a funding mechanism, while other Conventions do not. The governments, especially developing country parties, have to bear the costs of implementation of the obligations of the Conventions.

Therefore, there is a great need for all of the Conventions to be technically and financially supported through the GEF mechanism and extended to all developing country parties. CSD should ensure that the funding of the developing country Parties is made obligatory, without which the world's heritage is not likely to be conserved on a sustainable basis. Pakistan is a Party to the Convention on Biological Diversity and has taken up many measures before becoming a Party to this Convention. Pakistan is also a party to a number of nature conservation Conventions which include :

— The Convention on International Trade in Endangered Species of Wild Fauna and Flora (CITES)

— The Convention on Conservation of Migratory Species (CMS) - Bonn Convention

— The Convention on Wetlands of international Importance Especially as Waterfowl Habitat

— World Heritage Convention

— The Convention on Biological Diversity (CBD)

— The Framework Convention on Climate Change

— The Convention to Combat Desertification in Countries Experiencing Drought and/or Desertification, Particularly in Africa (CCD).

Current land use knowledge in Pakistan is based on Satellite Imagery Interpretation. Land degradation and human impact assessment have not yet been covered, although some surveys were done dating back to 1988. The International Convention to Combat Desertification in Countries Experiencing Drought and/or Desertification, Particularly in Africa was signed 15 October 1994 and ratified 24 February 1997. The United Nations Environment Programme is providing financial assistance of US$60,000 for the preparation of the National Plan for Combatting Desertification, a plan which will soon become operational. Pakistan has the objective of doubling its forest area, from the existing 5% to 10% of total land area. In order to meet this target, the Government has initiated various projects in an umbrella campaign of a Massive Afforestation Programme (MAP). This programme has five main components:

i) Mobilization of resources;

ii) Nursery development;

iii) Procurement of large forest lands;

iv) Ensuring adequate technical capacity; and

v) Monitoring plantations.

In Pakistan, forests are divided on the basis of whether they are state-owned or private-owned forests. The state-owned forests are again divided into four categories: reserved, protected, unclassified and resumed lands. Two-thirds of the public forest are non-commercial. The remaining one-third, located mostly on steep and unstable slopes of the Himalayas, is harvested. Production of timber from commercial forests is about 0.5 million m^3. The Rawal Lake has been selected for special attention concerning unsustainable activities, such as building latrines at specific locations and construction of septic tanks in the existing settlements. In addition, three projects have been recommended, concerning improvement of catchment areas and the provision of septic tanks and watershed management. A pilot project in Karachi has been cleared for implementation. The concept of the project is to recycle waste water by sewage collection and by conveying the waste water to irrigate areas via underground pipes.

Surface water from rivers is the primary source of water in Pakistan. Infiltration from rivers, canals, watercourses, and fields is the main source of groundwater, which is a secondary resource. The limitation on some of the water available cannot be facilitated through storage dams. Pakistan is struggling with the fact that only 30% of the diverted water at canal heads reaches crop roots. In general, Pakistan needs much integrated water and soil improvement. The Kabul and Ravi Rivers provide food, directly through fishing and indirectly through irrigation, as well as water for both drinking and industry.

In general, Pakistan needs to address a vast array of problems regarding water usage since, for example forty percent of urban deaths are caused by water-borne diseases. Special focus is also needed in terms of sodicity, water mining and the accumulation of salt in commercial crop roots. Pakistan also has an on-going research-project which aims at assessing the water requirements of different species. The idea is to use the information for various forest extension projects. The Asian Development Bank has worked with the Ministry of Environment, Urban Affairs, Forestry and Wildlife, under an Umbrella Technical Assistance Agreement, to study Rivers Kabul and Ravi and their environmental state. The initial study on River Kabul was conducted with the assistance of the

International Union for Conservation of Nature (IUCN). Pakistan faces a general lack of capacity of institutions to promote an integrated approach to the planning and management of land resources. The institutions responsible for mountain issues are the Governments of Azad Jammu & Kashmir; North West Frontier Province; Northern Area; Punjab and Sindh.

Pakistan is troubled by the lack of land-use planning and land-use control, uncertain land tenure and an inadequate policy on sustainable development in mountain areas. The mountain areas which are cultivated suffer from soil and water erosion, as well as limited infrastructure and marketing facilities. These problems lead to a need for sustainable economic diversification, especially since, despite intensification of the use of farmlands in the mountain areas, these lands will never be able to accommodate the additional population growth expected and already apparent. The environmentally sound management of toxic chemicals is a core issue of the National Conservation Strategy. Management of this type of waste has not yet been achieved. This committee is collaborating with the Ministry of Environment, Urban Affairs, Forestry and Wildlife, and they have launched a joint action plan.

The joint action plan to deal with medical wastes underlines the need for more training and education of relevant personnel, identification and strengthening of the proper institutions, and an initiative to raise awareness of problems. The projects aiming at reducing pollution from the industries, address toxic effluent reduction by using appropriate technology transfer, recycling chrome recovery, establishing institutions for in-house pollution control in the tanneries, and by establishing industrial complexes which provide the leather industry with the infrastructure and utilities required. Pakistan is suffering from the adverse soil, air and occupational effects caused by the use of chemicals in the textile and leather industries.

The privatization of solid waste management was initiated by the Ministry of Environment, Urban Affairs, Forestry and Wildlife. The Ministry is also responsible for the proposals in connection with the recycling of paper in Federal Government Offices. The National Environment Quality Standards have been implemented for issues related to this sector. This has led to some concrete measures; for example the waste problems of cement factories are being addressed by installing anti-pollution technology. The environmentally sound management of sewerage and solid waste is a core issue in the National Conservation Strategy of Pakistan. There is practically no solid waste management in Pakistan. Around 40% of the waste is discarded in the streets or at collection sites. Only half of the urban wastes is disposed in sewers, with most remaining untreated.

Solid waste treatment has been privatized in order to keep up with the demand for solid waste treatment services. Only Karachi and Islamabad have sewage treatment plants. Communities are being encouraged to participate in enhancing solid waste treatment capacities. The industrialization of Pakistan has had an effect on the environment, especially since the discharging of waste is being done without consideration of the treatment facilities that are required to maintain sustainability. Pakistan has implemented a Pollution Release Project to monitor select industries in the Province of Punjab.

Enviornmental Problems of Bangladesh

The Convention on Biological Diversity was signed by Bangladesh in 1992 and ratified in 1994. The Convention on International Trade in Endangered Species of Wild Fauna and Flora was signed by Bangladesh in 1973. Bangladesh is also a party to the Ramsar Convention and the World Heritage Convention. Conservation and sustainable use of biological diversity are applied to the following areas:

— terrestrial biological diversity,

— agricultural biological diversity,

— freshwater biological diversity and

— coastal and marine biological diversity.

Bangladesh signed The International Convention to Combat Desertification in Countries Experiencing Drought and/or Desertification Particularly in Africa in 1994 and ratified it in 1995. Programmes for human resource development and transfer of appropriate technologies are required for managing fragile eco-systems. Cooperation with international development financing agencies and development partners is needed. Financial and technical assistance is required from these international development agencies and development partners. Managerial and technical decisions needed for effective forest management are drafted and initiated by the Forest Department. After the approval of the Ministry of Environment and Forests, the Forest Department executes the decisions. Major financial and administrative decisions are taken by the concerned Ministries of the Government.

The Government of Bangladesh imposed a moratorium on tree felling in 1989 and declared that it would increase the protected area from 5% of total forest area to 10%. It envisages raising forest area to 20% within the next 15 years. Further policy and legal measures are under consideration in the Government in order to arrest the deforestation trend in the country. Institutional strengthening in the forestry sector is a major issue, and the modalities for institutional restructuring are under consideration in the Government in accordance with the guidelines provided by the 20-year Forestry Sector Master Plan. Government agencies such as the Environment Directorate, LGED, NGOs and major international development organizations are involved. Local people, including indigenous people, are also stakeholders in the afforestation programmes of the Government as well as the NGOs. The Forest Department (FD) takes up afforestation programmes covering the whole country and all forest types through participatory mechanisms in every year. Between 1974 and 1995, Bangladesh raised a total of 321,254 ha of plantations of various types.

Among these were 165,954 ha of hill forests, 28,208 ha of plain land Sal Forests, and 127,092 ha of littoral plantations. By using a social forestry approach, the Forest Department is mobilizing a movement involving people from all walks of life to plant trees. The Forest Department is presently pursuing the identified issues of human resource development through recruitment and training, infrastructure and logistics development, genetic improvement of trees through tissue culture and clonal propagation, computerized database development, appropriate technology for in situ and ex situ conservation, etc.

The Forest Department is carrying out an inventory of the Sundarban and Coastal plantations by using the Resource Information Management System (RIMS) facilities. This information will be used to implement the strategies identified under the Integrated Resource Management of Sundarban. RIMS will also be used in the subsequent inventory programmes of the hill forest and plain land Sal Forests. Being a computer-based facility RIMS will also enable the monitoring of changes in the forest resources of the country. The Forest Department is putting a special emphasis on genetic research to meet the growing demand of forest products as quickly as possible. In Bangladesh, National Water Council (NWC), chaired by the Prime Minister, takes decisions and provides policy guidance on key national issues relating to water resources. Decisions are also taken in the interministerial meetings where different agencies involved in water-related projects are represented. In 1983, the National Water Plan, started in 1983, focused on the assessment of water resources and demand by different users. It assembled a substantial amount of information, developed a range of planning models and analytical tools and recommended strategies and programmes, many of which were adopted by the Government.

The Plan also produced a water policy and other proposals to institutionalize the process of water planning and long-term water resources management. Despite these achievements the Plan fell short of a comprehensive national water plan. It was inadequate for evaluating large-scale programmes, impacts and requirements; failed to evaluate properly and integrate a number of major projects and programmes within the sector: inadequately addressed requirements in other

Ministries, viz. fisheries, navigation, public health, industries, municipalities, etc. Under the Flood Action Plan (FAP), a number of projects were evaluated at the prefeasibility level, and possible flood mitigation projects have been identified within a regional context. Implementation of a few priority projects are either under way or ready to commence. Amongst the considerable achievements have been the formulation of standard guidelines for project assessment, participatory planning and environmental impact assessment. On the basis of the FAP studies, a strategy for the development of water resources and the management of water and floods was approved by the Government of Bangladesh in 1995.

The major water user groups are farmers (marginal, landless), fishermen, boatmen, women, indigenous people and local communities. The groups' activities are organized by the local governmental agencies and NGOs. Participatory planning helps address issues of all Project-Affected People (PAP). However, significant use is required for salinity management in the coastal belt, where considerable fresh upland flow is needed during the dry season. In Bangladesh, land-based activities affecting oceans and coasts and needing to be implemented by Bangladesh include:

(i) alternatives for pesticides and insecticides for agriculture;

(ii) industries to be provided with waste recycling equipment;

(iii) new industrial machineries to be designed for producing minimum wastes;

(iv) facilities for storage, recycling and treatment of harmful wastes are to be built.

The Local Government Engineering Department (LGED) has been engaged in various Urban Services Projects with components of solid waste disposal, health and sanitation with other services. The projects through which these services are provided are the Secondary Towns Infrastructure Development Project (STIDP), the Secondary Towns Integrated Flood Protection Project (STIFPP), the Slum Improvement Project (SIP), the Municipal Services Project (MSP), the Urban Poor Reduction Project (UPRP) and the Urban Basic Services Project (UBSP). Technology is needed for recycling, transportation, disposal design improvement, and equipment. Capacity-building will be required at the following levels:

(i) Executive agency level: technical/technological issues, support to local governmental bodies, NGOs/CBOs, beneficiaries;

(ii) Local governmental bodies: technical/technological issues, equipment, linkage with governmental agencies and support to NGOs/CBOs.

Human resource development in the management of hazardous wastes and equipment for detection is necessary. Financial assistance from international development financing agencies and development partners is required for environmentally sound management of hazardous wastes. The Bangladesh Atomic Energy Commission (BAEC) is, in principle, responsible for developing and implementing a national strategy and the necessary infrastructure for the collection, handling, treatment, conditioning, transportation, storage and disposal of radioactive wastes in compliance with the regulatory requirements, duly considering local and socio-economic conditions of the country. Wastes are temporarily stored in the respective places of origin. The proposed waste processing and storage facility will be constructed at AERE, Savar, to meet the current national needs on approval by the competent authority.

Enviornmental Problems of Nepal

Nepal is a Himalayan terrain with hills and mountains covering three quarters of the country's total land area. Because of the pronounced steepness and fragility of the land, there are landslide and erosion problems which limit its productivity. Migration from the hills and mountains to the Terai is likely to continue as new infrastructure increasingly opens up in the south, and as the disparity between incomes in upland and lowland regions continues to grow. The hills and mountains need to be developed in an ecologically sustainable way with the development of watersheds and by providing hydropower to industrial establishments. Growing urbanization, markets and employment accelerate the economy in the hinterlands. This is still a matter of operational research and cautious practices.

The ecologically and economically strained hills and mountains have to develop their unique but intrinsic potential to support the population growth. In Nepal, the National Planning Commission (NPC) is the apex body formulating and monitoring the national plans on sustainable development. People, including farmers, NGOs, and the private sector are involved in this field. This is consistent with the efforts of Nepal which, after restoring a multi-party democracy, has been trying to practice decentralization through participatory decision-making. Agriculture is very important to Nepal as it alone contributes to about 60% of the GDP, and provides employment to nearly 80% of the entire population. The percentages of the total land area used for agriculture are 9.3% in the mountains, 43.1% in the hills and 47.6% in the Terai.

Nepal has to integrate a developmental dimension into land productivity within the Rural Development Programme as well as open up off-farm economic opportunities for industrial development based on the resources available in the mountain terrain. Some studies indicate that the pre- and post-harvest losses in food crops caused by pests and diseases range from 20 to 35%. In 1996, a severe outbreak of rice hopper affecting an area of about 2,000 ha was recorded in the main rice growing belt of the south causing a loss of an estimated NRs 50 million. Nepal may be among the few countries in the world where farmers use traditional botanicalpesticides with considerable success in crop protection. Exploiting these skills, His Majesty's Government of Nepal (HMG/N) has launched an Integrated Pest Management (IPM) Programme in the Kingdom, and IPM has now been endorsed as the national policy.

HGM/N is in the process of establishing a National Steering Committee for the effective launching of the IPM Programme. HMG/N has established Regional Plant Protection Laboratories in five different development regions, though there is still a lack of human resources, equipment and infrastructural support. Nepal is trying to become a member of the International Plant Protection Convention (IPPC), the Asian Plant Protection Convention (APPC) and similar international/regional agencies. Nepal is going to become a member of the WTO for which the Ministry of Agriculture has consituted a core group. The protection of the atmosphere is a worldwide concern and Nepal, as a Least

Developed Country, cannot afford to invest in this issue without compromising its economic growth and development.

With regard to the import and export of substances and products affecting the atmosphere, such as fossil fuels, industrial goods, agricultural chemicals and so forth, different governmental and non-governmental organizations make their own decisions depending on the national policies. There are no institutions or research groups with specific technology for improving the state of the environment. The Department of Hydrology and Meteorology has, to some extent, been supported by the US Government in assessing the nation's vulnerability to the impacts of climate change, and in preparing the national inventory of greenhouse gases.

The Government of Nepal has actively promoted the development of greenhouse gas-free hydropower energy. It is estimated that Nepal has a theoretical hydropower potential of 83,000MW, of which 42,000 MW can be generated according to the economic feasibility studies. The installed hydropower generation capacity in the country is around 233 MW which is less than 0.3% of the total theoretical potential. The Government policy for the massive production of hydropower energy in Nepal has largely been targeted to the vast village communities which otherwise depend on the already dwindling forests and woods which are also the potential carbon dioxide sinks.

Nepal signed the Montreal Protocol (1987) on 6 July 1994 and the London Amendment (1990) signed in 6 July 1994. It signed the United Nations Framework Convention on Climate Change on 2 May 1994. Nepal is trying to develop an innovative, decentralized decision-making process involving the Department for National

Parks and Wildlife Conservation (DNPWC), national NGOs, and international NGOs. The DNPWC needs to expand its staffing and training activities for effective conservation and management. Training of professional, technical as well as administrative staff is necessary in order to strengthen DNPWC's capacity. Nepal signed the Convention on Biological Diversity in 1992, and ratified it in 1993. The Convention on International Trade in Endangered of Wild Fauna and Flora was signed by Nepal in 1975, and the latest report was submitted in 1995.

In Nepal, the Ministry of Forests and Soil Conservation, the National Planning Commission, the Ministry of Finance (MOF), and the Ministry of Population and Environment; at the district level, District D C and District Soil Conservation Offices; and at the community level, user groups. NGOs, and GOs. Active participation of local people is important in land-use planning, forest management, and watershed development. Ecological rehabilitation and specific measures on land and resources have been the appropriate base for sustainable development.

Experiences to date show that planning, decision-making and implementation efficiency is to grow from the grassroots level. Policies for resource management, ecological balance and industrial growth prevail in a broader sphere of human undertakings. Updating policy formulations need to be in terms of achieving the objectives through ensured implementation and of strengthening regional cooperation in specific issues of concern. National and regional activities need to be active simultaneously and be directed towards providing capacity for resource management.

The Department of Soil Conservation is planning, implementing and monitoring the Soil Conservation and Watershed Management (SCWM) Programme through its District Soil Conservation Offices in 45 of 75 districts. The SCWM Programme includes land-use development and improvement, land productivity conservation, erosion hazard prevention, infrastructural protection, and community soil conservation and income generation activities. Nepal needs capacity-building for the technical and professional staff and, at the local level, awareness-building and transfer of technology. Nepal signed the International Convention to Combat Desertification in Countries Experiencing Drought and/or Desertification Particularly in Africa in 1994, and ratified it in 1996. Nepal took an active part in the UN Conference on Desertification, and in the formulation of the UN Plan of Action to Combat Desertification.

For Nepal, being a mountainous country, combating desertification is a matter of great concern both in developmental activities as well as in regional cooperation. Thirty-seven percent (5.4 million ha) of the total land area of Nepal is covered by natural forests, and another 16% is potentially suitable for forest development or for rangeland. Forests are the main natural resources of Nepal. Various programmes have been launched to develop the forestry sector, including forest management programmes under which, for example community groups have been formed. Other programmes have been designed for the production of saplings, for afforestation, and for the implementation of national and leasehold forestry programmes. Programmes related to forests, soil and watershed conservation, and to the production and processing of medicinal herbs, have also been undertaken.

Strengthening the capacities of both the governmental and semi-governmental organizations at all levels, from central to local level, is essential for the successful implementation of these programmes. Similarly, relevant laws and regulations are being reviewed and revised to meet operational needs. People are also more aware of the programme objectives and take more interest in the community forest management and in informing user groups. Nepal's water supply and sanitation authorities have not mobilized enough financial resources to enable them to operate and maintain their systems properly, much less contribute to investments. To make land use and environmental information effective, an appropriate institutional system will be developed under the National Planning Commission by integrating scattered units into a single unit.

Management of land resources has been deemed critical from the point of view of sustainable agricultural production. Improved agricultural output is the only way towards economic growth and poverty alleviation. Soil fertility is a crucial element in determining the productivity of the land. It has been noted that soil fertility is declining in many parts of Nepal, having a negative impact on the yield of the key crops. Changes in farming practices are needed to reverse this trend, and institutional improvements are imperative for agricultural research and extension.

Agricultural policies must be flexible in order to conform to the features of different agro-ecological zones and thus take maximum advantage of the diversity of natural resources. As Nepal adjusts to these essential requirements, the production of food grains, fruit farming and livestock farming will be gradually expanded. In addition, district level planning will have a significant role. Therefore, a mapping system for districts will be developed taking into account different agro-ecological zones. There is a great diversity in the nature of different geographical regions of Nepal. The Terai occupies 23.11%, whereas hills and mountains cover 35.21% and 41.68%, respectively, of the country's total land area.

Eighteeen percent of Nepal's land area is not in use, including barren land, land-slide affected areas, snow-covered land, etc. Of the remaining 82%, 20% is reserved for agricultural purposes. Appropriate programmes relating to mountaineering and other associated arrangements under the Development of Mountain Tourism Programme will be undertaken with the objective of protecting the environment and increasing local employment. Chemical manufacturing industries are now required to obtain a permit. The proponents need to submit IEE or EIA reports depending upon their annual production capacity. Importation of toxic chemicals also requires a permit from the Ministry of Home Affairs.

Among industrial users, to date, very little pollution abatement equipment has been used by industries in Nepal. Investors wishing to maximise profits have opted for the cheapest technology, which, unfortunately, often turns out to be the most polluting one as well. It is the people in general who have to face the consequences of such decisions. Therefore, industries need to adopt less polluting technologies, and for that, His Majesty's Government of Nepal (HMG/N) may need to offer a limited range of subsidies as well as provide the technologies directly. Research has already been carried out in Nepal to identify pollution prone industries. The cement, leather and tanning, paper and pulp, soap and chemicals, sugar and textile industries have all been identified as major sources of various kinds of pollution. HMG adopted the Pesticides Act in 1991, and Pesticides Regulation in 1993.

In accordance with these laws, Nepal has established the Nepal Pesticide Board which will assist the Government in formulating pesticide policies and in adopting regulatory measures for the safe use of these. There are about 10 major importers of pesticides in the country and nearly 100 domestic retail outlets. The predominant users of toxic chemicals, especially pesticides, are farmers who are also over 90% of the Nepalese population. Due to the lack of appropriate Integrated Pest Management technologies, farmers have been largely dependent on using these chemicals for pest control to obtain the expected yield. This has, in isolated cases, begun to cause health and environmental hazards.

Nepal has already prohibited some toxic chemicals like DINOSEB and dinoseb salts, fluoroacetamide, chlordane, chlordimeform, cyhexatine, edb, heptachlor, and mercury compounds. In Nepal, the National Council for Solid Waste Management is responsible for policy formulation at the national level and the Solid Waste Management and Resource Mobilization Center (SWMRMC) is responsible for landfill management in Kathmandu Valley. Local bodies are responsible in the field.

Nepal has a programme on waste management concentrating on street cleaning, waste collection, transport and landfill deposit activities. In urban and suburban areas, solid wastes have been identified as problematic. In 1987, an act was adopted with a view to systematizing waste management in Kathmandu and to seek possibilities of recycling solid wastes into economic resources. In accordance with the act, the Solid Waste Management and Resources Mobilization Center was established. Composting activities were carried out by the Center with successful results, but were dropped for various reasons after 3-4 years. At present, the Center is responsible for the management of sanitary landfill sites, and the rest of the waste management activities are undertaken by municipalities. His Majesty's Government (HMG) adopted a national policy for solid waste management in order to set standards for waste disposal, recycling and reuse. A National Council for Solid Waste Management has been set up under the chairmanship of the Ministry of Local Development.

In addition, the Ministry undertakes major activities in this field. The role of local governments needs to be strengthened as self-contained and active agencies in waste management. The Ministry of Population and Environment is responsible for decision-making on hazardous wastes. At present, Nepal does not perceive itself to have a hazardous waste problem. In the future, activities will be regulated in accordance with the Basel Convention. In November 1996, the Ministry of Population and Environment organized a one-day workshop on the Basel Convention and management of solid wastes in Kathmandu Valley. In the workshop, environmental experts and concerned officials from different governmental and non-governmental organizations discussed national policies and programmes for the control of transboundary movement of hazardous wastes and their disposal. In the conclusions of the workshop it was stressed that national policies need to be revised in accordance with the convention, and that the nature of toxic wastes should be identified so as to minimize their potential risks.

Wastes from hospitals, laboratories, pathological clinics, and the leather industry cause massive harm to human health. In addition, the experts stressed that it is important to see the issue of hazardous waste in a global context as well as a domestic context and to integrate this issue into overall sustainable decision-making.

Enviornmental Problems of Sri Lanka

Sri Lankan National Development Council has appointed a Task Force to recommend policy changes to address issues such as agriculture research, extension, marketing, pricing and the role of the State in providing services and inputs and the role of the private sector in providing inputs, and multiplication and distribution of seeds. Farmers' organizations have been established to strengthen their bargaining power. By the end of 1996, a total of 12,934 farmers' organizations had been established. Farmers' organizations and Samurdhi Animators focus on mobilizing the rural poor to upgrade their skills and create employment opportunities. The Ministry of Agriculture launched an island-wide food drive called 'Vaga Lanka' which aims at combining modern and traditional methods of agriculture. This involves agriculture and the adoption of integrated farming techniques.

The emphasis placed on integrated pest management contributed to a reduction in the use of pesticides in 1996. During this year, the Department of Agriculture conducted Farmer Field Schools for integrated pest management (IPM) in 21 districts and 3 Mahaveli Systems; 800 field-level IPM demonstrations have been conducted in selected areas. Rural credit schemes have provided agricultural loans. A number of policy measures are directed to give an impetus to agricultural exports. Plantation Sector Reforms (privatization) are expected to improve the productivity and efficiency of the Tree Crop Sector.

Agriculture continues to be an important sector in the economy of Sri Lanka, contributing 20 percent of the GNP. Between 1991 and 1995, the agriculture sector was able to absorb 89 percent of the public investments per annum. The Government implemented large irrigation projects, like the Mahaveli Programme, to increase food production and employment opportunities for the rural poor. The Ministry of Environment is the focal point for both Conventions. Interministerial committees have been set up to consider relevant issues and make recommendations. Important decisions need ratification by the Cabinet Ministers. Government Ministries, Departments Statutory Corporations, Universities and NGO groups, are involved in implementing the Montreal Protocol and the UNFCCC.

There was a regional programme on the impact of climate change under SAARC in 1992. Sri Lanka was also a participant in the Regional Study on Global Environmental Issues, funded by the Asian Development Bank in 1992-1993. Sri Lanka signed the Convention on Biological Diversity in June 1992 and ratified it in March 1994. Sri Lanka ratified the Convention on International Trade in Endangered Species of Wild Fauna and Flora on 4 May 1979, and the Convention on the Conservation of Migratory Species of Wild Animals entered into force on 1 September 1990. Major legislative enactments on the biological resources of Sri Lanka are the National Environmental Act 1980, Forest Ordinance, The Flora and Fauna Protection Ordinance, National Heritage Wilderness Areas Act, Botanic Gardens Ordinance,

Fisheries and Aquatic Resources Act, the Plant Protection Ordinance, and the Customs Ordinance.

The preparation of the Biodiversity Action Plan was undertaken in response to Article 6 of the Convention (CITES). While consolidating the ongoing efforts of conservation and sustainable use of biological diversity, the Action Plan aims at establishing a policy and programme regime, which brings national action to various aspects of the subject, including capacity-building and bio-safety measures, in tune with the articles of the Convention. The Government is to adopt this National Biodiversity Action Plan for the conservation and sustainable use of these resources in the near future. Wildlife preservation, in the form of zoos and national farms, is used for the ex-situ preservation of wildlife. Also, efforts are being made to strengthen the legislative framework to derive maximum benefit from biotechnology while minimizing its risks.

The lack of technology and technical capacity, as well as financial constraints, have weakened the national efforts to protect biodiversity. A network of over 100 NGOs has been built up, and biodiversity focal points have been established in development ministries and agencies for environmental advocacy in formulating biodiversity policies. Topographically the island consists of a south central mountainous region which rises to an elevation of 2,502 m and is surrounded by broad lowland plains at an elevation of 0-75 m above sea level. From the mountainous regions nine major rivers and 94 other rivers flow across the lowlands into the Indian Ocean.

Sri Lanka is one of the few countries in South Asia having a wealth of biodiversity. Within a land area of 25,000 sq. miles, this rich biodiversity is distributed within a wide range of eco-systems varying from rainforests to grasslands, freshwater bodies, wetlands and rivers, and coastal and marine eco-systems. An important feature of the climate is that there are two basic eco-zones: a wet zone and a dry zone. Since these two zones are not sharply distinct, there is also what may be termed, an "intermediate" zone gradually merging into the wet and the dry zones. These climatic conditions and the panorama of natural eco-systems in the country support over 3,800 species of flowering plants, of which 23% are endemic, 314 species of fern and derivatives of the fern family. Species diversity is also high among mosses and fungi. In addition, the country has a high faunal diversity.

The diversity of the country's biological resources has not yet been fully surveyed. Conservation and sustainable use of these resources based on the indigenous knowledge systems and practices is ingrained in Sri Lanka's ethos and way of life. The developed countries should ensure that benefits of biotechnology accrue to the country of origin of the biological resources; these benefits to include royalty payments and transfer of technologies to the countries of origin of the biological resources in accordance with the provisions of the Convention. The capacities of biodiversity-rich countries should be built up to enable them to carry out bio-prospecting and undertake technology assessment for protection of their resources.

The introduction of transgenic and alien species should be only with the requisite safeguards. Sri Lanka is trying to build up a bio-technology information network and capacity in the area of taxonomy. The facilities for cryo-preservation of germ plasma in the country are very limited. The Plant Genetic Resource Centre at Peradeniya is the only institution with such facilities and only a fraction of the range of the agricultural germ plasma available in the country is stored at this centre. It is necessary to build capacities and develop programmes for gaining a better understanding of the different components of the country's biodiversity. The country's capacity in the area of taxonomy needs to be built up. The opportunities available for training in this area are limited. The SAARC countries cooperate in identifying regional issues and taking regional and international measures for the conservation and sustainable use of biological resources. However, national action regarding conservation and sustainable use of biodiversity and an equitable share of benefits, demands contributory action on the part of the international community, particularly the developed countries.

The process of development and increase in the number of households is increasing the consumption of energy. It should be emphasized that the consumption of energy by an individual in South Asia is about one-twentieth that of a person in a developed economy. The Ministry of Forestry and Environment lays down policy in consultation with the Department of Forests. The Chief Conservator of Forests implements the programmes. The Cabinet approves major policies and investments on the recommendation of the Ministry. The Government's efforts to arrest deforestation through the enforcement of stringent laws, such as the Forestry Ordinance and the Wild Life Conservation Act, have resulted in limited success. A forestry sector Master Plan was prepared and it was revised in 1993, with the aim to protect and develop forest cover.

NGOs are involved in developing forestry development plans and they contributed in preparing the

5-year forestry development programme which commenced in 1997 with ADB assistance. Environmental groups exercise vigilance and assist law enforcement authorities in the prevention of illicit logging. Deforestation is one of the critical environmental problems in Sri Lanka. Forest cover which stood at 44% of the land area in 1956, declined to 27% by 1981, and the present forest cover is estimated at approximately 23% of the land area. This situation was brought about by both poverty and affluence. Nearly 70% of the people are rural and agriculture-dependent.

The rural poor destroy forests for cultivation and to meet energy needs. The affluent and the entrepreneurs use more and more timber without replacing the forests. The development process has also contributed to deforestation. Sri Lankan national tree planting campaigns are carried out by the Ministry of Forestry and Environment to increase the forest cover in urban areas and to mobilize the energies of school children and youth in promoting reforestation. The Department of Forests trains officials in forestry management. Youth and NGOs participate in tree-planting campaigns. Sri Lankan Water Resources Council is a coordinating body which was established to plan the water resources at the macro level. Decisions are made by respective agencies, and they follow a hierarchical order. All related agencies are represented in the Council and an integrated approach has been adopted for the protection of the quality and supply of freshwater resources.

The Central Environmental Authority (CEA) has published water quality standards as well as standards for industrial effluent that could be discharged into water bodies. Other agencies, such as the Department of

Irrigation and the Department of Agrarian Services, have been alerted to ensure quality water. The Water Resources Board is most concerned about the underground water supply and studies are being undertaken to ascertain the volume of water supplies. The main supplier of drinking water for the urban centres, namely, the National Water and Drainage Board, has a strong programme to monitor the water quality of the Kelani River, before releasing it for drinking purposes. The Community Water Supply and Sanitation Project is ongoing and has improved the sanitation facilities and raised awareness about the need for maintaining hygienic standards in water supply.

A Land-use Planning Unit has been established in the Ministry of Lands with a view to planning development in a sustainable manner and conserving natural resources. This Unit identifies different types of soil for agricultural purposes. There are coastal development laws in which lands are identified for development projects, such as the construction of hotels, taking into account the need to protect the marine environment.

The Department of Fisheries and Coast Conservation, under the Ministry of Fisheries, is responsible for policy-making and implementation. Sri Lanka signed and ratified UN Convention on the Law of the Sea in 1994. The Government of Sri Lanka has various laws, rules, and regulations for dealing with activities in the coastal zone. Regulations have been developed to prevent over-fishing, and the coastal management plan provides for zones to conserve marine species threatened by indiscriminate fishing and the use of inappropriate fishing techniques.

A Coastal Zone Management Plan has been prepared by the Ministry of Fisheries in order to adopt an integrated approach to the management of coastal resources and to involve local communities in the planning and implementation of programmes for the conservation and sustainable use of marine resources and the conservation of the coastline. The policy on coastal fishing has been oriented towards mitigating the adverse effects on the environment and maximizing the protection of fish in a sustainable manner.

A complete inventory of chemicals in use within the country was completed. The International Register of Potentially Toxic Chemicals (IRPTC) database on chemicals is also to be installed. The Ministry of Forestry and Environment is the focal point, and the Central Environment Authority is the competent authority for this convention. Decision-making is also the responsibility of the National Co-ordinating Committee for the implementation of the Basel Convention, chaired by the Secretary, Ministry of Forestry and Environment. Sri Lanka ratified the Basel Convention on the Control of Transboundary Movements of Hazardous Wastes and their Disposal in August 1992. The regulations for the internal management of hazardous waste were published in 1996, by the Ministry of Environment. Regulations for the transboundary movement of hazardous waste are being formulated and will be brought into operation under the Import and Export Control Act. In addition to that, several regulatory measures taken by the Government help indirectly to reduce the pollution caused by high- and medium- polluting industries.

3

Climate Changes in South Asia

Today, the south Asian community faces many risks from climate change. So that it is important to understand the nature of those risks, where natural and human systems are likely to be most vulnerable, and what may be achieved by adaptive responses. While dealing with the climatic changes of South Asia, it is important to consider the Asian continent as a whole, because the climatic changes of various regions of the continent are so interrelated. This chapter presents a detailed account of the reasons and vulnerabilities of climate change in the region and also examines the adaptive measures taken to control its ill-effects.

Asia is the most populous of the continents. Its total population in 1998 is estimated to be about 3,589 million, of which almost 65% is rural. The coastline of Asia is 252,770 km long. Based on broad climatic and geographical features, the Asian region can be divided into four subregions: boreal Asia, arid and semi-arid Asia, temperate Asia, and tropical Asia.

Boreal Asia is located on the northern margins of the Eurasian continent between 50°N and the Arctic Circle. Boreal forests cover most of this region. Siberia, which is a part of Russia, has a mean monthly temperature of about -50°C in January and is the coldest region of the northern hemisphere in winter. Three Siberian rivers-the Ob, the Yenissey, and the Lena-contribute about 42% of total runoff from all rivers of the Arctic basin. In the heart of this region is one of the world's largest and oldest lakes, Baikal, the age of which is estimated to be about 25-30 million years. Lake Baikal contains as much as 85% of Russian surface freshwaters. There is evidence of recession of permafrost in recent decades.

Arid and semi-arid Asia extends from 22°N to 50°N and from 30°E to 105°E; it includes more than 20 countries of the Middle East and central Asia. Many of the countries in the region are landlocked. Many storms develop locally over central Asia; some move into the region from the west. The maximum frequency of cyclones occurs in January and March. Despite this cyclonic activity, very little precipitation is recorded over most of the region because of the lack of moisture. Most of the region has a precipitation-to-potential evapotranspiration ratio of less than 0.45, which is typical of a semi-arid and arid climate. Grasslands, rangelands, and deserts dominate most of arid and semi-arid Asia.

Temperate Asia extends from 22°N to 50°N and from 105°E to 150°E; it includes eastern China, the Japanese islands, the Korean peninsula, Mongolia, and Taiwan. Geographically, the region is located on the eastern part of the Eurasian continent-the world's largest continent-and borders the Pacific, the world's largest ocean. The east-west distance of the area is about 5,000 km; its north-south extent is about 3,000 km. Much of the natural forest in the region has long been destroyed. Broad plains have been cultivated and irrigated, and natural grasslands have been used for animal husbandry for centuries.

Tropical Asia extends from 10°S to 28°N and from 50°E to 150°E; it includes several countries of south Asia, which are influenced predominantly by the monsoons. The region is physiographically diverse and ecologically rich in natural and crop-related biodiversity. Although the present population of the region is principally rural, the region includes seven of the 25 largest cities in the world.

Agriculture is the main industry in several countries of this region. Exploitation of natural resources associated with rapid urbanization, industrialization, and economic development has led to increasing air and water pollution, land degradation, and other environmental problems in countries of this region. Climate change represents a further stress. Over the long period of human occupation in the region, human use systems have developed some resilience to a range of environmental stresses.

Climatic Variations

Temperature

Climate differs widely within Asia. In boreal Asia, the climate generally is humid and cool; it is classified as continental type. Permafrost covers as much as 90% of boreal Asia. An average annual mean increase in surface air temperature of about 2.9°C in the past 100 years has been observed in boreal Asia. Warming was more pronounced during the period 1951-1995 in all of boreal Asia region except for the coast of the Arctic Ocean and Chukotka. The mean surface air temperature increase is most pronounced in the winter, at a rate of approximately 4.4°C over the past 100 years. Summer temperatures in central Siberia have exhibited decreasing trends, however.

The climate of arid and semi-arid Asia is the warm temperate type, with hot and wet or dry summers. The highest value of diurnal temperature range (DTR) is experienced in this region. A mean maximum temperature of >45°C in July is not uncommon in some parts of arid Asia. In most of the Middle East, the long time series of surface air temperature shows a warming trend. An increasing tendency in spatially averaged seasonal and annual air temperatures has been observed in Kazakhstan over the past century. Maximal warming has occurred in spring. The mean annual surface temperature has risen by about 1.3°C during 1894-1997; in the arid regions of China, air temperature has obviously increased since the 1970s. In Pakistan, annual mean surface temperature has a consistent rising trend since the beginning of 20th century.

In temperate Asia, the average annual mean surface temperature in Mongolia has increased by approximately 0.7°C over the past 50 years; consequently, noticeable changes have taken place in the length of the cold and warm seasons. Surface temperature in northeast China has increased in winter but decreased in summer since 1905; observations also reveal a 1-2°C decrease in temperature in some parts of southeastern China. In Japan, the surface air temperature has shown a warming trend during the past century.

Tropical Asia has a unique climatological distinction because of the pervasive influence of the monsoon. In tropical Asia , climate uniformity is differentiated by three factors: latitude, relief, and continentality. The entire tropical Asia region stretches over 38° in latitude, so the differences resulting from this factor are pronounced. In spite of some differences, the climates of countries have one factor in common: The Asian monsoon modulates them all to a large extent. For countries near the Equator, only small seasonal variations occur, although most countries in this region experience clearly marked cold and warm seasons. The spatial range of temperature in this region is significantly large during winter. Extreme temperatures of over 45°C occur over the northwest part of the region during May-June.

Several countries in this region have reported increasing surface temperature trends in recent decades. In Vietnam, annual mean surface temperature has increased over the period 1895-1996, with mean warming estimated at 0.32°C over the past 3 decades. Annual mean surface air temperature anomalies over Sri Lanka during the period 1869-1993 suggest a conspicuous and gradually increasing trend of about 0.30°C per 100 years. The warming trend over India has been reported to be about 0.57°C per 100 years.

Rainfall

Rainfall in boreal Asia is highly variable on seasonal and inter-annual as well as spatial scales. The time series of annual mean precipitation in Russia suggests a decreasing trend; these tendencies have amplified during 1951-1995, especially in warm years. In long-term mean precipitation, a decreasing trend of about -4.1 mm/ month/100 years has been reported in boreal Asia.

During the past 10-15 years, however, precipitation has increased, mostly during the summer-autumn period. As a result of this increase in precipitation, water storage in a 1-m soil layer has grown by 10-30 mm. The large upward trends in soil moisture have created favourable conditions for infiltration into groundwater. The levels of major aquifers have risen by 50-100 cm; the growth of groundwater storage has resulted in increasing ground river recharge and considerable low-water runoff.

Annual mean rainfall is considerably low in most parts of the arid and semi-arid region of Asia. Moreover, temporal variability is quite high: Occasionally, as much as 90% of the annual total is recorded in just 2 months of the year at a few places in the region. Rainfall observations during the past 50 years in some countries in the northern parts of this region have shown an increasing trend on annual mean basis. A decreasing trend in annual precipitation for the period 1894-1997 has been observed in Kazakhstan. The precipitation in spring, summer, and autumn, however, has shown slight increasing trends. In Pakistan, seven of 10 stations have shown a tendency toward increasing rainfall during monsoon season.

In temperate Asia, the East Asian monsoon greatly influences temporal and spatial variations in rainfall. Annual mean rainfall in Mongolia is 100-400 mm and is confined mainly to summer. Summer rainfall seems to have declined over the period 1970-1990 in Gobi; the number of days with relatively heavy rainfall events has dropped significantly. In China, annual precipitation has been decreasing continuously since 1965; this decrease has become serious since the 1980s. The summer monsoon is reported to be stronger in northern China during globally warmer years. On the other hand, drier conditions have prevailed over most of the monsoon-affected area during globally colder years.

In tropical Asia, hills and mountain ranges cause striking spatial variations in rainfall. Approximately 70% of the total annual rainfall over the Indian subcontinent is confined to the southwest monsoon season (June-September). The western Himalayas get more snowfall than the eastern Himalayas during winter. There is more rainfall in the eastern Himalayas and Nepal than in the western Himalayas during the monsoon season.

The annual mean rainfall in Sri Lanka is practically trendless; positive trends in February and negative trends in June have been reported, however. In India, long-term time series of summer monsoon rainfall have no discernible trends, but decadal departures are found above and below the long time averages alternatively for 3 consecutive decades.

Recent decades have exhibited an increase in extreme rainfall events over northwest India during the summer monsoon. Moreover, the number of rainy days during the monsoon along east coastal stations has declined in the past decade. A long-term decreasing trend in rainfall in Thailand is reported. In Bangladesh, decadal departures were below long-term averages until 1960; thereafter they have been much above normal.

Severe Weather Systems

Apart from intraseasonal and interannual variability in climate, extreme weather events such as heat waves associated with extreme temperatures, extratropical and tropical cyclones, prolonged dry spells, intense rainfall, tornadoes, snow avalanches, thunderstorms, and dust storms are known to cause adverse effects in widely separated areas of Asia. There is some evidence of increases in the intensity or frequency of some of these extreme weather events on regional scales throughout the 20th century, although data analyses are relatively poor and not comprehensive.

Some mountains in Asia have permanent glaciers that have vacated large areas during the past few decades, resulting in increases in glacial runoff. As a consequence, an increased frequency of events such as mudflows and avalanches affecting human settlements has occurred. As mountain glaciers continue to disappear, the volume of summer runoff eventually will be reduced as a result of loss of ice resources. Consequences for downstream agriculture, which relies on this water for irrigation, will be unfavorable in some places.

A large number of severe floods also have occurred in China, predominately over the middle and lower basins of the Yangtze, Huanghe, Huaihe, and Haihe Rivers. Severe flooding with daily rainfall exceeding 25 cm struck during July and August 1998 in Korea. In Japan, drought disasters are significantly more frequent during years following ENSO warm events than in normal years.

Floods, droughts, and cyclones are the key natural disasters in tropical Asia. The average annual flood covers vast areas throughout the region: In Bangladesh, floods cover 3.1 Mha; the total flood-prone area in India is about 40 Mha. In India, chronically drought-affected areas cover the western parts of Rajasthan and the Kutch region of Gujarat. However, drought conditions also have been reported in Bihar and Orissa States in India.

In Bangladesh, about 2.7 Mha are vulnerable to drought annually; there is about 10% probability that 41-50% of the country is experiencing drought in a given year. Drought or near-drought conditions also occur in parts of Nepal, Papua New Guinea, and Indonesia, especially during El Niño years. In India, Laos, the Philippines, and Vietnam, drought disasters are more frequent during years following ENSO events.

At least half of the severe failures of the Indian summer monsoon since 1871 have occurred during El Niño years. In the event of enhanced anomalous warming of the eastern equatorial Pacific Ocean, such as that observed during the 1998 El Niño, a higher frequency of intense extreme events all across Asia is possible.

Scenarios of Future Climate Change

Increases in atmospheric concentrations of GHGs from anthropogenic activities would warm the earth-atmosphere system. The radiative forcing inferred from likely future increases in GHGs and sulfate aerosols as prescribed under IS92a emission scenarios has been used in recent numerical experiments performed with coupled atmosphere-ocean global climate models (AOGCMs). Projections of future regional climate change and also most of the impact assessment studies for Asia cited herein are based on these numerical experiments.

To develop climate change scenarios on regional scales, it is first necessary to examine if the coupled AOGCMs are able to simulate the dynamics of present-day regional climate. The multi-century control integrations of AOGCMs unforced by anthropogenic changes in atmospheric composition offer an excellent opportunity to examine the skill of individual models in simulating the present-day climate and its variability on regional scales. A model validation exercise carried out for Asia and its subregions has indicated that each of these models shows large seasonal variations in surface air temperature over boreal Asia and only small seasonal variations over southeast tropical Asia.

Seasonal variations in observed precipitation over the South Asia region as a consequence of summer monsoon activity are poorly simulated by most of the models. Moreover, none of the seven models can reproduce the observed precipitation climatology over the Tibetan Plateau.

One important aspect of the observed temperature change over the globe during the past century relates to its asymmetry during the day and night. Observed warming in surface air temperatures over several regions of the globe has been reported to be associated with an increase in minimum temperatures and a decrease in DTR.

AOGCM simulations with increasing concentrations of GHGs in the atmosphere suggest relatively more pronounced increases in minimum temperature than in maximum temperature over Asia on an annual mean basis, as well as during the winter, for the 2050s and the 2080s-hence a decrease in DTR. During the summer, however, an increase in DTR is simulated-suggesting thereby that the maximum temperature would have a more pronounced increase relative to the minimum temperature.

The summertime increase in DTR over central Asia is significantly higher relative to that in other regions. Most of the subregions follow the same pattern of change in DTR, except south and southeast Asia. A marginal increase in DTR during the winter and on an annual mean basis is simulated over southeast Asia. Over the south Asia region, a decrease in DTR on an annual mean basis and during the winter and a more pronounced decrease in DTR during the summer are projected.

The significantly higher decrease in DTR over south Asia during the summer is a result of the presence of monsoon clouds over the region. In general, the decline in DTR is slightly moderated in the presence of sulfate aerosols. Changes in DTR over Asia in this case suggest a decrease in both seasons. Similar changes also are seen over boreal Asia and temperate Asia.

In general, all AOGCMs simulate an enhanced hydrological cycle and an increase in annual mean rainfall over most of Asia. An area-averaged annual mean increase in precipitation of 3±1% in the 2020s, 7±2% in the 2050s, and 11±3% in the 2080s over the land regions of Asia is projected as a result of future increases in the atmospheric concentration of GHGs. Under the combined influence of GHGs and sulfate aerosols, the projected increase in precipitation is limited to 2±1% in the decade 2020s, 3±1% in the 2050s, and 7±3% in the 2080s.

The increase in precipitation is maximum during NH winter for both the time periods. Clearly, intermodel differences in projections of precipitation are relatively large particularly during the winter even when they are averaged for the entire Asian continent-suggesting low confidence in projections of future precipitation in current AOGCMs. The increase in annual mean precipitation is projected to be highest in boreal Asia.

During the winter, boreal Asia and the Tibetan Plateau have the most pronounced increase in precipitation. Over central Asia, an increase in winter precipitation and a decrease in summer precipitation are projected. Because the rainfall over this region is already low, severe water stress conditions-leading to expansion of deserts-are quite possible with a rise in surface air temperature here. The area-averaged annual mean and winter precipitation is projected to increase in temperate Asia. The models show high uncertainty in projections of future winter and summer precipitation over south Asia.

The effect of sulfate aerosols on Indian summer monsoon precipitation is to dampen the strength of the monsoon compared to that seen with GHGs only. The overall effect of the combined forcing is at least partly dependent on the land/sea distribution of aerosol forcing and on whether the indirect effect is included along with the direct effect. To date, the effect of aerosol forcing (direct and indirect) on the variability of the monsoon has not been investigated.

Recent observations suggest that there is no appreciable long-term variation in the total number of tropical cyclones observed in the north Indian, southwest Indian, and southwest Pacific Oceans east of 160°E. For the northwest subtropical Pacific basin, Chan and Shi found that the frequency of typhoons and the total number of tropical storms and typhoons has been more variable since about 1980.

Several studies have considered likely changes in tropical cyclones. Some of these studies suggest an increase in tropical storm intensities with carbon dioxide (CO_2)-induced warming. Some of the most pronounced year-to-year variability in climate features in many parts of Asia has been linked to ENSO. Since the SAR, analysis of several new AOGCM results indicates that as global temperatures increase, the Pacific climate will tend to resemble a more El Niño-like state.

Collins finds an increased frequency of ENSO events and a shift in their seasonal cycle in a warmer atmosphere: The maximum occurs between August and October rather than around January as currently observed. Meehl and Washington indicate that future seasonal precipitation extremes associated with a given ENSO event are likely to be more intense in the tropical

Indian Ocean region; anomalously wet areas could become wetter, and anomalously dry areas could become drier during future ENSO events.

Several recent studies have confirmed earlier results indicating an increase in interannual variability of daily precipitation in the Asian summer monsoon with increased GHGs. Lal et al. also report an increase in intraseasonal precipitation variability and suggest that intraseasonal and interannual increases are associated with increased intraseasonal convective activity during the summer.

The intensity of extreme rainfall events is projected to be higher in a warmer atmosphere, suggesting a decrease in return period for extreme precipitation events and the possibility of more frequent flash floods in parts of India, Nepal, and Bangladesh. However, Lal et al. found no significant change in the number and intensity of monsoon depressions in the Bay of Bengal in a warmer climate. Because much of tropical Asia is intrinsically linked with the annual monsoon cycle, a better understanding of the future behaviour of the monsoon and its variability is warranted for economic planning, disaster mitigation, and development of adaptation strategies to cope with climate variability and climate change.

Although these AOGCMs treat the complex interactions of atmospheric physics and planetary-scale dynamics fairly well, coarse horizontal resolution in the models restricts realistic simulation of climatic details on spatial variability. Although most global climate models (GCMs) are able to simulate the large-scale monsoon circulation well, generally they are less successful with the summer monsoon rainfall. Since the SAR, nested modeling approaches have been followed to generate high-resolution regional climate scenarios with more realistic mesoscale details and the response of GHG forcings to the surface climatology over the Asian monsoon region.

Large-scale patterns of temperature change simulated by GCMs and nested regional climate models (RCMs) are found to be generally similar under 2 x CO_2 forcing, but the regional model results present some additional details associated with coastline and local topographical features. In addition, projected warming over eastern China region in the summer is less pronounced in the RCM than in the GCM and is characterized by a different spatial pattern. This is related to an increase in monsoon precipitation simulated by the RCM there and associated surface cooling induced by evaporation and cloudiness. Nonetheless, the GCM and RCM simulations suggest a general increase in warming toward higher latitudes and greater warming in winter than in summer. The RCM produces a more pronounced increase in winter precipitation over southeastern China than does the GCM in response to orographic lifting of stronger low-level southerly onshore winds. The RCM also simulates increased precipitation in the monsoon rain belt over east China, Korea, and Japan during the summer.

The increase in surface air temperature simulated by the RCM over central and northern India is not as intense as in the GCM and does not extend as far south. These anomalies are linked with changes in surface hydrological variables. Summer precipitation exhibits a more complex pattern of increases and decreases. Whereas an increase in rainfall is simulated over the eastern region of India, northwestern deserts see a small decrease in the absolute amount of rainfall in RCM simulation.

Changes in soil moisture broadly follow those in precipitation except in eastern India, where they decrease as a result of enhanced drainage from the soil. The largest reductions are simulated in the arid regions of northwest India and Pakistan. The projected increase in precipitation in flood-prone Bangladesh is approximately 20%. Nested RCM simulations have the potential to simulate the onset of the summer monsoon and its active/break cycle over India. The RCM captures the observed precipitation maximum over the southern tip of India during weak monsoon conditions, whereas the GCM does not. Given the current state of climate modeling, projections of future regional climate have only limited confidence.

The degree of confidence that could be attributed to RCM responses in terms of temporal and spatial changes resulting from GHG forcings would depend on more accurate simulation of the space and time evolution of large-scale monsoon circulation features in AOGCMs , as well as additional long-term RCM simulations with better skill.

Current efforts on climate variability and climate change studies increasingly rely on diurnal, seasonal, latitudinal, and vertical patterns of temperature trends to provide evidence for anthropogenic signatures. Such approaches require increasingly detailed understanding of the spatial variability of all forcing mechanisms and their connections to global, hemispheric, and regional responses. Because the anthropogenic aerosol burden in the troposphere would have large spatial and temporal variations in the atmosphere, its future impact on regional scale would be in striking contrast to the impact from GHGs. It has also been suggested that aerosols produced by tropical biomass burning could lead to additional negative radiative forcing. Considerable uncertainty prevails about the indirect effect of aerosols on tropospheric clouds, which could strongly modulate the climate. The implications of localized radiative forcing on deep convection in tropical Asia and on Hadley circulation are still not understood.

Vulnerabilities of Climate Changes

An examination and analysis of the climate change-induced vulnerabilities in Asia has to be undertaken against the backdrop of the physical, economic, and social environment of the countries in the region. They provide not only the benchmark against which vulnerabilities are to be assessed but also the potential for adaptation to them. Surface water and groundwater resources in Asian countries play vital roles in forestry, agriculture, fisheries, livestock production, and industrial activity. The water and agriculture sectors are likely to be most sensitive to climate change-induced impacts in Asia.

Climate change in boreal Asia could have serious effects on climate-dependent sectors such as agriculture, forestry, and water resources. Climate change and human activities, for example, may influence the levels of the Caspian and Aral Seas, with implications for the vulnerability of natural and social systems. The increase in surface temperature will have favourable effects on agriculture in the northernmost regions of Asia, and a general northward shift of crop zones is expected. However, as much as a 30% decrease in cereal production from the main agriculture regions of boreal Asia by 2050 has been projected.

A decrease in agriculture productivity of about 20% also is suggested in southwestern Siberia. Forest ecosystems in boreal Asia could suffer from floods and increased volume of runoff, as well as melting of permafrost regions. Model-based assessments suggest that significant northward shifts in natural forest zones are likely in the next 50 years. There also is growing anxiety that significant increases in ultraviolet radiation, as observed in recent years, could have serious implications for ecosystems along the Arctic shore of Siberia.

In arid and semi-arid Asia, the climate limits the portion of land that presently is available for agriculture and livestock production. Croplands in many of the countries in the region are irrigated because rainfall is low and highly variable. The agriculture sector here is potentially highly vulnerable to climate change because of degradation of the limited arable land. Almost two-thirds of domestic livestock are supported on rangelands, although in some countries a significant share of animal fodder also comes from crop residues.

The combination of elevated temperature and decreased precipitation in arid and semi-arid rangelands could cause a manifold increase in potential evapotranspiration, leading to severe water-stress conditions. Many desert organisms are near their limits of temperature tolerance. Because of the current marginality of soil-water and nutrient reserves, some ecosystems in semi-arid regions may be among the first to show the effects of climate change. Climate change has the potential to exacerbate the loss of biodiversity in this region.

The major impacts of global warming in temperate Asia will be large northward shifts of subtropical crop areas. Large increases in surface runoff-leading to soil erosion and degradation, frequent water logging in the south, and spring droughts in the north-ultimately will affect agriculture productivity.

The volume of runoff from glaciers in central Asia may increase three-fold by 2050. Permafrost in northeast China is expected to disappear if temperatures increase by 2°C or more. The northern part of China would be most vulnerable to hydrological impacts of climate change; future population growth and economic development here may exacerbate seriously the existing water shortage. Deltaic coasts in China would face severe problems from sea-level rise. Sea-level rise also will expand the flood-prone area and exacerbate beach erosion in Japan.

In monsoon Asia, the issue of sensitivity of physical and natural systems to the hydrological cycle is linked to major stresses caused by projected climate change on agricultural production and increased exposure of social and economic systems to impacts of extreme events, including forest die-back and increased fire risk; typhoons and tropical storms; floods and landslide; and human disease impacts. These stresses on physical systems translate into key social vulnerabilities, particularly in combination with unsustainable utilization of resources.

Conversion of natural forests to palm oil plantations in many southeast Asian countries during recent decades increased the probability of uncontrolled forest fires and increased health and biodiversity impacts during the 1997 ENSO event. The ecological security of mangroves and coral reefs may be put at risk by climate change. Sea-level rise could cause large-scale inundation along the coastline and recession of flat sandy beaches of south and southeast Asia. Monsoons in tropical Asia could become more variable if ENSO events become stronger and more frequent in a warmer atmosphere.

Vulnerability relates to social or natural systems and is delineated as such. The issues of social and physical vulnerability to climate change are directly related because the major sensitivities of ecological and natural systems across the regions of Asia translate into risks to socioeconomic systems. Social vulnerability is defined as the degree to which individuals or groups are susceptible to impacts; the determinants of social vulnerability are exposure to stress as a result of the impacts of climate change and the underlying social position.

Climate variability and change, both natural and anthropogenic, cause a wide range of direct and indirect impacts on natural and human systems. To understand which adaptation opportunities will be most cost-effective and have the greatest value, emphasis must be given to characteristics of system vulnerability, such as resilience, critical thresholds, and coping ranges, which are highly dependent on regions and nations. In this respect, lessons learned from past experiences regarding climate variability and change provide essential understanding of processes, actions, and successes.

The impacts of climate change and other drivers of environmental degradation are likely to be felt more severely in developing countries than in developed countries of Asia, irrespective of the magnitude of climate change, because of the poor resource and infrastructure bases. The developing countries need to scope the development of adaptation strategies incrementally to support development of existing policies that exploit "no regret" measures and "win-win" options. Detailed and reliable regional scenarios of climate change need to be developed and used in rigorous vulnerability analysis.

In developing countries, adaptation responses are closely linked to developmental activities. Consequently, there are likely to be large spillover effects between adaptation policies and developmental activities. Care in this regard must be taken in the evaluation of adaptation costs and benefits. In developing countries of Asia, options such as population growth control, poverty alleviation, and capacity building in food production, health care delivery, and water resource management hold great potential in creating more resilient social systems that are capable of withstanding the negative impacts of climate change.

Despite global technological and economic development, a large proportion of the nearly 1.5 billion people living in severe poverty at the dawn of the new millennium are located in Asia. Global per capita water supplies are declining and are now 30% lower than they were 25 years ago. By 2050, as much as 42% of the world's population may have to live in countries within sufficient freshwater stocks to meet the combined needs of agriculture, industry, and domestic use. The world's population will reach at least 8.9 billion by the middle of the 21st century.

India and China alone now account for 38% of the world's population. Most of the additional population would be in developing countries. These countries are likely to suffer adverse agricultural responses; significant changes in seasonal runoff; possibly severe vector-borne diseases; increased risks of severe tropical weather disturbances, including storms; vulnerability to sea-level rise; and other stresses.

Impacts on Ecosystems

Relatively hospitable mountain regions in Asia are under pressure from human settlements and commercial cultivation, which have led to land degradation and adverse effects on water supply. Ongoing changes in different mountain systems within Asia include those associated with high crop production and those characterized by extensive animal husbandry and pastureland.

Human encroachment in mountain regions has reduced vegetation cover, which has increased soil moisture evaporation, erosion, and siltation-with adverse effects on water quality and other resources. Changes in the snowfall pattern have been observed in mountain and highland systems, particularly in the Himalayas. These changes will have wider implications-from marked impact on the monsoon regime to seasonal runoff and vegetation cover, including agriculture. Changes in the hydrological regime also will trigger episodes of extreme events.

One-tenth of the world's known species of higher altitude plants and animals occur in the Himalayas. In addition, some countries in Asia are centers of origin for many crop and fruit-tree species; as such, they are important sources of genes for their wild relatives. Biodiversity is being lost in these regions because of human activities, especially land degradation and the overuse of resources.

In 1995, approximately 10% of known species in the Himalayas were listed as threatened, and the number of species on the verge of extinction has increased since then. As a consequence of global warming, the present distribution of species in high-elevation ecosystems is projected to shift to higher elevations, although the rates of vegetation change are expected to be slow and colonization success would be constrained by increased erosion and overland flows in the highly dissected and steep terrains of the Himalayan mountain range. Weedy species with a wide ecological tolerance will have an advantage over others.

High-elevation tree species-such as Abies, Acer, and Betula-prevail in cold climates because of their adaptations to chilling winters. In Japan, the area of suitable habitat at higher elevations has shrunk over the past 30 years, and the variety of alpine plants that grow there has been rapidly reduced. Increases in temperature would result in competition between such species and new arrivals. The sensitivity of alpine flora to climatic factors and, in particular, water stress in the summit region of Mt. Kinabalu-the highest mountain in southeast Asia-already have been demonstrated. The accumulated stresses of climate change are likely to disrupt the ecology of mountain and highland systems.

Impacts on Lakes, Streams, Rivers, and Glaciers

Lakes, streams, glaciers, and other freshwater ecosystems in Asia are highly diversified in terms of plant and animal species. These freshwater ecosystems have been stressed by environmental burdens, exploitation of natural resources, transformation of lands, and recreational activities. There is growing concern that climate change may accelerate the damage to freshwater ecosystems such as lakes, marshes, and rivers.

More than 50,000 ha of coastal territories, including 35,000 ha of delta in the Selenga River and 12,000 ha of delta in the Upper Angara River, have been damaged during the past few years by precipitation and riverflow increases. With an increased amount of precipitation likely in the future, more incidences of flooding and other adverse impacts are possible.

With a rise in temperature, a decrease in the amount of snowfall in the Lake Biwa catchment in Japan is projected-which might exacerbate the process of eutrophication. Deterioration of lake water quality also is suggested in Kasumigaura Lake in eastern Japan. The response of lakes and streams to climate change will involve complex interactions between the effects of climate on areal inputs, hydrology, and catchments and in-lake processes.

Many of the major rivers in Asia have long been targets for development projects related to the hydroelectric, water supply, agriculture, industry, and navigation sectors. As a consequence, there have been shifts between freshwater and estuarine conditions as a result of high freshwater flows during the rainy season and low to nonexistent freshwater flows in the dry season. Increasing literol vegetation is causing health risks for local habitats in many countries of south Asia.

Changes in aquatic habitat also have affected fisheries in lower valleys and deltas; the absence of nutrient-rich sediments has detrimental effects on fish productivity. Reduced flows in lower valley catchments also have resulted in eutrophication and poor water quality. Many rivers originate from the glaciers in the

Tianshan mountain range, which create wide alluvial fans at the foot of the northern Tianshan.

The Hindukush Himalayan ranges are the source of some major rivers. The total amount of water flowing from the Himalayas to the plains of the Indian subcontinent is estimated at about 8.6 x 10 6 m 3 per year. The Himalayas have nearly 1,500 glaciers; it is estimated that these glaciers cover an area of about 33,000 km^2. These glaciers provide snow and the glacial meltwaters keep major rivers perennial throughout the year.

In recent decades, the hydrological characteristics of watersheds in this region seem to have undergone substantial change as a result of extensive land-use change-leading to more frequent hydrological disasters, enhanced variability in rainfall and runoff, extensive reservoir sedimentation, and pollution of lakes. Almost 67% of the glaciers in the Himalayan and Tienshan mountain ranges have retreated in the past decade.

The mean equilibrium-line altitude at which snow accumulation is equal to snow ablation for glaciers is estimated to be about 50-80 m higher than the altitude during the first half of the 19th century. Available records suggest that Gangotri glacier is retreating by about 30 m yr^{-1}. A warming is likely to increase melting far more rapidly than accumulation.

Impacts on Forests, Grasslands, and Rangelands

Most of the frontier forests in Asia are endangered today by rapid population growth, ever-increasing demand for agricultural land, poverty, poor institutional capacity, and lack of effective community participation in forestry activities. Climate change is expected to affect the boundaries of forest types and areas, primary productivity, species populations and migration, the occurrence of pests and diseases, and forest regeneration.

The increase in GHGs also affects species composition and the structure of ecosystems because the environment limits the types of organisms that can thrive and the amount of plant tissues that can be sustained. Compositional and structural changes, in turn, affect ecosystem function. The interaction between elevated CO_2 and climate change plays an important role in the overall response of net primary productivity to climate change at elevated CO_2.

Climate change will have a profound effect on the future distribution, productivity, and health of forests throughout Asia. Because warming is expected to be particularly large at high latitudes, climate change could have substantial impact on boreal forests.

Global warming will decrease permafrost areas, improve growing conditions, and decrease areas of disturbed stands and ecosystems in a general sense, although impacts would be significantly different at various locations within the boreal forests. Moreover, forest fire is expected to occur more frequently in boreal Asia as a result of increased mean temperature. Pest activity also could increase with a rise in temperature, depending on the age composition of the boreal forests.

Asia's temperate forests are a globally important resource because of their high degree of endemism, biological diversity, ecological stability, and production potential. About 150 Mha of forests in central China have been cleared during the past several decades. Efforts are now underway to at least partially restore the area under forest cover in China through reforestation, soil recovery, and water conservation programs. Studies on projected impacts of climate change suggest that northeast China may be deprived of the conifer forests and its habitat, and broad-leaved forests in east China may shift northward by approximately 3° of latitude. These results are based on a 2°C increase in annual mean temperature and a 20% increase in annual precipitation.

Tropical moist forests have trees with higher densities of wood and larger proportions of branch wood relative to those in temperate forests. As many as 16 countries of tropical Asia are located within the humid tropical forest region. These forests and woodlands are important resources that must be safeguarded, given the heavy use of wood as fuel in some countries. Past policies in the humid tropics have focused mainly on natural forest protection and conservation. However, there is a need to shift emphasis from conservation alone to a strategy that involves sustained development, investment performance, and public accountability.

Encouragingly, the current annual rate of reforestation is highest in tropical Asia as a result of relatively high investments in reforestation schemes, including social forestry. Most semi-arid lands in Asia are classified as rangelands, with a cover of grassland or scrublands. Although the share of land area used for agricultural purposes is about 82% of the total area, it is mainly low-productive pastures. With an increase in temperature of 2-3°C combined with reduced precipitation as projected for the future in the semi-arid and arid regions of Asia, grassland productivity is expected to decrease by as much as 40-90%.

Approximately 70% of pastures are facing degradation, with dramatic decreases in fodder yield over recent decades in some parts of Mongolia. Rangelands in Nepal also have been subject to degradation in recent years. Climate change is likely to represent an additional stress to rapid social change in many of Asia's rangelands.

Impacts on Drylands

Precipitation is scarce and has a high annual variance in dryland areas. Very high daily temperature variance is recorded with frequent sand storms, dust ghost, and intense sunshine. Arid plants usually belong to drought escaper, drought evader, drought resister, or drought endurer categories. Evaporative losses and water limitations are the most prominent factors dictating animal life in arid environments. Low rainfall dictates the formation of shallow or extremely sallow soils that often are characterized by high content of airborne particles and small fractions of rock-erosion elements.

Most of the soils are poor in or completely devoid of organic matter, and the nutrient pools of the soils are low. Apparently, humans not only utilize the ecosystem services of this region but are also influencing the evolution of some of its important biotic elements.

Soils exposed to degradation as a result of poor land management could become infertile as a result of climate change. Temperature increases would have negative impacts on natural vegetation in desert zones. Plants with surface root systems, which utilize mostly precipitation moisture, will be vulnerable. Climate change also would have negative impacts on sheep breeding and lamb wool productivity. Just as shifts in vegetation belts are expected in non-drylands, in the drylands of Asia a shift in dryland types is expected as a result of climate change. Drylands are ranked along an aridity index, in relation to the ratio of precipitation to potential evapotranspiration. Because soil moisture is likely to decline in this region, the least-dry land type are expected to become semi-arid, and semi-arid land is expected to become arid.

Population pressure on dryland resources is reduced with increasing aridity, but resistance to degradation and resilience following degradation also is reduced with increasing aridity. Therefore, semi-arid drylands, which are intermediate in aridity as compared to arid drylands and dry subhumid ones, are most susceptible to becoming further desertified. Because semi-arid drylands are very common among Asian drylands, large areas will become not only dry but also desertified as a result of climate change.

Impacts on Permafrost

Permafrost is highly responsive to climatic fluctuations at several temporal and spatial scales. Evidence of spatially extensive episodes of permafrost thawing and poleward contraction has been documented. Depending on regional climate and local biological, topographic, and edaphic parameters, pronounced warming in the high latitudes of Asia could lead to thinning or disappearance of permafrost in locations where it now exists. Poleward movement of the southern boundary of the sporadic permafrost area is likely in Mongolia and northeast China. Large-scale shrinkage of the permafrost region in boreal Asia also is likely.

The development of thermokarst and thermal erosion because of perennial thawing and increase in the depth of seasonal thawing of ice-rich grounds and monomineral ice accumulations is a critical process in permafrost regions of boreal Asia . The change in rock temperature will result in a change in the strength characteristics, bearing capacity, and compressibility of frozen rocks, generation of thermokarst, thermal erosion, and some other geocryological processes.

In response to projected climate change, four main economic sectors in permafrost regions-surface and underground construction, the mining industry, heating energy demand, and agricultural development-will be affected. Because large quantities of carbon are sequestered in the permafrost of boreal peatlands and tundra regions, changes in distribution of frozen ground and systematic increase in the thickness of seasonally thawed layer are likely to result in the release of large amounts of CO_2 and possibly methane (CH_4) into the atmosphere.

The permafrost area on the Tibetan Plateau has an average altitude of about 5,000 m and is one of the several regions not significantly affected by direct human activities. Because of this area's thermal and moisture conditions are on the edge of the ecological limitations of vegetation, it is believed to be highly sensitive to global warming. The boundary between continuous and discontinuous permafrost areas on the Tibetan Plateau are likely to shift toward the center of the plateau along the eastern and western margins.

Impacts on Protected Areas

Protected areas usually are designated and managed to keep wild species that live within the area from becoming extinct. Even after an area has been set aside as protected habitat, extinction or population declines may still occur as a result of changes in environmental conditions related to climate change, land use in surrounding areas, or widespread pollution.

Climate change is likely to induce vegetation change that will force wild plant and animal species to shift their distribution in response to the new conditions. For example, a variety of changes in butterflies, dragonflies, beetles, and other migratory insects have been recorded in green corridors of Japan in recent years, and shifts have been recorded in the ranges of many North American, European, Arctic, and Antarctic bird and insect species.

If the protected area is not large enough to contain an area that will be suitable under the new climate conditions, a species may become locally extinct. In contrast, protected areas that are large enough to cover an elevation or a latitudinal gradient should allow species to make adjustments along the gradient as conditions change. In some cases, such as in coastal areas, habitat may simply be lost as a result of factors such as sea-level rise, with no potential area for species to migrate.

Frontier forests in Asia are home to more than 50% of the world's terrestrial plant and animal species. Risks to this rich array of living species are increasing. For instance, of the 436 species of mammals and 1,500 species of birds in Indonesia, more than 100 species each of mammals and birds have been declared threatened. Similar trends also are seen in China, India, Malaysia, Myanmar, and Thailand.

In India, as many as 1,256 higher plant species, of more than 15,000 species, are threatened. Coastal areas are likely to be at risk from climate change-induced sea-level rise. A rise in the water level of estuaries will reduce the size and connectedness of small islands and coastal and estuarine reserves and increase their isolation.

The Yangtze and Mekong deltas on mainland China and the Mai Po marshes in Hong Kong are refueling stops for migratory birds, especially ducks, geese, and shorebirds. The presence of these birds may be threatened by the disappearance of coastal marshes as a result of increases in sea level from global warming.

Similarly, the Rann of Kutch in India supports one of the largest Greater Flamingo colonies in Asia. With sea-level rise, these salt marshes and mudflats are likely to be submerged, which would result in decreased habitat for breeding flamingoes and lesser floricans. In addition, about 2,000 Indian wild asses in the Rann of Kutch could lose their only habitat in India to rising sea level.

The Sundarbans of Bangladesh, which support a diversity of wildlife, are at great risk from rising sea level. These coastal mangrove forests provide habitat for species such as Bengal tigers, Indian otters, spotted deer, wild boars, estuarine crocodiles, fiddler crabs, mud crabs, three marine lizard species, and five marine turtle species. With a 1-m rise in sea level, the Sundarbans are likely to disappear, which may spell the demise of the tiger and other wildlife.

Species that live in mountainous areas also are particularly at risk of losing habitat as a result of changes in climate. Extreme temperature conditions may cause these protected areas to undergo major changes, partly because of high rates of variation in habitat structure that naturally occur on mountain ranges as a result of changes in slope, steepness, and exposure. Protected areas also may be subjected to extreme surface runoffs because of rapid melting of winter snow. Because many Asian mountain ranges are east-west oriented, there will be little room for species to shift their ranges toward cooler mountainous habitat.

An additional barrier to wildlife movements in mountainous habitat derives from the fact that many of the larger reserves in central Asia are located along international borders. Depending on topography, if these borders are heavily fenced, most of the larger terrestrial vertebrates will not be able to respond spatially to changes in their environment.

Besides loss of habitat, wild species are at risk from changes in environmental conditions that favor forest fires and drought. For example, forest fires under unseasonably high temperatures in Nepal may threaten local extinction for red pandas, leopards, monkeys, deer, bears, and other wild animals. If the frequency of these extreme events increases, the frequency of fire also may increase. Similarly, increases in the frequency of dry spells and local droughts may decrease populations. For example, drought-related decreases in the density and persistence of Green Leaf Warblers have been recorded on their wintering grounds in the Western Ghats of south India.

In desert ecosystems, protected areas often are located around oases, which are the basis for the existence of much of the local fauna. Protected oases often are far apart, so droughts that cause a decline in local forage often cause mass mortality because animals may not be able to move on to adjacent oases. The frequency of these droughts therefore is a key component in the viability of populations in such protected areas.

Climate change is likely to act synergistically with many other stressors, such as land conversion and pollution, leading to major impacts on protected areas and species. Currently designated major protected areas in Asia need to be examined with respect to the ability of their species to shift in range in response to changing climate, as well as with respect to how much habitat could be lost. Many species-especially those in coastal areas and mountainous habitats-could experience large population declines; some may become extinct at least in part because of climate changes.

Impacts on Agriculture

Asia has the world's largest area under cereal cultivation and is the largest producer of staple foods. Present crop yields in Asia are comparable to those in Europe and South America. Within Asia, India has the largest area under cereal cultivation. The total production of cereals in China is twice that of India, as a result of higher average productivity. Most land that is suitable for cultivation is already in use; by 2010 per capita availability of land in developing countries of Asia will shrink from the present 0.8 ha to about 0.3 ha. Current rates of land degradation suggest that a further 1.8 million km^2 of farmland could become unproductive in Asia by 2050, adding stress to a system that must ensure food security in the context of a rapidly growing population.

Rice is central to nutrition in Asia. In 1997, rice provided about 700 kilocalories per person per day or more for approximately 2.9 billion people, most of whom live in developing countries of Asia and Africa. During the 1990s, rice production and productivity in Asia grew at a much slower rate than did population. Yield deceleration of rice in Asia has been attributed to water scarcity, indiscriminate addition and inefficient use of inputs such as inorganic fertilizers and pesticides, and policy issues and the reliance on a narrower genetic material base with impacts on variability. Several other factors also have contributed to productivity stagnation and the decline of rice (lower output/input ratio) in the intensive cropping system (two to three rice crops per year). Key factors currently contributing to the yield gap in different countries of Asia include biophysical, technical/management, socioeconomic, institutional/policy, technology transfer, and adoption/linkage problems.

Urbanization in Asia has accentuated increased demand for fresh vegetables; this demand is to be met by new production areas combined with more intensified horticulture crop management to raise the productivity per unit of land and water. In most cases, urban and peri-urban agriculture initiatives with uncontrolled use of agrochemicals are a high-risk activity.

Adequate steps need to be taken at regional and local levels to safeguard specialized and diversified urban production systems (vegetables, fruits, and root crops) through sustainable intensification of natural resource use and strengthening of decision support systems. Increased productivity and sustained production of food grains and legumes, industrial crops (oil, gum and resins, beverage, fiber, medicines, aromatic plants), and horticultural crops through crop diversification is critical for food and nutritional security in Asia.

Even minor deviations outside the "normal" weather range seriously impair the efficiency of externally applied inputs and food production. Moisture stress from prolonged dry spells or thermal stress resulting from heat-wave conditions significantly affect the agricultural productivity when they occur in critical life stages of the crop.

Stress on water availability in Asia is likely to be exacerbated by climate change. Several studies aimed at understanding the nature and magnitude of gains or losses in yield of particular crops at selected sites in Asia under elevated CO_2 conditions and associated climatic change have been reported in the literature. These studies suggest that, in general, areas in mid- and high latitudes will experience increases in crop yield, whereas yields in areas in the lower latitudes generally will decrease. Climatic variability and change will seriously endanger sustained agricultural production in Asia in coming decades. The scheduling of the cropping season as well as the duration of the growing period of the crop also would be affected.

In general, increased CO_2 levels and a longer frost-free growing season are expected to enhance agricultural productivity in north Asia. The area under wheat cultivation is likely to expand in the north and west. The increase in surface temperature also may increase the growing season in temperate Asia, thereby prolonging the grain-filling period, which may result in higher yields.

In tropical Asia, although wheat crops are likely to be sensitive to an increase in maximum temperature, rice crops would be vulnerable to an increase in minimum temperature. The adverse impacts of likely water shortage on wheat productivity in India could be minimized to a certain extent under elevated CO_2 levels; these impacts, however, would be largely maintained for rice crops, resulting in a net decline in rice yields. Acute water shortage conditions combined with thermal stress should adversely affect wheat and, more severely, rice productivity in India even under the positive effects of elevated CO_2 in the future.

More than 10,000 different species of insect pest are found in the tropics, 90% of which are active in the humid tropics. The occurrence, development, and spread of crop diseases depend on integrated effects of pathogen, host, and environmental conditions. The survival rate of pathogens in winter or summer could vary with an increase in surface temperature.

Higher temperatures in winter will not only result in higher pathogen survival rates but also lead to extension of cropping area, which could provide more host plants for pathogens. Thus, the overall impact of climate change is likely to be an enlargement of the source, population, and size of pathogenic bacteria. Damage from diseases may be more serious because heat-stress conditions will weaken the disease-resistance of host plants and provide pathogenic bacteria with more favourable growth conditions.

The population growth rate has been a primary factor in the increase in demand for food grains in Asia. Since the mid-1980s, rapid changes in food supply and demand structures have been observed in most developing countries. Declines in self-sufficiency for grains have been particularly dramatic in countries with advanced economies, such as Japan, South Korea, Taiwan (China), and Malaysia, where the grain self-sufficiency rate has fallen below 30% in recent years. The rapid decline in grain self-sufficiency in these countries is unprecedented in any region of the world. Between 1970 and 1996, grain self-sufficiency fell from 45 to 27% in Japan, from 68 to 31% in Korea, from 61 to 19% in Taiwan

(China), and from 60 to 25% in Malaysia. Declines in grain self-sufficiency also have been observed in the Philippines, Indonesia, and Sri Lanka.

Populous countries such as China, India, Bangladesh, and Pakistan have long maintained grain self-sufficiency of more than 90%, but as these countries shift to industrialization it is possible that declines will be observed there as well. In contrast, Thailand and Vietnam, which encompass the great grain-producing regions of the Menam and Mekong River deltas, continue to maintain better than 100% self-sufficiency for grains.

The annual per capita consumption of meat in principal Asian countries also has shown an upward trend in recent years. Since the 1970s, South Korea and China have reported the most rapid increases in meat consumption. In South Korea, per capita meat consumption grew about seven-fold, from 5.2 to 40 kg between 1970 and 1997; in China, it increased nearly five-fold, from 8.8 to 42.5 kg. During the same period, per capita meat consumption more than doubled in Japan and Malaysia.

Meat consumption in Sri Lanka, Bangladesh, and India grew only marginally, remaining below or at 5 kg even in 1997-considerably lower than the level in east Asia. The increasing trend in meat consumption in temperate Asia means higher demand for livestock feed for the production of meat. Demand for this feed in Asia increased from 25.2 Mt in the 1970s to 61.2 Mt in 1980, 147.0 Mt in 1990, and 163.0 Mt in 1999. The demand for feed grain in Asia has grown at an annual rate of about 6.6% and has been a principal factor in the rapid increase in demand for world grain imports.

The world is moving toward a tighter grain supply and demand, and instability in the world grain market is rising. At the same time, Asia is becoming increasingly dependent on the world grain market. The impact of global warming on the international supply and demand of rice and wheat has been evaluated by Nakagawa et al. through the use of a partial equilibrium-type dynamic model for world supply and demand. Based on a world rice and wheat supply and demand model and a unit harvest scenario, the study projected that the serious impacts of global warming would be felt as early as the year 2020. The study suggests that the early impacts will not be so severe that humans are unable to control them. However, the gap between supply and demand may grow in some regions of Asia, resulting in considerably increased reliance on imports. Furthermore, the problem of short-term fluctuations in the market because of an increased frequency of droughts, floods, and other extreme weather events will be exacerbated, making it necessary to promote measures to combat climate change on a global scale.

Food Security Issues

A major new challenge in future food production to meet the demand of the growing Asian population is in coping with the changing environment, which may alter the current optimum growing requirement of agricultural crops. The potential impacts of climate change on agriculture in Asia are crucial because of agriculture's ultimate role in providing food and fiber to Asia's human population.

Countries in south and southeast Asia have shown strong reductions in undernourished population in the

1990s. Even so, it has been estimated that almost two-thirds (more than 500 million) of undernourished people live in developing countries of Asia and the Pacific. South Asia accounts for more than one-third of the world total (258 million).

Another 64 million undernourished people live in southeast Asia; more than 160 million live in China. The undernourished population almost doubled between 1995 and 1999-from 6 to 12%-as a result of the economic crisis in Indonesia. With the highest incidences of undernutrition and a very large population of children under the age of five, south Asia accounts for almost half of the world's underweight and stunted children.

Ongoing studies on crop productivity in relation to global warming cover not only biophysical aspects but also socioeconomic drivers and consequences. The economic impacts of climate change on world agriculture are expected to be relatively minor because decreasing food production in some areas will be balanced by gains in others. Such findings however, should be viewed as aggregate results that mask crucial differences in inter-country and intra-country production impacts and the distribution of food resources.

In Asia, where rice is one of the main staple foods, production and distribution of rice-growing areas may be affected substantially by climate change. Disparity between rice-producing countries is already visible, and it is increasingly evident between developed and developing countries. The projected decline in potential yield and total production of rice in some Asian countries because of changes in climate and climate variability would have a significant effect on trade in agricultural commodities, hence on economic growth and stability.

Increasing population growth and changing dietary patterns in Asia have resulted in more and more land moving from forests and grasslands into agricultural production. Regardless of the increased use of chemical fertilizers and pesticides, in addition to changes in irrigation practices and improved seed stock, yields for major cereal crops have stagnated in many Asian countries during recent years; further intensification of agriculture on area in cropland is certain, and conversion of more land to agricultural use is likely, especially in the developing countries of Asia. Both actions will have far-reaching implications with regard to increased soil erosion, loss of soil fertility, loss of genetic variability in crops, and depletion of water resources. Soil degradation is seemingly irreversible unless remedied through painstaking reconstruction of soil health.

A clear understanding of the relationship between climatic variability, crop management, and agricultural productivity is critical in assessing the impacts of climatic variability and change on crop production, the identification of adaptation strategies and appropriate management practices, and the formulation of mitigating measures to minimize the negative effects of climatic variability on agricultural productivity. In the future, food security will be at the top of the agenda in Asian countries because of two emerging events: growing population, and many direct and indirect effects of climate change. Greatly enhanced efforts to understand the relationship between key climate elements and agriculture should provide a sound basis for meeting the challenges of optimizing the benefits of changing climatic resources.

In some Asian countries, the pace of food grain production has slowed in recent years as a result of depletion of soil nutrients and water resources, creation of salinity and water logging, resurgence of pests and diseases, and increased environmental pollution.

Many natural as well as environmental factors-such as extremely dry or cold climates, erratic rainfall, storms and floods, topsoil erosion and severe land degradation, and poor investment and lack of appropriate technology-have played limiting roles in the agricultural potential of most developing countries of Asia. For example, food grain production in Pakistan and India has continued to increase since the 1970s while it has stagnated in Bangladesh, largely because of increased losses to climate extremes and land degradation.

In India, the estimated total requirement for food grains would be more than 250 Mt by 2010; the gross arable area is expected to increase from 191 to 215 Mha by 2010, which would require an increase of cropping intensity to approximately 150%. Because land is a fixed resource for agriculture, the need for more food in India could be met only through higher yield per units of land, water, energy, and time-such as through precision farming.

To ensure food security in the developing countries of south and southeast Asia, it is necessary to expand agricultural production, develop the food distribution system, and promote nutrition education, as well as expand the economy and adjust the distribution of incomes.

Impacts on Hydrology and Water Resources

One-third of the world's renewable water resources are concentrated in Asia. Water availability varies widely across the different regions of Asia, however-from 77,000 m 3 yr^{-1} per capita to less than 1,000 m 3 yr^{-1} per capita.

The major share of Asian water resources (72%) is located in four countries: Russia, China, Indonesia, and India. Water resources of the two largest river systems of Asia—the Ganges (with Brahmaputra and Meghna) and the Yangtze —attain 1,389 km 3 yr^{-1} and 1,003 km^3 yr^{-1}. The runoff distribution within a year in Asia is most uniform in the rivers of southeast Asia. Over the rest of the continent, more than half of the annual runoff is discharged during the three summer months.

Water availability is expected to be highly vulnerable to anticipated climate change. Growing populations and concentration of population in urban areas will exert increasing pressures on water availability and water quality. Runoff generally is expected to increase in the high latitudes and near the equator and decrease in the mid-latitudes under anticipated climate change scenarios.

Some areas of the Asian continent are expected to experience increases in water availability; other areas will have reduced water resources available. Surface runoff is projected to decrease drastically in arid and semi-arid Asia under climate change scenarios and would significantly affect the volume of water available for irrigation and other purposes. Sensitivity of Japanese rivers and lakes also are sensitive to climate change. Recent studies suggest that, on average, a 3°C increase in temperature coupled with a 10% increase in precipitation will increase river flows by approximately 15% in water abundant areas. An increase in temperature also accelerates snow melting, which increases river flows from January through March but decreases flows from April through June.

The perennial rivers originating in the high Himalayas receive water from snow and glaciers. Snow, ice, and glaciers in the region are approximately equivalent to about 1,400 km 3 of ice. The contribution of snow to the runoff of major rivers in the eastern Himalayas is about 10% but more than 60% in the western Himalayas. Because the melting season of snow coincides with the summer monsoon season, any intensification of the monsoon is likely to contribute to flood disasters in Himalayan catchments. Such impacts will be observed more in the western Himalayas compared to the eastern Himalayas because of the higher contribution of snowmelt runoff in the west.

An increase in surface runoff during autumn and a decrease in springtime surface runoff are projected in highland regions of south Asia. The increase in surface temperature also will contribute to a rise in the snowline-which, in effect, reduces the capacity of the natural reservoir. This situation will increase the risk of flood in Nepal, Bangladesh, Pakistan, and north India during the wet season. No significant changes are projected for annual mean surface runoff in southeast Asia; an increase during winter and a decrease during summer season is likely, however.

Available data on the dynamics of freshwater use by natural-economic regions of Asia suggest that freshwater use-in terms of total water withdrawal and water consumption-have increased significantly in recent decades in all regions and is projected to increase further in the 21st century.

At present, approximately 57% of total water withdrawal and 70% of water consumption in the world occurs within the countries of Asia. Agriculture accounts for 81% of total water withdrawal and 91% of water consumption in Asia. The area of irrigated lands in Asia currently amounts to 175 Mha and may increase to 230 Mha by 2025.

The two most populated regions of south and southeast Asia account for about 68% of water withdrawal and about 69% of water consumption in Asia More than 75% of the total water available in India currently is used for irrigation. As much as 20% is required to meet domestic and municipal needs-leaving just 5% for industrial needs. The only river in north India that has surplus water to meet future needs of the country is the Brahmaputra. This river, however, is an international river; other countries such as Bangladesh may not approve of building a dam across some of its tributaries.

In peninsular India, only the Mahanadi and Godavari have surplus water, but conveying it to drought-prone areas of the south is problematic. Many states in India need to adopt measures for restricting the use of groundwater to prevent a water famine in the future. China's rapid economic growth, industrialization, and urbanization-accompanied by inadequate infrastructure investment and management capacity-have contributed to widespread problems of water scarcity throughout the country.

Taking into account projected dynamics of economic development in the temperate, tropical, and arid and semi-arid regions of Asia, combined with the climate change-imposed effect on hydrological regimes, agriculture and the public water supply would require priority attention in these regions to secure sustainable development and avoid potential intersectoral and international water conflicts. Radical changes in water management strategies and substantial investments will be required in Asia to cope with water problems in the 21st century.

Adaptation measures will include legal, institutional, and technical initiatives such as modifying existing and constructing new infrastructure, introducing water-saving technologies, upgrading efficiency of irrigation systems, enhancing waste-water recycling systems, introducing low water-use crops, and implementing groundwater protection programs.

At least 14 major international river watersheds exist in Asia. An integrated and decentralized system of restoration and conservation of the water cycle in these drainage basins is vital to mitigate the negative consequences of natural and externally imposed perturbations. Watershed management is challenging in countries where the people-to-land ratio is high and policy and management are inadequate, prompting use of even the most fragile and unsuitable areas in the watersheds for residential, cultivation, and other intensive uses. This is particularly true for countries such as Bangladesh, Nepal, the Philippines, Indonesia, and Vietnam, where many watersheds suffer badly from deforestation, indiscriminate land conversion, excessive soil erosion, declining land productivity, erratic and unreliable surface and groundwater resources, and loss of biodiversity.

Many watersheds in Asia already are stressed by intensive use of the land and other resources and by inhospitable climate, beyond their ability to adequately supply water, prevent floods, and deliver other goods and services. In the absence of appropriate adaptation strategies, these watersheds are highly vulnerable to climate change.

Impacts on Oceanic and Coastal Ecosystems

In line with global trends, more than half of the region's population-1.7 billion people-presently resides in the coastal zone of Asia. Given the relentless and cumulative process of global environmental change driven by, among other factors, demographic changes, urbanization and industrial development, trade and transport demands, and lifestyle changes, the coastal zones of Asia are under increasing anthropogenic pressures. The consequences of this process pose a significant threat to environmental and socioeconomic systems located in Asian coastal zones. All coastal areas are facing an increasing range of stresses and shocks, the scales of which now pose a threat to the resilience of human and environmental coastal systems and are likely to be exacerbated by climate change.

Climate impacts on coastal zones of Asia include accelerated sea-level rise and more frequent and severe storm events. Large populations in coastal areas of southeast and south Asia are vulnerable to pressure from unsustainable resource use and environmental degradation. These areas already are subject to numerous climate change-related stresses, including loss of coastal mangroves that act as major environmental determinants of coastal fisheries.

Major delta areas of Asia are likely to be subjected to stresses associated with sea-level rise, changes in water regimes, saltwater intrusion, siltation, and land loss. Low-lying coastal cities will be at the forefront of impacts; these cities include Shanghai, Tianjin, Guangzhou,

Jakarta, Tokyo, Manila, Bangkok, Karachi, Mumbai, and Dhaka-all of which have witnessed significant environmental stresses in recent years. In addition, increases in temperature can lead to increased eutrophication in wetlands and freshwater supplies.

Tropical Asia experiences the impact of present-day climate variability associated with ENSO, therefore is more prone to changes in ENSO-related impacts with global climate change. The ENSO phenomenon is a major cause of year-to-year variability in the number of cyclones in the Asia Pacific region. The numbers are higher during La Niña events, particularly late in the season over southeast Asia. The 1982-1983 El Niño caused a decline in rainfall and associated impacts over large areas, including parts of Indonesia. El Niño events are known to have significant impacts on coastal areas and water resources in southeast Asia through decreased precipitation in El Niño years and increased frequency of typhoons in subsequent La Niña years.

Sea levels of interior seas in arid and semi-arid Asia have dramatically changed, driven either by climatic or anthropogenic factors. The level of the Caspian Sea lowered by about 4 m from 1930 to 1977; since 1978 it has begun rising. The coastline also propagated landward by 20-40 km; 2 Mha of farming land and more than 100 oil wells have been inundated.

Many cities in the coastal zone, such as Makhachkala and Kaspisk, are seriously damaged. The Volga delta propagated 17 km during the period of lowering sea level but has retreated 12-15 km during the period of the rise in sea level. Caspian Sea level fluctuations are attributed mainly to the Volga water discharge controlled by climate anomalies in its catchment area. The Aral Sea area also reduced, from 60,000 to 28,500 km^2, in the period 1960-1989; the exposed seabed (particularly deltas) now have frequent dust and salt storms, and there are shortages of freshwater.

River-borne sediments have formed at least 10 deltas in the coastal zones of Asia with an area of more than 10,000 km^2 each. Delta and estuarine ecosystems are sensitive to complex responses to agents associated with climate change. Low-lying deltas are especially vulnerable to sea-level rise and increasing shoreline wave action.

A decrease in river water discharge, as projected under some climate change scenarios, could lead to hindrance of delta progradation and increase the risk of irreversible change for the ecosystem in estuarine-deltaic areas. Tidal rivers and estuaries will become more prone to saltwater intrusion as a result of projected sea-level rise. Sea-level changes associated with global warming would be exacerbated by tectonic submergence, ground subsidence as a result of groundwater withdrawal, rise of water level created by delta progradation, and eustatic sea-level rise.

Low-lying muddy coastlines associated with large deltas form a significant resource and support large human populations. Beach erosion is widespread in the coastal zone of Asia and has been reported in China, Japan, Indonesia, Sri Lanka, Thailand, Bangladesh, and Malaysia.

Coastal wetlands frequently are associated with deltas, estuaries, lagoons, and sheltered bays. Tidal flats of the muddy coast in Asia constitutes the main part of the coastal wetland. Large-scale wetland reclamation in the major deltas has taken place during the past few decades. Lagoons, which are important wetlands, are located across the coastal regions of India, Sri Lanka, Malaysia, Indonesia, China, and Russia. The transitional area between uplift and subsidence belts has favoured the formation of lagoons along China's coastline. These lagoons tend to be decreasing in area as a result of silting of sediments and plant growing. Sea-level rise and reduction of river-borne sediments will decelerate delta progradation and wetland renewal. The rich biodiversity of wetlands in Asia is seriously threatened by loss of wetlands from sea-level rise.

Mangroves are made up of salt-adapted evergreen trees; they are restricted to the intertidal zone along the vast coastlines of tropical countries in Asia and extend landward along tidal rivers. The Sundarbans in Bangladesh and adjacent areas in India, covering about 6,000 km^2, are the largest mangrove forests in the world. Depletion of mangrove forests by anthropogenic pressures has become a serious problem.

Approxmately half of mangrove forests in Thailand were reduced by 56% during 1961-1996. In the Philippines, more than 75% of the mangrove forests have been lost in less than 70 years. Destruction of Indonesia's estimated 44,000 km^2 of mangroves has taken place mainly since 1975.

Mangrove forests are highly vulnerable to climate change-induced sea-level rise because it will change the salinity distribution and hence productivity. Large-scale changes in species composition and zonation in mangrove forests also are expected as a result of changes in sedimentation and organic accumulation, the nature of the coastal profile, and species interaction.

Impacts on Coral Reefs

Coral reefs play a crucial role in fishery production and in protecting the coastline from wave action and erosion. Southeast Asia has almost one-third of the world's mapped coral reefs; these reefs extend to the northern extreme range in Japan. Coral reef productivity is a function of their structure, biological recycling, and high retention of nutrients. Reefs in Indonesia and the Philippines are noted for extraordinarily high levels of biodiversity: Each contains at least 2,500 species of fish. Severe coral bleaching can occur as a result of seawater warming and clear skies.

Major coral bleaching events have occurred in 1983 (Japan, Indonesia), 1987 (Maldives), 1991 (Thailand, Japan), 1995 (Thailand, Philippines), and 1998 (Maldives, Sri Lanka, India, Indonesia, Thailand, Japan, Malaysia, Philippines, Singapore, Vietnam, Cambodia). As a result of the major 1998 coral bleaching in the south Asia region, many reefs dominated by branching species have been severely damaged, with high mortality of these species. In coastal seas around the Maldives, Sri Lanka, the Andaman Islands of India, and Japan, reef community structure has switched from dominance by fast-growing branching species to monopolization by the more physically rigorous and slow-growing massive corals.

Deforestation in many island countries of Asia and quarrying of live corals for manufacture of calcium carbonate have led to significant coral decline or severe damage to the entire ecosystem. Studies show that a moderate rise in sea level around the coast of Thailand would stimulate the growth of coral reef flats and extend corals shoreward. The enhanced growth potential is likely to be restricted by human infrastructure and development along the coast.

Asia's coral reefs are undergoing rapid destruction in terms of habitat richness as a result of several factors, including extreme temperatures and solar irradiance, subaerial exposure, sedimentation, freshwater dilution, contaminants, and diseases. The increase in atmospheric CO_2 concentration and consequent rise in sea surface temperature (SST) is likely to have serious damaging effects on reef accretion and biodiversity.

Impacts on Fisheries and Aquaculture

Asia dominates world aquaculture, producing four-fifths of all farmed fish, shrimp, and shellfish. Farming of fish, shrimp, shellfish, and seaweeds has become a vital source of food supply in Asia in recent decades. Fishery products are staples for the Asian population and are embedded in its culture. Fish, an important source of food protein, is critical to food security in many countries of Asia, particularly among poor communities in coastal areas. The annual fish catch and aquaculture production in Asia reached a peak at about 20.7 and 19.1 Mt, respectively, in the year 1998. Japan has the largest distant-waters fishery production. Inland fishery production is dominated by China and India, which have shown increases in recent years as a result of stock enhancement practices.

Fish farming requires land and water-two resources that already are in short supply in many countries in Asia. Nearly half of the land now used for shrimp ponds in Thailand was formerly used for rice paddies; water diversion for shrimp ponds has lowered groundwater levels noticeably in coastal areas of Thailand. In China, concern over the loss of arable land has led to restrictions on any further conversion of farmland to aquaculture ponds. Intensive production systems and large-scale facilities used to raise high-value shrimp, salmon, and other premium species has taken a heavy toll on coastal habitats, with mangrove swamps in southeast Asia being cleared at an alarming rate. Thailand lost more than 15% of its mangrove forests to shrimp ponds from 1987 to 1993. Destruction of mangroves has left these coastal areas exposed to erosion and flooding, altered natural drainage patterns, and increased salt intrusion.

The fishery resources of Japan, China, and many other countries of Asia are being depleted by overfishing, excessive use of pesticides, industrial pollution, red tide, and even construction of dikes and other coastal structures. Loss of inshore fish nursery habitats to coastal development, as well as pollution from land-based activities, causes significant change to ecosystems supporting fisheries. Marine productivity is greatly affected by temperature changes that control plankton shift, such as seasonal shifting of sardine in the Sea of Japan and induced during the cyclical occurrence of the ENSO in low latitudes.

The impact of global warming on fisheries will depend on the complicated food chain, which could be disturbed by sea-level rise, changes in ocean currents, and alteration of mixing layer thickness. Anomalies in the water temperatures of major oceanic currents have resulted in low commercial fish catch in recent years. The steady wintertime decrease in mean wind speed observed over the Sea of Japan between 1960 and 1990 has accelerated surface temperature increase and stagnated bottom water formation in recent years.

Fish production of certain species may decrease because of the decline of river volume. Increases in marine culture products and declines in marine fishery output are current trends in most south Asian countries that are engaged in commercial fishery activity. It is likely that increased surface run-off and higher nutrient load might lead to potentially beneficial increases in plankton within the coastal zone of boreal Asia. However, increased frequency of El Niño events, which are likely in a warmer atmosphere, could lead to measurable declines in plankton biomass and fish larvae abundance in coastal waters of south and southeast Asia. Such declines in lower levels of the food chain will have negative impacts on fisheries in Asia.

Tropical Cyclone and Storms

Asia is close to the warm pool of the west equatorial Pacific Ocean, and tropical cyclones and associated storm surges strongly affect coastal zones of tropical and temperate Asia. Tropical cyclones and storm surges are one of most critical factors affecting loss of human lives in India and Bangladesh. Approximately 76% of the total loss of human lives from cyclonic storms has occurred in India and Bangladesh. Several Asian countries are faced with cyclones and associated storm surges every year, which causes serious economic losses.

There is concern that global warming may affect tropical cyclone characteristics, including intensity, because SST plays an important role in determining whether tropical disturbances form and intensify. Several researchers have used modeling techniques to examine the possible effects of global warming on tropical storms.

Lighthill et al. conclude that there is no reason to expect any overall change in global tropical cyclone frequencies, although substantial regional changes may occur. Recent studies indicate that the maximum potential intensities of cyclones will possibly undergo a modest increase of as much as 10-20% in a warmer atmosphere. More recent analyses support the possibility of an increase in cyclone intensity. Coastal erosion in Asia should increase with sea-level rise, and storm surges could still exacerbate hazards, even if the number and intensities of tropical cyclones do not change.

Coastal Zone Management

Climate-related stresses in coastal areas include loss and salinization of agricultural land resulting from changes in sea level, likely changes in the intensity of tropical cyclones, and the possibility of reduced productivity in coastal and oceanic fisheries.

Human activities, including protection facilities themselves, aggravate the vulnerability of the coastal regions to climate change and sea-level rise. There are complex interrelationships and feedbacks between human driving forces and impacts, on one hand, and climate- and sea level-induced changes and effects on the other. At the interface between ocean and terrestrial resources, coastal ecosystems undergo stress from competing multi-usage demands, while having to retain their functional diversity and resilience in the face of global environmental change.

To enhance coastal resilience and facilitate adaptation, integrated management of coastal zones must take into account the multiple resource demand and variety of stakeholders, as well as natural variability, recognizing the importance of the institutional, cultural, and historical context.

Integrated coastal zone management (ICZM) is an iterative and evolutionary process for achieving sustainable development by developing and implementing a continuous management capability that can respond to changing conditions, including the effects of climate change. Essentially, ICZM is a cooperative effort on the part of coastal zone stakeholders that results in a "win-win" outcome. ICZM already has been developed and implemented in some Asian countries for the allocation of environmental, sociocultural, and institutional resources to achieve conservation and sustainable multiple use of the coastal zone.

Sri Lanka conserves coastal tourism resources by using ICZM principles. Coastal natural conservation parks have been established in Bangladesh, Thailand, China, and other countries. However, land ownership and management responsibility issues in Bangladesh have inhibited coastal zone management. Similarly, privatization and decentralization of storm protection systems in Vietnam have created a vacuum for strategic management and increased the potential impacts of climate variability. Given that many potential climate change impacts on coastal zones feature irreversible effects, surprise outcomes, and unpredictable changes, the appropriate policy response should be to maximize flexibility and enhance the resilience and adaptation potential of these areas. By contrast, coastal management in Asia to date more often than not has been dominated by policies that have sought to buffer socioeconomic activities and assets from natural hazards and risks via hard engineering protection.

Health Impacts

A remarkable increase in the number of heatstroke patients and mortality was observed when maximum daily temperatures in Nanjing, China, exceeded 36°C for 17 days during July 1988. In Japan as well, intense heat in summer is now becoming more common in large cities. The numbers of heatstroke patients are reported to have increased exponentially with temperatures of more than 31°C in Tokyo, Japan, and 35°C in Nanjing, China. Beyond a maximum daily temperature of 36°C, a remarkable increase in the number of heatstroke patients and deaths caused by heatstroke has been observed. Typical hyperthermia occurs during hot days and during physical exercise in the summer.

Climate change will have a wide range of health impacts all across Asia. Although a reduction in health stresses and wintertime deaths is anticipated as a result of less frequent occurrence of extreme cold temperatures in boreal and temperate Asia, an increase in the frequency and duration of severe heat waves and humid conditions during the summer will increase the risk of mortality and morbidity, principally in older age groups and urban poor populations of temperate and tropical Asia. Heat stress-related chronic health damages also are likely for physiological functions, metabolic processes, and immune systems.

Adverse health impacts also result from the build-up of high concentrations of air pollutants such as nitrogen dioxide (NO_2), ozone, and air-borne particulates in large urban areas. Combined exposures to higher temperatures and air pollutants appear to be critical risk factors for cerebral infarction and cerebral ischemia during the summer months. The heat index and the concentration of

NO_2 are shown to be significant risk factors for heatstroke in males age 65 years and older residing in Tokyo, Japan. The number of heatstroke emergency cases per million residents is found to be greater in males than in females in the same age groups. Global warming also will increase the incidences of some diseases, such as respiratory and cardiovascular diseases, in arid and semi-arid, temperate, and tropical Asia.

Health impacts secondary to the impacts of climate change on ecological and social systems should include changes in the occurrence of vector-borne infectious diseases in temperate and tropical Asia. The distribution of diseases such as malaria is influenced by the spread of vectors and the climate dependence of infectious pathogens.

In recent years, the resistance of anopheline mosquito to pesticides and of malaria parasites to chloroquine has affected eradication activities. Malaria still is one of the most important diseases in countries in tropical Asia such as India , Bangladesh, Sri Lanka, Myanmar, Thailand, Malaysia, Cambodia, Laos, Vietnam, Indonesia, Papua New Guinea, and Yunnan, China as a result of the presence of the mosquito vectors and the lack of effective control. With a rise in surface temperature and changes in rainfall patterns, the distribution of vectors such as mosquito species may change.

Changes in environmental temperature and precipitation could expand vector-borne diseases into temperate and arid Asia. The spread of vector-borne diseases into more northern latitudes may pose a serious threat to human health. Climate change is likely to have principal impacts on epidemics of malaria, dengue, and other vector-borne diseases in Asia. The epidemic areas of vector-borne diseases in Asia would depend on many demographic and societal factors, as well as environmental hygiene for vector control, available health infrastructure, and medical facilities.

Depletion of stratospheric ozone that normally filters out ultraviolet radiation in sunlight in the region from 280 to 320 nm has been linked to widespread use of volatile halogenated organic compounds, particularly chlorinated and brominated methanes and chlorofluorocarbons. Some of these compounds also are effective GHGs and therefore contribute to global warming as well. The quantitative relationship between U V-B dose and its physiological effect varies with the wavelength of UV-B exposure. These effects include melanoma and non-melanoma skin cancers, cataracts and other ocular diseases, and dysfunction of the systemic and cutaneous immune systems. The known effects of UV-B on the eye include inflammatory reactions from acute exposure, snow blindness, and long-term damage to the cornea and lens from chronic exposure. It has been demonstrated that damage to melanocytes in human skin initiates the progression of changes leading to melanoma skin cancer. Suppression of the immune response by UV-B radiation involves damage to Langerhans cells and subsequent activation of T-lymphocytes, thus increasing the severity of certain infectious diseases.

The impacts of greater exposure to shorter wavelength UV radiation on human health are cumulative and, for some effects, may have long latencies. Noticeable increases in UV-B radiation over high and mid-latitudes as a result of depletion of stratospheric ozone have occurred in recent decades. Climate change could make conditions for the spread of diseases associated with higher UV-B doses more favourable.

The distribution of water-borne infectious diseases is influenced mainly by the hygienic circumstance of water. Water-borne diseases-including cholera and the suite of diarrheal diseases caused by organisms such as giardia, salmonella, and cryptosporidium-are common with contamination of drinking water quality in many countries of south Asia.

Higher SSTs and rich nutrient load in major river deltas would support extended phytoplankton blooms in selected coastal areas of temperate and tropical Asia. These phytoplankton blooms are habitats for the survival and spread of infectious bacterial diseases. The cholera outbreak in Bangladesh during 1994 has been attributed to the presence of extended phytoplankton blooms. The aforementioned water-borne diseases could become more common in many countries of south Asia in a warmer climate.

For preventive actions, impact assessments are necessary on various aspects such as the nutritional situation, drinking water supply, water salinity, and ecosystem damage. Water-borne infectious diseases, natural disaster, environmental migration, nutritional deficiency, and environmental pollution should be major risk factors for human health. The risk factor of diseases also will depend on infrastructure, economic conditions, the hygienic situation, and medical facilities. Risk could be reduced by awareness in the communities that are more vulnerable to instability in the future environment.

In Asia, economic and population growth will expand rapidly during the 21st century in many countries. The rapid increase in population will be accompanied by migration from rural communities to overcrowded large cities. Disasters linked to climate extremes such as floods and droughts also would impact local and regional populations and enforce migration. The huge energy consumption by the expanding population in urban cities would result in degradation of air and water quality, whereas rapid expansion of the economy will bring about improvements in living standards, such as improved environmental sanitation, hygienic practice, and medical treatment facilities. Therefore, better understanding of the interaction among climate change and environmental and health status in communities at regional and local scales is crucial to forge physiological acclimatization and social adaptations in the future.

Socioeconomic Impacts

The impacts of climate change on Asia will place additional stress on socioeconomic and physical systems. These pressures may induce change in demographic processes. Demographic trends, including the stability and size of populations, will be influenced directly through the impacts of climate change on human health and indirectly through the impacts of climate change on food security and the viability of natural resource-based economic activity.

A further demographic response will come about through the risk of extreme events on human settlements. If the incidence and magnitudes of events such as droughts and coastal floods increase, there could be large-scale demographic responses-for example, through migration. Migration in itself is not necessarily a signal of vulnerability to present-day extreme events. Motivations for migration are diverse; much rural-to-urban migration in Asia takes place as a result of increased economic opportunities in megacities. Future increases in the frequency and intensity of severe weather systems as a consequence of climate change can trigger mass migration, however.

The annual rate of growth in migration on a global scale has been greatest in developing countries of south and southeast Asia. For instance, population growth and land scarcity has encouraged the migration of more than 10 million Bangladesh natives to neighbouring Indian states during the past 2 decades. This migration has been exacerbated by a series of floods and droughts affecting the livelihoods of landless and poor farmers in this region.

Many south Asian countries increasingly expect the number of internally displaced persons to rise in future. Immigrant labour often benefits both the donor and the host cities/ countries. However, perceptions of regional/ national identity, language/cultural differences, and fears of unemployment may contribute to increased hostilities between immigrants and nationals in years to come. Climate change will act in parallel with a complex array of social, cultural, and economic motivations for and impacts of migration.

Irrespective of resource constraints in developing countries of Asia, they have to better equip themselves through appropriate public education and awareness programs with disaster preparedness measures, including infrastructures for effective resettlement of displaced people as a consequence of weather calamities.

The urban population in Asia is growing at four to five times the rate of the rural population. At this rate, more than 60% of the people in Asia will be living in towns and cities by 2015. An estimated 80% of the increase will occur in developing countries. The number of megacities in Asia would grow to at least 23 of the world's 36 by the year 2015.

Urbanization is rapid in fast-growing economies of south and southeast Asia, where the average annual urban growth rate is more than 4%. The current pace and scale of change often strains the capacity of local and national governments to provide even the most basic services to urban residents. An estimated 25-40% of urban inhabitants in developing countries today live in impoverished slums and squatter settlements, with little or no access to water, sanitation, or refuse collection.

Basic infrastructure demand in urban corridors is likely to increase dramatically in the future. Already governments in several developing countries of Asia are introducing suites of acts and laws to ensure provision of adequate public services and minimize adverse effects on surrounding communities and ecosystems. For instance, Indonesia introduced the Spatial Use Management Act in 1992 for the identification of environmentally sensitive areas-where development activities would be restricted-and for improved planning for the location and support of activities such as industrial development.

Developing countries in Asia would soon need to develop new priorities and policies that try to address demands created by the increasing number of people in cities while capitalizing on the benefits of urbanization, such as economic growth and efficient delivery of services. Climate change has the potential to exacerbate basic infrastructure demands of urban inhabitants in many countries of Asia.

In many cities in the developing countries of Asia, movement of the labour force from dispersed agricultural centers to concentrated industrial sectors has increased urbanization and expansion of the suburban area where industries are located. This situation has caused serious traffic, housing, and sanitary problems. Moreover, a substantial share of industrial growth in developing countries revolves around the transformation of raw materials into industrial products such as steel, paper, and chemicals.

Production of industrial chemicals has been shifting from developed countries to developing countries of Asia in recent years. Not only are these processes resource-intensive, in addition, industries such as electricity generation, chemicals and petroleum refining, mining, paper production, and leather tanning tend to produce a disproportionately large amount of hazardous and toxic wastes and already have caused serious air and water pollution. Moreover, because of poor regulatory capacity, developing countries have become targets for dumping of toxic wastes such as polychlorinated biphenyls (PCBs) by multinational companies.

In developing countries of Asia, an increase in paper consumption of more than 80% is expected to occur by 2010. However, a shortfall in the supply of all wood products and especially pulp and paper is likely in the 21st century as a result of declines in natural vegetation productivity. This trend will put immense pressure on unmanaged forests of Asia. Some countries in Asia have resorted to agroforestry and farm woodlots to meet their increasing demand for pulp and paper on a near-term basis. Over the long term, however, anticipated growth in demand for wood products of all types probably will necessitate changes in forest management practices such as greater reliance on industrial plantations. Heat stress to livestock herded in open areas would reduce animal weight gain, dairy and wool production, and feed conversion efficiency in arid and semi-arid Asia. An increase in the frequency of drought and heavy rainfall could result in a decline in tea yield in Sri Lanka. Climate change could have adverse impacts on agroindustries such as food, beverages, tobacco, natural fiber textiles, leather, wood, and rubber.

The manufacturing industry could be affected indirectly through the availability of water, energy supply, and transportation systems throughout Asia. Mining operations, which are required to produce raw materials such as coal (practiced intensively in China and India because of heavy demand), exposes sulfur-and iron-bearing rocks to weathering and erosion that would be aggravated by global warming. Mineral industries discharge large amounts of waste ore known as tailings. Manufacturing industries release effluent to the air and water during production processes. For instance, cement production and foundry operations release particulates; metal industries release SO_2, CO_2, HF, and organic solvents; and chemical plants release particulates, SO_2, and various hydrocarbons. Food processing, pulp and paper industries, brewing, and tanning industries release effluents in the form of contaminated water and sediments. This degradation of the environment may be exacerbated by climate change.

Climate change will adversely affect hydroelectric energy generation in Asia, exacerbating already depleted water resources in several major rivers in Asia. Increased humidity and hence more cloudiness in a warmer atmosphere could inhibit direct solar radiation. Photovoltaic technology, which is used extensively in

Indonesia and a few other south Asian countries for remote area electrification programs, could be jeopardized.

Changes in wind patterns could affect existing windmill installations. Availability of biomass, particularly fuel wood, depends on forest area and the quantity of rainfall. In areas with excess rainfall, CO_2 enrichment and higher temperatures could increase fuelwood production and supply. Geothermal resources also may be affected by changes in precipitation patterns. For instance, an increase in rainfall could increase recharge of groundwater for most geothermal fields.

In general, no major impacts of climate change on the production and distribution facilities of fossil fuels are likely, other than policies aimed at reducing GHG emissions from burning of fossil fuels. However, offshore exploration, production, and distribution facilities of oil and natural gas would be influenced by sea-level rise and extreme weather events such as cyclonic storms and associated surges that are likely to be exacerbated by climate change. Most power plants and oil refineries in Asia also are located along the coastlines to facilitate transportation and easy access to cooling water supply. Construction of seawalls will be needed to protect these facilities against sea-level rise.

Energy demand for heating, cooling, and agriculture activities can be influenced by climate change. Global warming would increase energy demand for cooling in the tropical Asia region and reduce energy demand for heating in boreal Asia. A similar pattern could be observed in temperate Asia, either in summer or winter. For agricultural activities, more energy would be needed for irrigation pumping during warmer weather as the soil becomes drier.

Tourism and outdoor recreational activities are likely to be disrupted in pattern by climate change. Global warming is expected to shorten the skiing season in many areas and affect the feasibility of some ski facilities. Summer recreational activities in coastal recreational areas may be affected with the inundation of beaches.

Imapcts on Finance Sector

The financial services sector typically includes banking, insurance, stock exchanges, and brokerages, as well as financial services firms such as investment banks, advisory services, and asset management, among others. Banking crises, currency speculation, and devaluation have become common in recent years in Asia and now are key policy concerns. Climate change could have serious consequences for this sector because many adaptation and mitigation measures such as crop insurance against floods or droughts are mediated or implemented through this sector. The implications and role of risk management techniques such as derivatives, options, and swaps are some of the new developments in financial services to dampen the impact of disasters on national finances.

There is a growing body of literature on the economic impacts of global warming that takes adaptation into account in estimating the imposed costs of climate change, but these studies fall short of specifically estimating the costs and benefits of adaptation. The basis for estimating adaptation costs is the economic opportunity cost of a product or activity. Estimating this cost requires price and other data from market transactions such as sectoral coverage and assumptions about markets, behaviuors, and policy instruments in addition to economic growth path as a function of socioeconomic conditions, resource endowment, and government policies. Multiple baseline choices are critical in the estimation and evaluation of the financial costs, based on accurate reporting of financial flows.

Although global gross domestic product (GDP) has increased by a factor of three since 1960, the number of weather-related disasters has increased four-fold, real economic losses seven-fold, and insured losses 12-fold in the same period. These losses have had some notable regional impacts-particularly in developing countries of Asia, where the impacts of climate change are expected to be greatest in terms of loss of life and effects on investment. Individual large events have shown visible short-term impacts on insurance profitability and pricing and public finance.

There is only limited penetration of or access to insurance in developing countries. This situation makes them more vulnerable and will impair their ability to adapt. The property/casualty insurance segment and small specialized or undiversified companies have greater sensitivity. Coping mechanisms and adaptation strategies will depend largely on public or international support. Given finite financial resources and international aid, increased climate-related losses would compete with development efforts.

Adaptation to climate change presents complex challenges to the finance sector. Increasing risk could lead to a greater volume of traditional business, as well as development of new risk and financing products (e.g., catastrophe bonds). However, increased variability of loss events would result in greater actuarial uncertainty. The design of an optimal adaptation program in any country would have to be based on comparison of damages avoided with the costs of adaptation. Other factors, particularly in developing countries with incomplete markets, also enter the decision-making process-such as the impacts of policies on different social groups in society, particularly those that are vulnerable; employment generation and opportunities; improved air and water quality; and the impacts of policies on broader concerns such as sustainability.

Adaptive Capacity

The adaptive capacity of a resource system or a human society depends on the resilience of these systems. Resilience in the face of climate change, as with resilience to present-day hazards such as floods and droughts, therefore depends on the scale, intensity, and rate of change of the climate system, as well as the inherent ability of ecosystems or communities to adjust to new circumstances.

Resilience is the ability of a system to return to a predisturbed state without incurring any lasting fundamental change. Resilient resource systems recover to some normal range of operation after a perturbation. The processes of short-term adjustment to changes in land productivity and food scarcity in traditional societies of Asian countries are resilient to perturbations. This resilience has been demonstrated in a range of resource systems throughout Asia, including highland agriculture, large-scale irrigated agriculture, and fishery-dependent communities.

Long-term adaptation to climate change requires anticipatory actions, which would require considerable investment of capital, labour, and time hence diversion from scarce available resources, existing services, and infrastructure. Constraints on such resources clearly are more acute in the developing countries of Asia. The three crucial sectors of land resources, water resources, and food productivity are of highest priority for planned adaptation, particularly for the poorer resource-dependent countries.

Adaptation to climate change in Asian countries depends on the real cost of adaptive measures, the existence and engagement of appropriate institutions, access to technology, and biophysical constraints such as land and water resource availability, soil characteristics, genetic diversity for crop breeding, and topography. Demand for land and water already is increasing to support growing populations, increased agricultural activities, and expanding modern urban infrastructure.

Most developing countries in Asia face significant impacts from present-day climatic hazards. Faced with impending floods, the economic insecurity of communities and rural households, lack of timely warnings, ignorance of the severity of danger from flood, and lack of efficient transport systems, some developing countries of Asia often choose not to evacuate homes to avoid climate-related disasters. Such circumstances also act as constraints for the alleviation of poverty and hence reinforce social vulnerability.

For many developing countries in Asia, climate change is only one of a host of environmental problems; these countries have to individually and collectively evaluate the tradeoffs between climate change actions and nearer term needs. Adaptation measures designed to anticipate the potential effects of climate change can help to offset many of the negative effects.

Adaptation measures that ameliorate the impacts of present-day climate variability include sea defenses, institutional adaptations, plant breeding, and adoption of new technologies in agriculture. Many countries in Asia already commit significant resources to ameliorating climate-related hazards. Development and broad application of integrated modeling efforts and modeling approaches that are particularly applicable at the regional scale warrant increased attention.

Sustainable development within Asia's agroecosystems is crucial to provide adequate food security for traditional farming communities in the lowlands and the uplands in developing countries and to ensure in situ conservation of crop biodiversity for sustaining high-input modern agriculture itself. However, conserving biodiversity with concerns for higher production from these complex agroecosystems is a challenging task, for which novel development alternatives are required

Traditional societies have always manipulated biodiversity to ensure ecosystem resilience and to cope with uncertainties in the environment, rather than to increase production on a short-term basis. There is increasing evidence now to suggest that we could learn from their traditional ecological knowledge base for coping with uncertainties associated with global change. The resilience of agricultural practices in the face of climate change depends on the nature and magnitude of region-specific climate change, regional sensitivity, or the threshold and social resilience and adaptive capacity of agricultural communities.

Adjustment of planting dates to minimize the effect of temperature increase-induced spikelet sterility can be used to reduce yield instability. for example, by avoiding having the flowering period to coincide with the hottest period. Adaptation measures to reduce the negative effects of increased climatic variability may include changing the cropping calendar to take advantage of the wet period and to avoid extreme weather events (e.g., typhoons and storms) during the growing season. Crop varieties that are resistant to lodging (e.g., short rice cultivars) may withstand strong winds during the sensitive stage of crop growth.

A combination of farm-level adaptations and economic adjustments such as increased investment in agriculture infrastructure and reallocation of existing land and water resources would be desired in the agriculture sector. Increasing demand for water by competing sectors may limit the viability of irrigation as a sustainable adaptation to climate change. Expansion of irrigation as a response to climate change will be difficult and costly in many of the countries in Asia even under favourable circumstances. Mounting societal pressures to reduce environmental degradation will likely foster an increase in protective regulatory policies, further complicating adaptations to climate change.

A commonly prescribed adaptation to climate change in the water sector is to enhance characteristics that offer flexibility hence enhancing resilience. Flexibility issues are particularly important with regard to the development of water resources for industry or agriculture. Major projects such as dams actually may limit flexibility if they lose effectiveness as regional hydrological water balances undergo major changes. With likely changes in climate variability, dams and sea defenses built to withstand a 100-year extreme event may not be adequate thus leading to a risk of major catastrophe. If hydrological patterns change markedly and irrigated agriculture is required to relocate in response, prior investments may be lost as existing infrastructures become obsolete, and additional investments will be needed. This necessitates critical scrutiny of a range of available choices that incorporate economic and environmental concerns. The potential for adaptation should not lead to complacency. Some adaptive measures may have detrimental impacts of their own. The issue of natural resource management in Asia has a highly complex set of interconnections between natural and social systems.

Natural resource management in largely rural tropical environments must reconcile ecological and social processes that operate at a range of scales, from species up to the landscape level. Studies have shown that ecologically important keystone species often are socially selected by many rural societies. The possibility for species selection for rehabilitating a degraded ecosystem should be based on a value system that the local people understand and appreciate; therefore, their participation in the process of developmental activity is important. Community perceptions of soil and water management can be a powerful agent for sustainable management of natural resources.

Major fishery-related environmental issues include the effects of trawling on sea-bottom habitats and the detrimental effects of catches of nontarget species on populations and ecosystems. Fishery resources also are threatened by activities other than commercial fishing. Loss of inshore fish nursery habitats from coastal development and pollution from land-based activities cause significant change to ecosystems that support fisheries. Effective conservation and sustainable management of marine and inland fisheries are needed at the regional level so that living aquatic resources can continue to meet regional and national nutritional needs. Asian economic growth has failed to alleviate poverty for a large share of Asian people to date.

Achieving economic and industrial growth in Asia that is sustainable-both ecologically and economically viable over the long term-would require more than just cleaner, more efficient industrial processes; it demands a reorientation toward becoming less material-intensive and attempting to contribute toward protecting our environment and ecosystem.

Regions of the Asian continent differ widely in their biophysical characteristics hence in their physical vulnerability to climate change. Different regions also experience highly differentiated social vulnerability. Adaptation strategies therefore will be differentiated across regions and sectors, depending on their vulnerability profiles.

The vulnerabilities and related adaptation strategies for four broad regions of Asia and for selected sectors are discussed below.

Boreal Asia: At present, only areas of sporadic permafrost are used for agriculture. Global warming should play a positive role for agriculture in boreal Asia. The growing season is likely to expand by 1-1.5 months by 2100. The increase in mean monthly air temperatures during the summer will increase active soil temperatures. In addition, winter air temperatures will substantially increase. Shifts in the limit of the permafrost zone to the north, formation of vast areas of perennial ground thawing, and better soil climate will contribute to a northward shift of agriculture boundary. The key step for an agriculture adaptation strategy could be the choice of suitable crops and cultivars. Shifts in sowing date of spring crops will allow more effective use of the soil moisture content formed by snow melting. The dates of spring crop sowing could be moved forward in a crop rotation calendar in southern regions, and farmers could plant a second crop that could even be vegetable with a short growth period. Optimum use of fertilizers and ecologically clean agrotechnologies would be beneficial for agriculture.

Climate change has the potential to exacerbate water resource stresses in some areas but ameliorate them in most parts of boreal Asia. The increase in surface temperatures will have considerable effect on the timing of snowmelt hence the timing of the flow regime. Diversions of water systems would adversely impact fisheries and fishery habitat in the region. A decrease in water flow during the dry summer season is likely in some parts of boreal Asia. Extraction of groundwaters from deep aquifers has been proposed as an option, keeping in view the likely surface water quality deterioration during dry periods. It would be necessary to increase the capacity of recycled water supply systems and autonomous water-use systems. However, even with water-saving measures it may be necessary to cut water intake for industry needs during dry periods to meet increasing demand in the future. Bottom-deepening along navigation channels may be required to facilitate the transport of goods and material through rivers.

Arid and Semi-Arid Asia: The major impact of climate change in arid and semi-arid Asia is likely to be an acute shortage of water resources associated with significant increases in surface air temperature. Conservation of water used for irrigated agriculture therefore should be given priority attention. With increased evapotranspiration, any adaptation strategy in agriculture should be oriented toward a shift from conventional crops to types of agriculture that are not vulnerable to evapotranspiration. These strategies entail either intensive agriculture in greenhouses-within which rates of evapotranspiration are much reduced-or developing alternatives such as aquaculture that will partly replace agriculture. All of these organisms are of high yield; they enjoy solar radiation and often heat, and they do not evaporate or transpire water. Expansion of commercial and artesian fisheries also could help reduce dependence on food productivity. Protection of soils from degradation should be given serious consideration.

Climate change would exacerbate threats to biodiversity resulting from land-use/cover change and population pressure in Asia. Ecosystem services can be impaired by loss of key species in arid and semi-arid Asia. Because intraspecies variation in response to environmental stress usually exists in populations subjected to year-to-year climate change, some genotypes in such populations are expected to be more resistant to climate change than others. Such genotypes are more common in peripheral populations than in core populations of species.

Although the core population may become extinct because of global warming, resistant types in peripheral populations will survive and can be used to rehabilitate and restore affected ecosystems. The geographic locations of the peripheral species population usually coincide with climatic transition zones, such as at the edges of drylands or along the transition between different types of drylands. Many countries in the region have more than one dryland type and hence should have peripheral populations-especially in desert and nondesert transitions, which often occur within semi-arid drylands. Identifying regions with concentrations of peripheral populations of species of interest and protecting their habitats from being lost to development therefore can play a role in enhancing planned adaptation for natural and semi-natural ecosystems.

Temperate Asia: Projected surface warming and shifts in rainfall in temperate Asia are significant and will induce increases in photorespiration, maintenance respiration, and saturation deficits-causing stomatal closure and decline in productivity. An adaptive response in the agriculture sector should be an effort to breed heat-resistant crop varieties by utilizing genetic resources that may be better adapted to warmer and drier conditions. Improvements in farming systems, fertilizer management, and soil conservation form major adaptation strategies. Research is needed to define current limits to heat resistance and the feasibility of manipulating such attributes through modern genetic techniques.

Crop architecture and physiology ma_. be genetically altered to adapt to warmer environmental conditions. The genetic resources of seeds maintained in germplasm banks may be screened to find sources of resistance to changing diseases and insects, as well as tolerances to heat and water stress and better compatibility with new agriculture technologies. Genetic manipulation also may help to exploit the potentially beneficial effects of CO_2 enhancement on crop growth and water-use efficiency. The process of rapid urbanization and industrialization in several Asian megacities has placed enormous stress on urban infrastructure, human well-being, cultural integrity, and socioeconomic arrangements. These urban cities are giant resource sinks and create a large "ecological footprint" on the surrounding countryside.

The negative environmental impacts of expanding cities are already large; as they continue to grow and become more prosperous, these impacts are likely to increase. Rising levels of air and water pollution in many of the large cities are considerable. Production and consumption systems that sustain life in cities are largely responsible for many of these changes.

As climate changes, the demand for basic infrastructure facilities such as housing, electricity, food supply and distribution, and drinking water supply will increase, and municipalities would have a difficult time managing waste recycling and waste disposal. Development policies that mitigate or avert some of these long-term problems would have to be country-specific and depend heavily on the availability of infrastructure resources, the size of the floating population, and sustainable behavioural changes in society.

Climate change will impinge on a diverse, complex, and dynamic form of climatic hazards such as floods, droughts, sea-level rise, and storm surges in the countries of temperate Asia. Preparation for changes in climate variability should include provision for the possibility of increased flooding, as well as incidences of drought. The present path of development in this region is placing more fixed infrastructures and economic activity within the coastal zone. This trend seems to offer limited scope for adjustments against flooding in the coastal zone resulting from sea-level rise.

The likelihood of damage to infrastructure and loss of human life because of unexpected extreme events will rise. A wide range of precautionary measures at the regional and national levels-including awareness, perception, and the acceptability of risk factors among regional communities-are warranted to avert or reduce the impacts of such disasters on economic and social structures. Many current technical and socioeconomic barriers will need to be overcome to prevent risks to human health resulting from increases in disease incidences associated with climate change.

Tropical Asia: Agricultural adaptation to climatic variability is an evolving process. Planned interventions through research, extension, or pricing or marketing policies can have inadvertent detrimental impacts for poor farmers. Agricultural productivity in tropical Asia is sensitive not only to temperature increases but also to changes in the nature and characteristics of monsoons. An increase in leaf surface temperatures would have significant effects on crop metabolism and yields, and it may make crops more sensitive to moisture stress.

Cropping systems may have to change to include growing suitable cultivars (to counteract compression of crop development), increasing crop intensities (i.e., the number of successive crops produced per unit area per year), or planting different types of crops. Farmers will have to adapt to changing hydrological regimes by changing crops. For example, farmers in Pakistan may grow more sugarcane if additional water becomes available, and they may grow less rice if water supplies dwindle. The yield ceiling must be raised and the yield gap narrowed while maintaining sustainable production and a friendly environment.

Development of new varieties with higher yield potential and stability is complementary to bridging the yield gap. Efficient production of a socially optimal level of agricultural output in this region ultimately may depend on biotechnological applications, but only if these applications prove to be environmentally sustainable.

Groundwater is the main source of freshwater in many parts of tropical Asia, particularly in semi-arid regions. Water resources already are limited in terms of supply and demand in this region. The aquifers in most countries have been depleted by high withdrawal and low recharge rates, and significant draw down problems exist. Even with increases in precipitation, surface runoff may diminish in some river basins under projected climate change scenarios because of greater evaporation in a warmer atmosphere (higher hydrological elasticity).

Increased runoff in some river basins can cause deleterious effects such as greater flooding, waterlogging, and salinity. More than 25% of the irrigated land in the Indus basin already is affected by waterlogging and salinization. Freshwater availability in the coastal regions is likely to undergo substantial changes as a result of a series of chain effects. Improvements in runoff management and irrigation technology (e.g., river runoff control by reservoirs, water transfers, and land conservation practices) will be crucial.

Increasing efforts should be directed toward rainwater harvesting and other water- conserving practices to slow the decline in water levels in aquifers. Recycling of waste-water should be encouraged in drought-prone countries in tropical Asia. However, major water development decisions to augment water supplies may have greater relative hydrological, environmental, and social impacts than climate change per se in the shorter term. Climate change will affect the benefits to be accrued by future water development projects and therefore should be taken into consideration in the context of water resource policies and planning.

With rapid development of the economy in several countries in tropical Asia during recent decades, the patterns of land use and land cover have been modified significantly; a sequence of transitions and conversions is discernable. As a result of different natural and socioeconomic conditions, the speed and scale of land-use change is very diverse in different parts of Asia. This process has contributed to significant losses in total forest cover; changes in standing biomass and the soil carbon budget; extinction of mammals, birds, and vascular plants; soil degradation; and threats to food security.

Excessive human and livestock population pressure in association with inappropriate agricultural extension activities also lend an explanation for widespread land degradation in tropical Asia. Salinization and acidification of soil in low-lying coastal areas would adversely affect cropland in addition to land losses from permanent inundation of deltas from anticipated sea-level rise.

Many of the major rivers originating in mountains and highlands are charged with sediments, depending on the types of land uses in the watersheds. Marginalization of production areas in highlands will continue to increase soil losses, land slips, and slides in the region. It has been suggested that upland micro-watersheds can be hydroecologically sustainable only if good forest cover and dense forests are maintained. Under changing climate conditions, the pressure toward small-and large-scale transfers of land for agricultural and urban uses may grow.

Sea-level rise poses the greatest threat and challenge for sustainable adaptation within south and southeast Asia. The sea level already is rising in many locations, primarily as a result of geological processes and anthropogenic manipulations. Projected sea-level rise along the Asian coastlines represents an increase of three to four times over present rates.

The potential impacts of accelerated sea-level rise include inundation of low-lying deltas and estuaries, retreat of shorelines, and changes in the water table. Episodic flooding from high storm surges would penetrate much further inland. Salinization and acidification of soil in low-lying coastal areas will adversely affect agricultural production, in addition to land losses from permanent inundation of deltas from anticipated sea-level rise. The impacts will vary from region to region because of local factors such as land subsidence, susceptibility to coastal erosion or sedimentation, varying tidal ranges, and cyclonicity.

The Ganges-Brahmaputra in Bangladesh, the Irrawaddy in Myanmar, the Choo Phraya in Thailand, and the Mekong and Song Hong in Vietnam are among the key low-lying river deltas in tropical Asia that are most vulnerable to sea-level rise. Local-level social and institutional adaptations in sensitive regions and development and promotion of risk management can potentially prevent accelerated impacts to these deltas through protection of the ecology of the region from further human interventions so they can sustain themselves at least in a short time horizon.

4

Environment Management

Despite progress since the early 1990s on economic reforms and developments in environmental institutions, countries in the South Asian region are still plagued by huge problems. Among them is the limited progress made on trade liberalization; on enabling environments for private sector participation, including the rule of law; on fiscal and financial policies; and on openness and accountability of public institutions. Poor economic management is also reflected in the large subsidies and the lack of economic pricing of natural resources, including water, energy, agricultural land, and other inputs. In addition, many state-owned industries—for example, in steel, fertilizer, and petrochemicals—and private manufacturing industries, such as leather, textiles, sugar, and pulp and paper, have prospered as a result of strong government protection policies and lack of compliance with environmental regulation. In this context, reform agendas, including deregulation and fiscal efficiency, often conflict with political institutions and interests.

South Asia stands out as the region most vulnerable to natural disasters such as floods and cyclones, which affect the region regularly. From 1990 to 1998, the region accounted for over 60 percent of disaster-related deaths worldwide. Over the 1965Œ 98 period, India accounted for about 64 percent and Bangladesh for 25 percent of the damages arising from natural disasters. Floods, cyclones, hurricanes, and typhoons were responsible for 86 percent of the damage in those countries during this period. The causes of resource depletion and environmental degradation include lack of incentives for resource conservation and protection, lack of institutional frameworks for the integrated management of natural resources, inadequate legal and policy frameworks, weak governance, low institutional capacity, subsidies and policy distortions, lack of public awareness of the value of healthy and sustainable ecosystems, and limited data on resources and environmental quality.

Assistance from International Agencies

Programmes of IDRC

The International Development Research Centre (IDRC) promotes environmental and natural resource management in South Asia through activities that support equitable and sustainable access to, and use of, natural resources by local communities. The emphasis on equity calls for an interdisciplinary approach that integrates gender, ethnicity, age and socioeconomic issues into natural resource management. Given that women comprise a large mass of the rural poor and are often most directly impacted by natural resource degradation (because of their role in gathering fuel, fodder, natural products and water), gender integrated activities are crucial. The emphasis on sustainability requires an approach that targets fragile ecosystems and remote regions and recognizes the critical role of local communities in managing their resources to meet their livelihood needs. The Environment and Natural Resource Management Program builds on community based knowledge and participation in the sustainable management of resources and aims to inform policy and institutional frameworks that govern resource management.

IDRC recognizes that natural resource degradation is inextricably linked with widespread rural poverty and inequitable access to basic resources in the region. Supporting initiatives that promote food and livelihood security based within the diversity of biological resources, is therefore, a key priority. The program supports the roles of farmers as experimenters and innovators in meeting their food needs and acknowledges the importance of medicinal plants and nontimber forest products (NFTPs) for meeting local health and livelihood needs.

One of the social costs of widespread environmental damage in the region has certainly been on human health. The Centre has begun to address this through research on better environmental management, including pesticide use, waste management and water pollution. The Environment and Natural Resource Management program is increasingly emphasizing the interrelationship between health, environmental management, sustainable livelihoods and local governance and decision making.

Program Initiatives

1. Community Based Natural Resource Management (CBNRM)

The Community Based Natural Resource Management (CBNRM) Program Initiative develops and transfers technical, methodological, analytical, social/institutional and policy innovations for more productive, equitable and sustainable natural resource use. CBNRM particularly targets communities in ecosystems facing environmental stress and degradation. In South Asia, this includes the uplands and coastal areas. While policies and research have typically discounted the role of local people in designing and implementing solutions for these problems, CBNRM proposes an alternative approach. The initiative works with those local men and women most directly involved with natural resource management. This often includes the poorest of the rural poor and ethnic minorities, both of which are politically, economically and/or geographically isolated. The program initiative aims to assist women and men living in ecosystems that face increasing resource exploitation, to manage and use their natural resources sustainably. This is done with a recognition that men, women, ethnic groups, and different social classes use natural resources in diverse ways and for distinct purposes.

The CBNRM program initiative follows a research approach which relies on the appropriate integration of social and natural sciences. The program supports research that generates insights and innovations in community-level resource management and leads to more sustainable food production and improved local livelihoods. Research innovations are directed to improving local interventions by:

— Transferring knowledge to enhance local understanding of the ecological value of productive resources and to ensure experts from outside the community recognize the scientific and development value of local knowledge;

— Improving production technologies to reduce degradation and increase productivity by optimizing interactions between different production elements (e.g. soils, agroforestry, livestock, irrigation);

— Supporting innovative organisational or management systems (related to common property resources) to foster local decision-making processes, resource inventories, allocation and monitoring mechanisms, capacity-building for disadvantaged groups and conflict resolution;

— Promoting policy innovations to develop local regulatory mechanisms and enforcement, support local government interventions on natural resource policies (e.g. land use and tenure policies), explore economic incentives for sustainability such as taxation, and increase policy responsiveness to local resource conflicts;

— Improving interaction and integration to strengthen communications and information flows between different actors, identify and integrate underlying causal factors into research programs, and improve verification of resource status, plans, processes and outcomes.

2. *Sustainable Use of Biodiversity*

Due to a multitude of factors, sources of biodiversity are disappearing at unprecedented rates. Each gene, species, or ecosystem lost reduces IDRC's options for adapting to change. This loss is compounded by the even more rapid disappearance of knowledge of biodiversity, especially among peoples with a close relationship to complex natural ecosystems.

The goal of the Sustainable Use of Biodiversity (SUB) Program Initiative is to promote, through research, the conservation and sustainable use of biodiversity by indigenous and local communities. This goal is operationalized by applying gender considerations and indigenous and local knowledge to the development of appropriate technologies, local institutions and policy frameworks.

SUB believes that supporting peoples' own technologies, innovations and management practices, through participatory scientific investigation and policy development, will empower communities to conserve and sustainably use biodiversity. The Program promotes the role of farmers as innovators, explores the tensions between resource use and conservation, and supports the creation of incentives for sustainable conservation and management. The SUB program initiative supports research on:

— Indigenous and local community knowledge, innovations and practices, that conserve and sustainably use biodiversity;

— Models for policy and legislation that recognize the rights of indigenous and local communities to genetic resources and to the equitable sharing of resource-use benefits in the context of intellectual property regimes;

— Community-based participation in *in situ* biodiversity conservation and management strategies, through gender sensitive incentives, methods, livelihood options and policies, and;

— Income generating incentives and strategies for the sustainable use of the products of biodiversity, especially medicinal plants.

3. Ecosystem Approaches to Human Health (EcoHealth)

The Ecosystem Approaches to Human Health (EcoHealth) Program Initiative is founded on the idea that the world is subject to the influences of many complex factors that are undermining the health of all living beings and cannot be understood or controlled by medical approaches alone. The EcoHealth approach constitutes a bridge between strategies for integrated management of the environment (healthy ecosystems) and a global, ecological approach to promoting human health. The EcoHealth PI supports interventions that will lead to better management of ecosystems in order to improve human health and well-being while simultaneously maintaining or improving the health of the ecosystem as a whole. The challenge lies in satisfying human needs while ensuring that the sustainability of the entire system is not jeopardized in the long term.

The goal of this Program Initiative is to improve human health by supporting multidisciplinary research on the structure and function of stressed ecosystems that people depend on for their lives and livelihoods. The program supports the use of participatory, transdisciplinary and gender sensitive methodologies to generate a better understanding of local determinants of human health. Understanding that local knowledge is the foundation for the development of appropriate and effective interventions and policies, is key to the

EcoHealth program. The program focuses particularly on agricultural, mining, and urban ecosystems.

Specific EcoHealth objectives include to:

— Develop and test research tools and methods on the application of ecosystem approaches to human health that incorporate societal needs;

— Develop and test ecosystem approaches for assessing causal linkages between human health and the natural and anthropogenic environments;

— Develop appropriate ecosystem management approaches to improve human health in the context of sustainable ecosystems, with particular emphasis on the use of participatory methods; and

— Disseminate the concept of improving human health through better ecosystem management that respects human development imperatives.

Programmes of USAID

Protecting the environment is essential for sustainable development. The US Agency for International Development (USAID) accomplishes this through activities carried out in concert with nongovernmental organizations (NGOs), the private sector, universities, other U.S. government agencies and donors, and partner countries. The six performance goals are:

— The world's environment protected for long-term sustainability

— Conservation of biologically significant habitat improved

— The threat of global climate change reduced

— Urban population's access to adequate environmental services increased

— The use of environmentally sound energy increased

— Sustainable management of natural resources increased

The World's Environment Protected for Long-Term Sustainability: The indicator for this goal is a 20-point index that includes national environmental action plans, or similar strategies, and participation in international environmental treaties: the Biodiversity Convention, the Framework Convention on Climate Change, the Convention on International Trade in Endangered Species (CITES), and three other environmental treaties. This index is a proxy: having an environmental action plan or ratifying a treaty does not necessarily mean that a country is willing or able to carry it out According to this indicator, there is a medium level of commitment across all regions.

Threat of Global Climate Change Reduced: Global climate change is an issue that cuts across science, politics, public policy, economics, finance, and health to affect all aspects of life. Studies show current levels of carbon dioxide to be the highest in 200,000 years. Levels will soon reach double the concentrations of the preindustrial age. Global warming appears inevitable. Given current trends, by 2035 developing countries stand to surpass industrial countries in their emission of greenhouse gases. Moreover, developing countries are most vulnerable to the adverse effects of climate change, including famine, coastal drought, coastal flooding, natural disasters, and higher incidence of climate-related disease.

Through its climate-change initiative, USAID continues to promote sustainable development by providing assistance geared toward reducing the economic, social, and environmental threats posed by global climate change. Given the breadth of its impact, mitigating the threat of climate change requires the participation of many sectors, including energy services, natural resources, and urban development. Included in the Agency's initiative are those sector activities that help in decreasing countries' greenhouse gas emissions or lessening their vulnerability to climate change.

India, Indonesia, and the Philippines are priority countries in USAID's climate-change initiative. Energy consumption in all three countries is growing rapidly, so the thrust of USAID's efforts to reduce greenhouse gas emissions will continue to be in the energy sector. USAID efforts to restructure the power sector, improve the efficiency of electricity generation, and expand the commercialization of renewable energy will reduce emissions of CO_2 and other pollutants, while also improving energy efficiency. ANE is continuing with clean energy, energy efficiency, and power sector reform in South and East Asia. The South Asia Regional Environmental Initiative is working with the private sector on clean power systems. The U.S.-Asia Environmental Program continues to address power sector reform and provide technical assistance for clean and efficient energy.

USAID's climate-change initiative in this region concentrates on Poland, Russia, Ukraine, and the Kazakhstan. The Agency hopes to reduce greenhouse gas emissions by improving efficiency in the energy sector. E&E is emphasizing legislative and power sector reform and development of institutional capacity but is mindful of the need for continued sustainable economic development. To achieve climate-change objectives, the Agency is using a variety of tools. They include credit instruments, policy reform, technological cooperation, donor coordination, private sector partnerships, institutional capacity-building, and the collection and dissemination of information. USAID's environmental programs in Brazil, Mexico, and the Central American region are designed to reduce the growth rate of CO_2 emissions by reducing tropical deforestation and promoting the use of "clean" energy technologies.

Urban Population's Access to Adequate Environmental Services Increased: Urban population's access to adequate environmental services has improved despite rapid migration to cities. Currently, 17 of the world's 21 cities with populations over 10 million are in developing countries. In the Asia-Pacific region, the annual urban growth rate is more than 4 percent, but at 5 percent a year Africa has the highest urban growth rate of all regions. Unless cities can properly manage their environmental problems, opportunities for sustainable development, economic growth, and social equity will be lost. The Agency's goal is to improve access to water and sanitation services. USAID has two indicators for sustainable urbanization:

— Percentage of urban population with access to safe drinking water

— Percentage of urban population with access to sanitation services Sub-Saharan Africa.

The Agency has significant programs in water resource management in the Middle East, where the degradation and depletion of water resources pose the most critical challenges to sustainable development. USAID activities seek to improve the management of freshwater supplies and to improve the quantity and quality of wastewater treatment.

Use of Environmentally Sound Energy Increased: Energy is a critical economic factor as well as being crucial to providing services that sustain and improve the quality of life of the average citizen. However, energy production and use are a major source of pressure on the environment. More efficient use and provision of energy services and increased reliance on environmentally clean and renewable energy sources are therefore critical for achieving environmentally sustainable development.

Sustainable Management of Natural Resources Increased: Sustainable natural resource management is essential for economic sustainability. Among the problems USAID's programmes are:

— Loss of forests, which affects watersheds, biodiversity, and climate change

— Competition artisanal fisheries face from commercial trawlers

— Problems with water consumption and management

— Declines in wildlife populations.

The Agency's strategy addresses sustainable management in five critical areas: forests, water resources, coastal zones, agriculture, and community-based natural resource management. To promote better resource management, programs work at both national and local levels to devolve ownership and control of natural resources to local communities. Linking resource management with local empowerment-developing local structures for natural resource management-has also contributed to civil society objectives. Long-term studies have shown that natural resource management spreads rapidly once the key enabling conditions-policies, institutions, and approaches-are established.

Sustainable Management of Natural Resources Increased: Sustainable management of natural resources is perhaps USAID's most diverse and historically its oldest program cluster. It yields a wide range of indicators at the program and strategic level. For example, strategies and programs that fall under this objective include measures of the number of farmers and households adopting improved agricultural processes. They also include improvements in coastal zone management, better soil conservation techniques, use of integrated pest management, enhanced watershed management, and the strengthening (environmental education, skills upgrades, civil society training, structural and functional help) of community-based natural resource organizations. No single indicator (or even two or three indicators) is likely to capture this diversity of the Agency's on-the-ground efforts.

Natural forest and planted trees (plantation) are very different kinds of land cover. Such distinctions are often defining characteristics of where USAID targets its programs. Measurement reliability is also an issue. According to the World Bank, data on forest cover may be especially unreliable because of changing definitions, varying in-country data reporting procedures, and reporting intervals that vary from nation to nation. Further limiting interpretation of these data is the fact that for some countries the data sets use different baselines or standard reference years.

The Agency's programs are diverse, and they include sustained emphasis on community-based natural resources. More than half the Agency's operating unit-level programmes have a natural resource management strategic objective. Regional differences in emphases, further complicate the choice of indicators. For example, Africa concentrates heavily on capacity-building, while Latin America and the Caribbean has worked extensively on upgrading park management. Several programs have a strong policy emphasis, while others are targeted directly to farmers and rural households. Close to half of all operating units with a natural resource objective use the number of families or households adopting sustainable agriculture practices as an indicator for better management practices. More than a third of operating units use one or more of the following indicators:

1) area of forest, water resources, or coastal zone under resource management plans,
2) area of land under sustainable agricultural practices,
3) number of policies implemented or supported that promote better management of natural resources.

One or more of these lower level indicators may be substituted for the current Agency-level performance goal indicators as the result of ongoing discussions among USAID's technical staff. More than 40 percent of field missions or operating units have strategic environmental objectives that address some element of policy formulation. Many of these field-based activities support the development of a national commitment to the environment. Policy related strategic objectives vary from 50 percent in energy to just over 30 percent each in biodiversity and urban programs.

Ten operating units have strategic objectives directly related to strengthening the policy environment. Progress in strategic objectives is measured mainly by assessing enactment of specific legislation and national policy formulation. Other strategic objectives measure whether citizens and nongovernmental organizations have accurate environmental information and are involved in decision-making about the environment. USAID works with two givens:

1) the range of USAID's environmental portfolio (energy, biodiversity, etc.) is wide, and
2) the earth's natural resources continue to decline. With that in mind, the Agency continues to emphasize getting the right environmental policies in place at the national level.

Since many operating units are engaged in activities related to environmental policy, USAID continues to seek the best formulation of a policy performance measure.

Biological Diversity Conserved: USAID's on-the-ground biodiversity strategies and activities are very diverse. There is often a long lag time before new data are available. Questions arise as to how to accurately measure the health of plant and animal biodiversity. For example, habitats that are "protected" can be rich in biological diversity or, in stark contrast, such habitats can be void of the critical animals and unique plants that made it biologically diverse in the first place. It is difficult to define indicators for the richness of animal and plant life within the protected areas.

That is, designating land as "protected" does not necessarily mean that protection has occurred or is currently in force. From a monitoring perspective, no single indicator can capture the complexity and ingenuity of USAID's wide-ranging efforts to conserve biodiversity or provide any real insight into habitat sustainability. Also, in some cases the Agency has directed its attention to areas of less than a thousand hectares (four square miles). That falls below the landmass defined as a "protected area."

Threat of Global Climate Change Reduced: Carbon dioxide emissions account for the largest share of greenhouse gases associated with the threat of global warming. CO_2 emissions result primarily from the burning of fossil fuels and from producing cement and other manufacturing processes. For example, tax policies change, world fuel prices fluctuate, a nation's economy undergoes structural changes. Sharp and sometimes prolonged declines in energy demand for manufacturing often stem directly from civil strife and economic downturns. Such downturns occurred last year, for example, in Asia and in some states of the former Soviet Union. They led to dramatic reductions in CO_2 emissions.

Distinguishing among these causes of decreased CO_2 emissions is not easy. Reliable emissions data are often available only on a national level (or adjusted per capita). This contrasts with USAID's efforts, which are much more localized and typically occur in only a very limited way, in a few key countries. CO_2 data are not current. They have at least a five-year lag time. This means that emissions projections are by default often used for both target-setting and actual data, leaving the so-called results open to question. Carbon dioxide emissions data do not really capture the kinds of programs and strategies the Agency employs. USAID activities in global climate change have so far involved four activities:

1) promoting energy efficiency, renewable energy, and clean energy technologies in power generation, and in industrial and urban applications;
2) reducing net emissions through sustainable forest management, agroforestry, reforestation, and sustainable agriculture activities;

3) increasing participation in the Framework Convention on Climate Change by supporting the development of national environmental action plans, joint implementation, and technology cooperation; and
4) maintaining a portfolio of cross-sectoral vulnerability and adaptation activities, including strengthening capabilities for disaster assistance planning and mitigation.

Assistance to Bangladesh

USAID/Bangladesh has recently restructured its natural resources management efforts to create a specific "Strategic Objective" covering environmental management. The timing of this assessment was useful to place these national activities—mostly on sustainable inland fisheries, watershed management and forest conservation—in a regional context.

USAID/Bangladesh's new strategy adds forest conservation efforts in response to Bangladesh's participation in the debt buy-back program under the US Tropical Forest Conservation Act. There also is an active bilateral assistance program in the energy sector—relating primarily to natural gas development—that has many environmental dimensions. These bilateral energy activities are being closely coordinated with those supported by the new South Asia Regional Initiative/ Energy (SARI/E). Four areas of high priority emerged and are presented below, roughly in order of their perceived degree of significance:

1.Water Management. Resting at the confluence of three of the world's largest rivers—the Ganges, the

Brahmaputra and the Meghna—much of Bangladesh is an enormous flood plain. Several severe flooding events over the past 15 years have spurred donor support for rethinking of national approaches to water resources planning. Improving water management remains a top social, economic, and political priority in the country.

Increasing emphasis in the USAID/Bangladesh program as well as in within the Government of Bangladesh is being given to managing water at the local level, especially to improve understanding of catchment area or watershed capacities and boundaries. As urban and industrial growth continues, these sectors are bringing high value water uses to the bargaining table to compete with agriculture for water supply. They also present increased threats to water quality from municipal wastewater and industrial pollution, with associated risks to human health and economic productivity.

Bangladesh has less than 10 percent of its area within the river basins that provide more than 90 percent of its water, giving the country little control over the waters entering its borders. The 1996 Treaty on the Sharing of the Ganga Waters at Farakka Barrage was a step forward in this regard, and there is a desire to go further with neighbouring countries to enact additional agreements and otherwise cooperate on water management schemes.

However, there remains a widespread perception among environmental professionals and officials in Bangladesh that the country is adversely affected by poor forest and other land use practices in neighbouring upstream states. Further, there is risk of outright conflict over water management—as witnessed by the current tensions along the border with Myanmar/Burma, derived in considerable measure, from disputes over water. Although the Indo-Bangladesh Joint Rivers Commission provides a useful institutional mechanism for bilateral discussions on such topics (the two countries share 54 rivers), it is considered very slow and cumbersome. Institutions are needed for concrete multilateral dialogue involving Bangladesh, India, Nepal, Bhutan, China and Myanmar/Burma, but the lack of political will and openness to this dialogue presents formidable challenges.

2. *Disaster Management*. Bangladesh is subject to drought, flooding from monsoon rains, typhoons (and associated wind damage), and earthquakes (particular concern was voiced about the risk of major rivers shifting courses, as has occurred in the past). The extremely high population densities in the country compound the risks of natural disasters. While considerable attention has been given to physical and institutional preparations for disasters (especially floods), there is a belief that more can and should be done to reduce the human costs of extreme natural events.

A particular gap relates to flood prediction and warning capacity—especially because it rests on inter-country information sharing. Strong disaster preparedness is dependent upon good land use planning, and efforts to address the former at the country level could improve understanding and application of sound rural and urban resources planning principles. There is also a sense that attention to this topic could provide a non-contentious vehicle for improving regional cooperation with Bangladesh's neighbours on broader natural resource management issues.

3. *Arsenic Contamination of Drinking Water*. While many questions remain unanswered about the causes of,

and possible remedies for, arsenic poisoning of tubewells in Bangladesh (as well as in West Bengal and the Terai of Nepal), the calamitous extent of the exposure is now becoming apparent. It is a problem that will draw the attention of water managers, geologists, health experts and others concerned with the sustainable development of Bangladesh's rural areas for years to come. The problem must be addressed as a central issue in national and regional water management planning and development. On the positive side, it has the potential to improve regional relations, as it could draw together the governments of West Bengal State and Bangladesh to cope with, and find solutions to, this common problem.

4. Coastal and Marine Resource Management. Bangladesh's coastal regions receive little concerted management attention at present, other than for fisheries production. With the prospect of significant offshore gas exploitation over the next decade, there are rising concerns in the environmental and business communities about the need for adequate environmental safeguards. Oil spill contingency planning appears to be of high priority.

As in many countries, there are a plethora of institutions with overlapping mandates relating to coastal and marine resource management in Bangladesh. Though USAID/Bangladesh has no explicit coastal resources management activities, the Asian Development Bank (ADB) is currently considering a regional project on coastal resources management in cooperation with IUCN. However, this institutional complexity has contributed to its decision, thus far, not to include Bangladesh among the participating countries (at present plans are to work in the Maldives, Pakistan, Sri Lanka, and Kerala State in India). The ADB also is supporting forest and protected area management in the Sundarbands coastal region. Despite these constraints, further attention to improving the management of Bangladesh's coastal and marine resources may be warranted.

Assistance to India

As the second most populated and seventh largest country in the world, India faces an entirely different scale of environmental challenges than its neighbours. The combination of these characteristics, and its decentralized form of government, means that the neighbouring countries often have closer working relationships with adjacent state governments than with central government agencies.

However, the size of the country's tax base and budget and the relatively high availability of well-trained environmental and economic experts mean that more resources are available to these central government bodies in terms of staff and access to information. The country is also able to command an influential place on the world stage.

As USAID/India is currently preparing a new assistance strategy, this assessment offers an opportunity to provide useful input on environmental and natural resources management issues in the country and within the regional context.

The quality of urban environments is deteriorating throughout India, with rising levels of air and water pollution, and weak provision of sanitation services. These factors contribute to high human costs through negative impacts on human health and morbidity. Delhi, Mumbai, and Chennai rank among the top ten most polluted cities in the world, and several others are close behind. The urbanization trend is a direct result of national policies promoting industrialization as the principal path to economic development. The subject of urbanization in India-its underlying causes, relationships with unsustainable rural resources management and the associated and growing pollution problems connected to both settlements and industrialization-are the subject of some analysis by USAID/India and the US-Asia Environmental Partnership (US-AEP) as part of the current strategic planning exercise at the country level.

USAID/India (and the USG generally) has identified the consequences of urbanization as a focus area for environmental assistance in the country. Program responses have included the introduction of innovative financing approaches for the provision of urban environmental infrastructure and a range of efforts in collaboration with chambers of commerce to promote cleaner production practices in the private sector.

In recent years, this assistance also has included a strong emphasis on reducing greenhouse gas emissions (due, in part, to sanctions imposed after India's nuclear weapons test). The addition of the South Asia Regional Initiative for Energy (SARI/E) will complement USAID/India's ongoing support for power sector restructuring and the promotion of cleaner and more energy-efficient industrial production. This "brown" emphasis of US government assistance programs in India means that relatively little current attention is being given by USAID and others to "green" problems of natural resource degradation—except through indirect efforts to stabilize population growth. The EPIQ team was struck with consistent concerns raised about a nexus of agriculture, population and environment issues.

Rural population pressures are outstripping gains from agricultural intensification such that the natural resource base is deteriorating in many places. Out-migration from such areas either to cities or regions with higher agricultural productivity is generating another set of environmental and natural resources challenges. There may be too much of a split in thinking between the "green" and "brown" sides of the equation. It is obvious that the two are intertwined, most notably through the potentially positive release of pressure on rural resource systems from well planned urban and industrial growth. Further analysis on this subject would seem warranted.

Three main topics were identified as potentially of high significance beyond the urban, industrial, and energy problem areas already being addressed by USAID/India's programs:

1. Competition Over Scarce Water Resources. Whether in the wet or dry areas of the country, or in urban or rural settings, competition over the allocation and management of water resources is emerging as a top environmental issue. With wide biogeographic, socio-economic and cultural variation, it is difficult to generalize about the nature of these issues in India—each area of the country seems to have a unique set of water management challenges. The decentralized form of government also means that the management of watercourses shared by multiple states within India's boundaries may present some of the same challenges inherent in "transboundary" river basin management involving multiple nations. Water management in India is a rising crisis that already affects national and regional economic and political stability.

In partial response to the "agriculture-population-environment nexus" mentioned above as well as these issues, USAID/India has identified the "water-energy nexus" as an area of emerging priority for mission support. The principal context is given in analysis provided by USAID/India below, juxtaposing simultaneous crises relating to water and power:

— Water Crisis and Need for planning

— Limited Renewable Water Resources

— High Population Growth

— Lack of Integrated Water Resources Planning and Management

— Increasing Cost of Water Supply Expansion

— Deteriorating Water Quality

— *Power Sector crisis and Need fro Reform*

— Low Capital Productivity in the Power Sector

— Poor Technical and Management Performance

— Halting Power Sector Reforms

— Power Shortages and High Losses

It remains to be seen how this new area of assistance will respond to the broader set of forces increasing by linking rural and urban populations. However, the initial emphasis on simultaneously improving the efficiency of pump irrigation and urban water supply seems promising.

2. *Environmental Determinants of Human Health in Urban Areas.* India's rapid urban growth is leading to enormous health problems derived from environmental causes. Rigorous studies have recently underscored

previous conclusions based on anecdotal evidence that environmental factors-ranging from indoor and outdoor air pollution to a scarcity of clean water supplies-are creating staggering social costs through increased disease and morbidity. The poor and socially weak suffer the most. Regional activities of USAID on urban development and on urban and industrial environmental management (through US-AEP) are addressing certain aspects of these problems. However, there would appear to remain scope for improved coordination between US government health, child survival, and environmental programs in understanding and responding to the environmental determinants of human health in urban and rural areas.

3. *Disaster Preparedness, Response and Links to Natural Resources Management*. Like Bangladesh, India is a disaster-prone country. It is subject to droughts, floods, wind damage, and earthquakes. The legacy of Bhopal also has left sensitivity to the threat of man-made disasters. Many leading scientists involved with climate change research believe that, at least for typhoons, the combined effects of more intense storms and sea level rise will lead to even higher damage.

There is a call for greater attention to be given to disaster forecasting and advance warning systems in India, and to both physical and institutional preparations and responses. As elsewhere in the region, there are clear opportunities for complemetarity between disaster preparedness and improved rural and urban development planning. As noted, India's neighbours believe that attention to the topic of weather and flood data sharing could provide a non-contentious vehicle for improved regional cooperation on broader natural resources management issues-especially those dealing with transboundary water resources.

Assistance to Nepal

USAID/Nepal has a new assistance strategy covering the period of 2001-2005. It emphasizes provision of improved family planning and health services as well as forest and water management, especially helping the country develop its considerable hydropower potential in an environmentally and socially sound manner. Both the community forestry and hydropower activities have explicit environmental dimensions. The former is gradually being phased out, while the latter is on track for further expansion.

As Nepal remains extremely poor with a weak and fragile government, USAID and other donors play a vital role in supporting basic services for the population. As in Bangladesh, the heavy donor influence in Nepal can also be a point of contention, especially with regard to the existence of dependency relationships or other disincentives for positive change.

But the role of the donors appears to be minor compared to other social and economic forces at work. Already heavy and still growing population pressure on a natural resource base limited by mountains in the north and India to the south exerts a fundamental influence on the country's development pattern. A Maoist insurgency is severely restricting the provision of government services in several parts of the country, and is underscoring wider calls for improved governance, and greater attention to equity and transparency in the development process.

The country's environmental and natural resources issues may be described according to the two major geographic zones, distinguishing between the mountainous region (where the emphasis is on environmentally sound tourism development), and the middle hills and terai zones (where there is significant in-migration, expanding small and medium-scale industrial development, growing land alienation and other land management problems and where relations with India exert heavy influence on resource use patterns).

While it was noted that forests are recovering in parts of the mid-Western region of the country, protected areas (conservation reserves and forest lands) are under severe pressure elsewhere in the middle hills and terai zones. It is also clear that the poor, women and those of low caste pay the highest price for environmental degradation-whether in rural or urban settings.

The government is currently preparing its Tenth Five-Year Development Plan, and there is at least a stated intent to include environmental planning and management in a more prominent manner than in previous development strategies.

Three topics are be identified as potentially worthy of further attention or emphasis:

1. Demographics and Land Degradation in the Middle Hills and Terai Zones. There is a need for stronger attention and a better understanding of how to respond to links between rural poverty alleviation and sustainable natural resources management. There has been some success with community forestry efforts in recent years (USAID assistance is being planned out), but even this appears to be having some negative consequences for those who depend upon the availability of grazing lands for their livelihoods. The middle hills and terai regions of the country face both rapid in-migration and high natural population growth coupled with weak infrastructure and access to government services. This contributes to the underpinnings of the Moaist insurgency, and it is a fundamental environmental and development challenge facing the country. Given the links with India, solutions will necessarily require a regional dimension, if not response.

2. *Ecotourism Development in the Mountain Zone.* Despite growing pollution in Kathmandu and congestion in some top tourist destinations, Nepal's reputation remains largely intact as one of the world's premier locations for nature-based tourism. The draw of its mountain ecosystems and unique cultural heritage is subject to increasing constraints due to poorly planned tourism development and growing strains on infrastructure. Since nearly all international tourists pass through Kathmandu, any improvements in the city's environmental quality will benefit not only its citizens but also the tourism industry. Micro-hydropower projects being supported by Norwegian and German aid among others are getting high marks, but this is not fully meeting the need nor tapping the potential. Such projects should be complemented by larger mini-hydropower investments as a way to reduce land pressures from fuelwood consumption and otherwise to improve rural infrastructure in support of ecotourism and other economic activity.

3. *Environmentally and Socially Sound Hydropower Development.* As evidenced by USAID/Nepal's current programs, there is widespread agreement that development of the country's significant hydropower resources lies at the core of the national development

strategy. While this topic is largely addressed by these USAID programs, it was mentioned often enough in discussions to bear repeating. Furthermore, expanded demand for clean energy within the South Asia region (especially for export to India) presents opportunities for regional and global economic and environmental benefits.

Involvement of US businesses in the exploitation of this potential offers further links to US interests. Somewhat ironically, a principal constraint to further development lies in the need to proceed in an environmentally and socially responsible manner. The recent release of a comprehensive set of reports by the World Commission on Dams establishing internationally recognized norms for such actions should be met with relief by those who have previously been confused about how to proceed without drawing the ire of environmentalists and others concerned with social justice. It would be in the Government of Nepal's best interests to embrace these standards so that they now can move ahead with environmentally and socially sound hydropower development. Unfortunately, sentiments within the Electricity Development Center and even the Ministry of Environment remain unnecessarily defensive.

Assistance to Sri Lanka

Discussions were held with both USAID/Colombo and embassy staff responsible for environmental issues. In addition, extensive interactions with government officials and both NGO and private sector representatives took place, particularly as afforded by participation by one EPIQ team member in the January 2001 "Workshop on New Directions in Land and Other Natural Resources

Management" sponsored by Asian Development Bank. A thorough review of Sri Lanka's policies and institutional capacities for natural resources management has recently been completed under the ADB's Sustainable Natural Resources Management for Development (SUNREM) Project. At present the ADB plans or has underway more than $200 million in natural resources management projects, covering forestry, coastal resources, water management and biodiversity conservation. A further ADB assistance program to improve land resources management—as a complement to assistance from the World Bank and Australia—is in the design stage.

Given the scale of these investments relative to Sri Lanka's size, there has been considerable interest of late and positive movement toward the reform of natural resources management policies and institutions. While no similarly concerted effort is underway with regard to urban and industrial pollution management, there is growing public and official awareness of the trade-offs between urban and industrial expansion and environmental quality.

The ADB took over the role of lead donor on the subject of environment from USAID after completion of USAID's Natural Resources and Environmental Policy (NAREP) Project in 1996. Since that time, US environmental assistance has been very limited and has mostly come through the US-AEP under the rubric of enhancing the competitiveness of key Sri Lankan economic sectors in the global marketplace. USAID is scheduled to phase-out its bilateral activities in 2002, after which time a foundation or other institution will be established to protect the "legacy" of US assistance. In the meantime, the Mission remains eager to actively participate in US-AEP and SARI/E.

Despite the ongoing civil strife associated with the separatist movement in the north and east parts of the country, Sri Lanka has continued to enjoy relatively rapid economic growth. However, if the country is to hold together, the devolution process outside of the conflict zone will need to set an example for provincial autonomy—including, significantly, the management of land and other natural resources. Together with demands for greater transparency and public consultation in government decision making, this has pushed governance issues to the forefront of natural resources and environmental policy discussions. In addition to the ongoing natural resources sector reforms mentioned above (covering forests, coasts, water, biodiversity and land), two additional and complementary topics were identified:

1. Environmental Information for Enhanced Transparency and Better Management Decisions. As evidenced by the frustrations encountered by SACEP/UNEP in trying to prepare a "State of the Environment" report for Sri Lanka, there is precious little reliable information available on current trends and conditions regarding environmental quality and the health of natural systems. The last such review was conducted in 1990 under USAID's NAREP Project, and the Sri Lankan National Science Foundation's current attempt to update the study appears to suffer from both a lack of good data and any concerted effort to evaluate trends in environmental quality or resource degradation. At the same time there are increasing calls for greater transparency in the handling and public disclosure of environmental information as well as improvements in both public consultation and participation in the design and implementation of environmental programs and policies.

2. *Environmental Dimensions of a Looming Energy Crisis.* The country is facing a severe electrical energy supply problem. It has exploited its considerable hydropower potential to the maximum extent possible subject to environmental, social and economic constraints. The last project proposed was turned down on environmental grounds, because it would have resulted in the loss of a number of culturally and aesthetically significant waterfalls.

Numerous attempts to construct new thermal power supply generating plants have been thwarted over the past 15 years by a combination of weak political leadership and even weaker environmental and social analyses. There has also been some discussion about the possibility of buying power and/or coal from India. The result is a country of 19 million people that currently is at the mercy of the monsoon rains. If they should fail to fill the hydropower reservoirs, the nation would face a major energy crisis that would cripple the economy. The solution will lie in a combination of demand management and supply expansion. There remains considerable scope for energy efficiency improvements, and power supply expansion must still pass through the strongest environmental impact regulations in the region and a political system that, thus far, has failed to exert sufficient vision and leadership on this subject.

Assistance to Bhutan

Information on Bhutan was collected from secondary sources. As mentioned, Bhutan's experiment with hydropower development in close cooperation with India is being carefully observed in Nepal. The country has a noteworthy and unique approach to development—

applying strict cultural and nature-based controls. But it is a model that Nepal, its most similar neighbour, would be hard pressed to emulate.

Despite its small size and isolationist policies, Bhutan cooperates productively in regional and global forums. For the moment at least, the country appears to have achieved a reasonable balance between environmental management and economic development. However, both the negative and positive external forces of globalization—together with growing internal pressures on the country's fragile mountain ecosystems and its still undemocratic political structures—may be difficult to control beyond the next decade. Bhutan receives no direct US environmental assistance .

Assistance to Maldives

Based on discussions in the region (the Maldives are covered by the US Embassy in Colombo), it is clear that this island nation has become very actively engaged with other small island states in international forums calling for attention to the threats from global climate change (particularly those associated with sea level and temperature rise). Their economy depends largely on fisheries and tourism-both of which are directly dependent upon healthy and productive coastal and marine ecosystems.

Attention to wise natural resources management—both within the borders of the archipelago and in the global commons—is a matter of high national priority. Despite the small population, environmental issues are given strong attention. There is strong interest in supporting such efforts at the US post in Colombo (in part because of the prospects for supportive positions in international forums), but assistance resources are extremely limited. The Maldives is in active discussions with the ADB (and IUCN) about participating in a new regional initiative on coastal resources management. Other environmental issues of greatest note are the supply of fresh water, sanitary disposal of solid wastes and efforts to develop renewable energy resources.

Assistance to Pakistan

Discussions with an IUCN staff member from Karachi were held at the GIN-Asia Conference, and an EPIQ team member also travelled to Pakistan in a private capacity affording an opportunity for further discussions with NGO representatives. A representative from the Karachi US Consulate attended the Kathmandu SA-ESTOC meeting.

Pakistan is facing concerns similar to those in neighbouring countries relating to population pressures on the natural resources base. However, the major issues in Pakistan appear tied to the environmental consequences of unplanned urban and industrial development. Though statistical analysis for the country remains weak, there is growing evidence of the heavy cost to human health paid by urban populations subject to severe air and water pollution. At present, there is no direct US assistance to Pakistan on environmental matters.

Programmes of World Bank

In the early 1990s, most environmental projects in the region dealt with natural resource issues. They included water resource management projects in Bangladesh and India, forestry and fisheries projects that addressed both production and resource degradation issues in Bangladesh, India, and Pakistan, and irrigation and drainage projects that focused on soil salinity and land degradation in India and Pakistan. As pollution concerns worsened, an increasing share of projects dealt with urban and pollution problems.

In the mid-1990s, the World Bank increased its emphasis on improving environmental management by supporting more effective policies, regulations, and procedures, as well as pollution prevention and control in Bangladesh, India, Pakistan, and Sri Lanka. The Bank sought to integrate environmental issues into other sectors, including transport, fisheries, and education. The mid- to late 1990s also saw increased attention to projects that focused on global and transboundary issues. For example, the Bay of Bengal Environment Program, which addresses fisheries research, environmental emergencies, large marine ecosystems, and coastal zone management in and around the Bay of Bengal, involves numerous riparian countries.

The Bank is currently emphasizing development outcomes and, specifically, ensuring that environmental programs benefit the poor. Programs and policy reforms are increasingly focused on reducing environment-related health risks; improving livelihood systems, particularly in rural areas; reducing vulnerability to natural and environmental disasters; and improving governance.

The Bank has continued to promote a coordinated and holistic approach to development assistance, by building partnerships and integrating environmental issues into sectoral and thematic strategies. The environmental portfolio is thus beginning to reflect issues highly relevant to poverty outcomes. This can be seen in two major areas.

First, the Bank is supporting innovative analytical work on the role of water supply and sanitation and reduced air pollution in achieving health outcomes in urban settings. For example, a study in Andhra Pradesh, India, designed to assist in the preparation of a State Environmental Action Plan, is assessing the overall burden of ill health associated with lack of water and sanitation infrastructure and with exposure to indoor air pollution as a result of the use of wood and dung for fuel.

Second, there is a sharper focus in all project development objectives on poverty impacts; examples include projects on sodic lands reclamation, joint forestry management, integrated watershed development, and fisheries management.

Strategic Priorities and Action

Consistent with the principles of the CDF, the present Strategy builds on the results of three years of realignment of environmental work in South Asia to focus primarily on development outcomes and the quality of operations and business procedures. The Strategy, while supported by a number of country and regional studies, also incorporates the results of continuous learning and interaction with clients and partners, including the recently held consultations in South Asia on the emerging Bank Environment Strategy.

The Strategy has extensive overlaps with all of the main pillars of the Bank's development approach, including:

(a) efficiency (with a particular focus on power, water, and petroleum sector reform measures);

(b) poverty (given that economic and social savings gained through improved environmental management have been shown to be highly progressive in both urban and rural areas); and

(c) governance (since public sector performance, rather than additional financial resources, is the key to improving environmental management).

Because South Asia is among the most populated and impoverished regions in the world, World Bank's Strategy focuses on contributing to making a difference in the quality of life of poor people by improving their health and livelihood systems and reducing their vulnerability to changes in environmental conditions. In addition, since equitable and sustained economic growth remains essential for substantially improving the quality of life of poor people in the region, the Strategy contributes to the development of policies and enabling conditions that support long-term quality of growth. Finally, the Strategy seeks to improve the quality of the regional and global commons in order to capture a significant part of their benefit flows locally, with the help of international financing mechanisms, and contribute to lessening the vulnerability of the region's poor to the effects of global environmental deterioration, for example, climate change.

Improving the quality of people's lives through better environmental conditions: The Strategy will continue the Bank's efforts over the past three years to promote environmental improvements as a fundamental part of development outcomes by supporting initiatives, programs, and policy reforms designed to:

— Improve livelihood systems, particularly in rural areas, through

(a) better management and improved productivity of the natural resources on which the poor depend;

(b) support for institutional reforms, incentive structures, and improved governance, particularly decentralization efforts;

(c) improved infrastructure, including access to markets, access to safe drinking water, and access to water for agriculture;

(d) improved access to agricultural technology, such as more productive, drought-resistant cropping systems;

(e) improved access to credit (for example, through microfinance);

(f) improved access to energy and to alternatives to solid fuels;

(g) improved educational and information services, including female education and extension services; and (h) support for initiatives to eliminate the gender gap and foster inclusive institutions

— Reduce environmentally related health risks by

(a) reducing exposure to indoor and outdoor air pollution;

(b) providing access to a safe and reliable drinking water supply;

(c) providing access to sanitation and solid waste services; and

(d) supporting mass hygiene and education programs.

Among the key areas of the World Bank's focus will be institutional reforms to improve service delivery, fiscal sustainability, and public-private partnerships.

— Reduce vulnerability to natural and environmental disasters through support for changes in land-use planning, disaster preparedness, community involvement and education, water conservation and management, and emergency-phase interventions.

— Refocusing the Bank's strategy in order to contribute to poverty reduction outcomes will also require addressing issues related to governance and supporting the emergence of institutions that can help empower the poor. Recent experiences with Bank projects and local success stories are providing evidence that social capital and participatory processes are as crucial to poverty reduction as are financial resources and development programs. Environmental institutions in the region are particularly weak and inefficient and would require reform and continued strengthening in order to become contributors to development outcomes.

Improving the quality of growth to support long-term sustainability. Because of the region's enormous environmental challenges and continued pervasive poverty, equitable and sustained economic growth is essential for producing lasting improvements in quality of life, particularly among the poor. In this context, policies and enabling conditions have been a major focus of every country program. The Bank's interventions will focus on two main areas:

1. Integrating environment into Country Assistance Strategies. This will be accomplished in three ways:
   (a) deepening macro-economic and sectoral reforms;
   (b) mainstreaming the environment into sector operations, including provision of operational support for the implementation of the safeguard policies; and
   (c) strengthening the analytical and empirical basis of the Bank's operational work.

   Recent and ongoing CAS work in India, Nepal, and Pakistan provides examples of this approach.

2. Enhancing project quality through strengthened implementation of safeguard policies. The overall emphasis in the region is on enhancing project quality by aiming for the most appropriate environmentally sustainable outcomes. Although a strong emphasis on safeguard policies may have a constraining effect on efforts to mainstream the environment, the focus on overall quality would not only ensure compliance on environmental safeguards but would also enhance environmental management in South Asia.

The shift in Bank lending operations toward a greater emphasis on programmatic lending has enhanced the promotion of strategic sectoral and regional environmental assessments to ensure adequate attention to environmental safeguards and good practice. Examples include sectoral assessments for energy reform projects in India and regional assessments for watershed projects in India and Pakistan. In addition, more attention is being given to integrating social and environmental assessments because of the intertwined nature of the issues involved. Combined environmental and social sectoral assessments for transport, urban, and rural development projects are now routinely being conducted in South Asia. Furthermore, there is increasing emphasis on environmental monitoring and evaluation, taking advantage of modern information management tools and human resources.

The Bank is placing a strong emphasis on local ownership and consensus building among its clients in South Asia to help them strengthen their environmental safeguard systems and practices. For example, the Bank is working collaboratively within the region and with the Asian Development Bank on the development of new resettlement polices in Pakistan and Bangladesh.

Enhancing the quality of the global and regional commons. The degradation of the region's global commons can constrain economic development because of its huge opportunity cost and threat to political security, The region's water resource systems, for example, are highly interdependent. The Bank's focus is on achieving global environmental objectives as a by-product of promoting local development benefits.

The management of shared river basins and seas poses an important challenge for the South Asia Region. The Bank has been involved in the past in helping to facilitate a robust agreement between India and Pakistan on the Indus River basin. The region could derive substantial benefits from greater cooperation among riparians on other internationally shared river basins, primarily the Ganges-Brahmaputra-Meghna basin.

South Asia is important from a climate change point of view in two respects. First, it is poised to become a major contributor to greenhouse gas emissions. Although per capita emissions in the region are currently very low, with total production of carbon dioxide representing only about 5 percent of global emissions, they are increasing at a rate of about 7 percent per year twice the average rate. Second, the impacts of climate change could be significant in the region, especially because of its extensive low-lying areas.

Small-scale renewable energy supplies may be the most cost-effective solution to providing reliable electricity in rural areas not connected to the grid and in some urban areas, and the use of cleaner fuels could have a concomitant impact on indoor air pollution. In the medium term, opportunities exist for building consensus on reform in the power sector that would promote energy efficiency and conservation and the application of renewable energy for rural and urban communities and industrial uses.

The custodians of South Asia's biodiversity are largely the rural poor, who often depend directly on these resources for their livelihood and sustenance. Efforts will therefore focus on finding effective mechanisms to channel available global resources—including GEF'to local communities in order to provide adequate incentives for changes in their patterns of resource use, and on broadening the scope of the GEF portfolio to promote biodiversity conservation over whole landscapes.

To enhance the quality of global and regional commons in South Asia, areas of focus will include:

— *Enhanced use of international financial assistance*: The integration of GEF into the Bank portfolio includes co-financing arrangements, as in the Bangladesh

Fisheries IV Project and the Pakistan Protected Area Management Project. Serious efforts are under way to better understand the tradeoffs and synergies between local and global environmental outcomes and to enhance the effective use of GEF resources to support mainstream Bank environmental activities.

— *Montreal Protocol activities.* The ongoing Montreal Protocol Program in South Asia has continued to expand. In India, as the Bank's portfolio of sub-projects has matured, approximately 3,000 tons of ODS chemicals have been phased out, of which sub-project completions in 1999 accounted for 580 tons. In addition, a major initiative to phase out production of all CFCs in India (one of the world's largest remaining producers of these chemicals), was agreed and began implementation in 2000.

Implementation Arrangements. The present Bank Environment Strategy for South Asia applies to the work being done by sector units throughout the Region, as well as to the work of the regional environment unit itself. More specific arrangements for effectively implementing the strategy include:

— Exercising selectivity in investment operations by:

(a) relying less on stand-alone environmental management projects implemented by central government agencies and more on mainstreaming the environment into sector operations;

(b) promoting participatory and community-driven development approaches (particularly in watershed management, irrigation and drainage, and area-based poverty reduction initiatives), and private sector participation, particularly in urban water supply, independent power production, and transport; and

(c) using GEF resources, when appropriate, to support the sustainable management of natural resources on which vulnerable groups depend (protected area management, medicinal plants, and solar thermal power).

Enhancing project quality by implementing the Bank's safeguard polices—a key pillar of strategy implementation. To this end, the World Bank have initiated the following activities:

(a) establishment of an independent safeguard review and compliance monitoring team;

(b) systematic upstream review and input into project design beginning with the project concept stage;

(c) a project risk management and compliance monitoring system, linked to the Bank's project document system;

(d) thematic joint social and environment reviews focusing on specific sectors such as water resources, transport, and health,

(e) periodic skills enhancement for all regional staff;

(f) enhancement of local ownership and consensus building; and

(g) strengthening the clients' capacity through policy dialogue and training

Intensifying the use of sectoral-regional environmental and social assessments by building on the experience of the past three years in the water, roads, and power sectors to enhance the environmental content of sector policies and institutions.

Strengthening analytical and advisory activities:

(a) filling critical gaps in knowledge and information by undertaking new analytical work on indoor air pollution (in at least two countries), clean fuels (in at least two countries), and NRM and rural livelihoods (in at least one country), in collaboration with the Energy and Rural Development Units;

(b) addressing institutional priorities by focusing on helping build client capacity in critical areas such as policy, incentives, and monitoring and enforcement; and

(c) promoting techniques that foster cross-sectoral integration, such as improved monitoring and evaluation of poverty impacts and spatially based analysis of projects and policies.

5

Sustainable Development in South Asia

Over the last decade, virtually all South Asian countries have made Environmental Impact Assessment (EIA) mandatory, especially for the larger projects. There have also been pioneering attempts at waste minimisation, clean technologies and initiatives, common effluent treatment and urban solid waste management. The need for conservation of biological diversity has been much more recognised and is visible in the several new initiatives including protection of National Parks and Sanctuaries.

Countries like Maldives and Sri Lanka have also taken the lead in demonstrating to the rest of the region that it is possible to achieve nearly 100 percent literacy and basic child immunization even with all the social, economic and other constraints. Sri Lanka has been particularly successful in arresting the population growth rate. The need for people's participation in policy formulation, programmes is increasingly being recognised by national and provincial governments. More than 70,000 people participated in the evolution of the National

Environment Management Action Plan (NEMAP) of Bangladesh. Experience from the Community Forestry Programme in Nepal, the Joint Forest Management Programme in India, and the Bangladesh Flood Action Plan indicates that several hurdles, including capacity building and empowerment, are yet to be crossed before meaningful participation is possible. The 73rd and 74th Constitutional Amendments in India have been a bold step towards empowering local self-governments in the rural and urban areas. More recently Pakistan has also enacted legislation to empower local governments.

Civil society groups in the sub-region, well known for their unique and pioneering contributions from the 'Chipko' movement to micro-credit systems, continue a diverse range of activities aimed at capacity building and service delivery to poorer communities. However issues of social justice and equity are still not adequately addressed in the sub-region. The larger and more global players among the corporate sector in the sub-region are recognising the need to be more explicit about their environmental and social responsibility. However, the vast majority is still driven by only the financial bottom line. They are yet to be influenced by environmental management measures that reduce waste and consumption, and the social norms, traditions and cultural values that cherish the natural resource base.

The globalisation process over the last decade has forced the academia in the sub-region to be less dependent on state funds and generate earnings through research for corporates. This has taken its toll on rigorous academic research on environmental and social issues. On the other hand, the globalisation process has increased manifold opportunities and space in the media—especially television. A number of capsules and programmes generated indigenously and also adapted from global operations contribute immensely to generate awareness on sustainable development concerns. Regional initiatives to address sustainable development concerns are also moving slowly, yet forward. The Male' Declaration on Control and Prevention of Air Pollution and its Likely Transboundary Effects for South Asia is a significant step in this direction. Other sub-regional Mechanisms like South Asian Association for Regional Cooperation (SAARC) and South Asian Preferential Trade Agreement (SAPTA) are also gradually beginning to focus on more concrete issues after going through the initial processes of confidence and institutional building. Most initiatives have been very successful on a micro-scale. The challenge is to set up and sustain systems that facilitate these initiatives on a much wider scale.

The enthusiasm of the civil society, considered efforts of the governments, dynamism of the media and cautious initiatives of the corporations in the sub-region have not been dampened by unfulfilled promises of the global community. Yet the unfulfilled promises are an important factor to be reckoned with in global deliberations on environment and sustainable development.

There are two main vehicles were designed at Rio for financing environmental protection and ensuring that the development process continued unhindered. The first was increased ODA flows to developing nations. The United Nations Conference on Environment and Development (UNCED) Secretariat had estimated that US$600 billion would be required each year between 1993 and 2000 to implement Agenda 21 in the low-income countries. Of this, US$125 billion was supposed to come from international donations or concessions. Towards this end, the high-income countries reaffirmed their commitment at Rio to reach the UN target of providing 0.7 percent of their Gross National Product (GNP) as Decreasing Overseas Development Assistance (ODA).

The reality however has been that ODA flows have failed to reach the 1992 figure of US$ 60 billion which is less than half the requirements. In fact the OECD records that ODA fell to its lowest of less that US$ 48 billion in 1997. The second vehicle was in the form of additional investment flows to the developing nations, through the Multi-lateral Environmental Agreements (MEAs) that were signed and agreed to during Rio. The only visible financial outcome of Rio is about $5 billion worth of commitments, mostly for the Global Environment Facility. Of this only $2 billion has been actually spent. In addition, there have been increased private sector investments into the low-income countries. However these have been concentrated in countries like China and India.

Most countries in the sub-region do not have the enabling conditions to attract large quantums of private sector investments. On the other hand, despite financial constraints, countries in the sub-region have increased their domestic investments in social and environmental sectors by initiating measures like tax reforms, environmental taxes and reducing perverse subsidies.

The Rio process deliberated considerably on the ways and means by which developing nations can have better access to technologies available with their industrialised counterparts. In the absence of firm commitments, there was a general understanding that various measures will be initiated to forge technology cooperation among the nations. The United Nations Commission of Sustainable

Development (CSD) was mandated to lead the process globally while the United Nations Asian and Pacific Centre to Technology Transfer (APCTT) was to complement this effort in the region. It clearly indicates that a wide range of activities have been initiated by most of the UN agencies to facilitate technology transfer, cooperation and capacity building in the developing world especially over the last decade.

However, the fact remains, that a decade after Rio, all developing nations and regions including South Asia still continue with obsolete technologies even as the rhetoric of technology transfer and cooperation continues. There are no firm commitments from the industrialised nations and thereby no compliance mechanisms within the international system to forge meaningful North-South technology cooperation. Probably, it may just be better for the developing nations and regions to pool in their resources for South-South cooperation in technologies. Technology cooperation with industrialized countries would be welcome on the basis of a clear understanding that they will be on mutually favourable terms and promote sustainability.

Another distressing factor for developing regions like South Asia has been the inadequacy of multilateral coordination and monitoring systems. There has been very little responsibility and accountability towards global conventions and obligations like Agenda 21. Follow-up mechanisms like the United Nations Commission on Sustainable Development (CSD) and other United Nations Agencies have little choice but to focus on softer issues of the agreements and commitments. As such they are not adequately empowered to ensure compliance and often are forced to be driven by concerns and changing policy directions of a handful of rich countries. While these agencies are pushed to the corner, developing nations quite helplessly watch and wait for the best. The marathon experiences at the Conference of Parties to the United Nations Framework Convention on Climate Change (UNFCCC) is adequate evidence.

Challenges to Sustainable Development

Sustainable development in the South Asian sub-region, and also globally, still remains a dream. Although countries like Sri Lanka and Maldives have reached a remarkable milestones in literacy, child immunisation and population control, poverty in the sub-region is chronic, population pressures are uncontrollable and the natural resource endowments are further being degraded and depleted. At the same time institutions and policies in the sub-region are not able to respond to emerging requirements. Chronic poverty are:

- — More than half a billion of its people living on less than a dollar a day
- — More than half the sub-region's children are malnourished
- — Almost half the people are illiterate
- — Nearly one-third of the people are unemployed

At the same time, the consumption patterns of the rich minority in the sub-region are moving rapidly towards unsustainable trends.

Population Pressures

- — South Asia, with its highest density of population in the world, is unable to support its unskilled people in agrarian activities

— Rural to urban migration has led to almost half of every city and town turning into slums and shanties

— Physical infrastructure and social facilities in both urban and rural areas are thus over stressed and very often dysfunctional

— Basic health and well-being of a majority of the population is constantly under threat Depleting and degrading natural resource endowments

— Almost half the land area in the sub-region is degraded in one form or another

— Most part of the sub-region are highly vulnerable to natural calamities like floods, earthquakes, cyclones, landslides and droughts

— With over-exploitation, the water resource base in the sub-region is under severe threat and nearly a fourth of the population do not have access to safe drinking water

— Reduction in the natural habitat, loss of species and depletion of genetic diversity characterise the plight of biodiversity in the sub-region

South Asia has witnessed a steady worsening of governance standards, essentially because of mutual distrust and threats from internal and external sources. In fact, institutional and policy shortcomings, have been one of the major causes behind overall sustainable development failures. The sub-region has suffered from lack of continuous focused attention to environmental and resource management by the national governments. At the national level, an encouraging trend in recent years has been that environment ministries and state agencies have been restructured and empowered with greater institutional strength to promote better vertical and horizontal co-ordination amongst different agencies. New legislations, including strengthening of existing laws has empowered executives and also enabled judicial institutions to oversee the effective enforcement of environmental measures.

The prominent transnational arrangements for strengthening the sub-regional institutional framework for sustainable development are the South Asian Association for Regional Co-operation (SAARC), South Asian Co-operative Environmental Programme (SACEP) and South Asian Preferential Trading Arrangement (SAPTA). In addition, there are regional (South East Asia, Asia Pacific) and global institutional arrangements, through various treaties and conventions that have significant impacts on the decision-making processes in the South Asian sub-region.

On the other hand, institutional shortcomings in South Asia include political instability, failure of commandand- control regimes and improper valuations that ignore costs to the environment. It is true that the region has received only a small fraction of what was promised at Rio. Yet, this can be no reason to justify institutional shortcomings in setting up the appropriate financial engines to lead the region into a sustainable future.

Ten years after Rio, a majority of the countries of South Asia remain the poorest in the world. The SAARC countries—with one fifth of the world's population and one third of Asia's—contribute just one per cent of the world's and five per cent of Asia's Gross Domestic Product. Agenda 21 was taken fairly seriously by the countries in South Asia who put in efforts consistent with their development priorities and fiscal constraints. However, the sub-region was unable to reverse degradation of natural resources but could slow down the rates of deterioration in some aspects. It also appears that the sub-region would have done better if some of the promises of aid flows mentioned in Agenda 21 had materialised. But, they are now confronted with new assessments in aid strategies with emphasis on private flows which are volatile.

The countries of South Asia should continue their war against poverty to improve the environment on their own with only a modest expectation of external aid which often comes with conditionalities and doses of advice. Experience over the last few decades, including that after Rio, echoes a very clear message. Developing countries and regions need to identify their own priorities and initiate concerted action with maximum selfreliance and minimal external assistance to retard the poverty and environmental degradation. The emerging sub-regional thematic priorities based on various regional and national assessments appear to be broadly as follows:

— Eliminating poverty and creating human security

— Managing population growth and its impact

— Conserving the natural resource endowments

— Securing the economic base.

A variety of experiences at different levels in the sub-region aimed at poverty eradication indicate that food and income securities are the two essential priorities that need to be directly addressed. Simultaneously, local communities need to be protected from devastation caused by regular natural disasters. While government and civil society organisations traditionally played a pivotal role in this effort, the importance of more proactive action by the private sector is being recognised. Some of the specific actions essential for creating human security in the sub-region are outlined below:

— Ensure food security through well-planned sustainable food production and distribution strategies:

— Emphasize self-sufficiency in food grains as a means of poverty reduction and livelihood for the 70 percent people who live in the rural areas

— Promote co-operative systems for aggregation of small land-holdings

— Strengthen research, information, infrastructure and incentives especially for small farmers

— Create a favourable and stable macro-economic environment for farmers

— Ensure accessibility and affordability of food grains, besides its availability

— Income security is intricately linked to explosive growth rates of the population in the sub-region.

— Promote income generating micro-enterprises as a means of livelihood and population control

— Strengthen micro-financing mechanisms by creating stronger ties between the small-scale enterprises and the formal sector

— Develop more effective marketing and distribution links with medium and large-scale industries

— Enhance the role of private sector as the main engine for economic growth and employment opportunities

— Facilitate the required reforms in the financial and capital markets to enable the effective functioning of the private sector.

— Ensure security from natural disasters. Prevent natural disasters through large-scale afforestation, rehabilitation of degraded lands, hazard resistant structures and other long term measures

— Strengthen preparedness for disasters through risk assessment, mapping, monitoring and vigilance systems

— Ensure that timely relief is available to disaster victims anywhere in the sub-region

Evolve policies and strategies that guarantee recovery and rehabilitation of victims affected by natural disasters The World Bank Regional Environmental Strategy notes that between 1990 and 1998, the sub-region accounted for more than 60 percent of disaster related deaths worldwide. These measures can ensure that the half a billion people in the sub-region vulnerable to regular natural calamities can be less prone and also have the security of long term rehabilitation.

South Asia cannot afford the annual 1.8 per cent population growth rate. The impacts are already visible with pressures on land, water and other natural resources. Cities and towns are bulging through the seams, and the infrastructure and facilities are over stressed. Arresting population growth is a priority for the survival of all the countries in the sub-region. It is important to learn from the experiences of Sri Lanka and Maldives. While population growth has to be directly addressed, experience shows that indirect measures are often more practically feasible and effective, though they may take a little longer to generate desired results. Some of the important measures that can be adopted are outlined below:

— Promote population control directly through large-scale awareness generation and small family incentives

— Reduce pressure on land by enabling rural communities to undertake non-farm income generating activities

— Provide livelihood security through food, water, energy, income and decentralised production systems

— Create sustainable cities by new management approaches that provide for the needs of the urban residents and at the same time protects the environment

— Strengthen infrastructure for health, education especially of women, drinking water, sanitation, transport, energy, and other public systems through conscious community participation and involvement

— Reformulate policies and strategies to encourage waste minimisation and pollution prevention by all stakeholders in society

Most countries in the sub-region are regularly confronted with poverty and survival issues. As a result, their financial and economic foundations are very fragile. The long-term sustainability of the South Asian subregion is critically dependent on a firm and secure financial and economic base. Each country in the sub-region has to strengthen its financial and economic systems. Considerable mutual support and assistance is possible through technology cooperation and sub-regional trade arrangements.

Countries in the sub-region, like their counterparts in the developing world, have quite naturally looked towards the industralised nations for state-of-the-art technologies. Experience clearly indicates that only second grade, or even obsolete, technology is often passed on. Countries in the sub-region need to focus seriously on indigenous technology development and sharing. Developing regions and sub-regions need to clearly demonstrate the potential and strength of South-South technology cooperation. Some of the vital steps in this process are:

- Identify the value addition and technology needs of the sub-region
- Initiate research and development through mutual support
- Create a South Asian Technology Bank
- Formulate agreements for technology sharing

Bangladesh, India and Pakistan have common interests in textiles and leather. It is only logical to cooperate in research and development for value added products. The opportunities become immense to compete in the global market. The sub-region needs to build up its capacity to negotiate with the industrialised world for specific technologies where it is critically required. The North-South technology cooperation should continue where it confers tangible and sustainable benefits to both the parties.

With acute poverty at one end, South Asia is also rated as the second fastest growing economic zone in the world (over 5% per annum), next only to the East Asian tigers. Unfortunately countries in the sub-region have not fully recognised and taken advantage of this latent potential. South Asia, with a consumer base of over 4257 million people in the middle class bracket—larger than any other economic bloc of the world— can contribute a great deal to the ever evolving global economy. Hence considerable rationalisation is required within the sub-region to tap this potential.

The countries in the sub-region need a much more liberalised trading regime among themselves. The South Asian Preferential Trade Agreement (SAPTA) and the proposed South Asian Free Trade Area (SAFTA) are important steps in this direction. However, these need to be strengthened and accelerated aggressively with several associated initiatives. For example, countries in the sub-region can accord "Most Favoured Nation (MFN)" status to each other to boost trade and their economies. Similarly, a single currency for the subregion may soon become inevitable.

Countries in the sub-region also need to pursue measures that reduce production and trading costs through sharing of basic resources. Pakistan has surplus power while Bhutan and Nepal have not harnessed their energy potential. On the other hand India and Bangladesh are power deficient. Subregional sharing of energy, besides rationalising peaks, can reduce costs and demand for power. Similarly, sharing of water and other natural resources may be considered for the mutual benefit of collaborating nations.

While strengthening preferential trade within the sub-region, South Asia also needs to build up its bargaining power as an economic bloc in the global trade negotiations. The sub-region has several unique products and services to be offered to the rest of the world. These include its rich traditional knowledge, practices, relatively pristine tourism destinations, biological diversity, arts and crafts, besides 'modern' industrial products and services and pool of contemporary brain power. The sub-region needs to carefully valuate these products and services as a bloc and negotiate with other regions from a position of strength.

In all international deliberations, developing countries are seen to be negotiating for more development assistance, besides technology. It is clear that overseas development assistance has been decreasing over the years and the likelihood of its increasing substantively is remote. In fact, many a developing country has been gradually dragged into the debt trap. Countries in South Asia need to consciously look at developing themselves with minimal overseas development assistance. With technology and trade cooperation, the economies in the sub-region can be bootstrapped. The sub-region also needs to seriously consider setting up a South Asian Development Bank, with equity contribution from the member countries and other multilateral, bilateral and private institutions. There is growing recognition in the South Asian sub-region that the priorities of eliminating poverty, managing population growth, conserving natural resources and building macro-economic stability can only be addressed if the development process is fundamentally reoriented so as to focus on them directly. It is also widely recognized that this can only be achieved if there is a clear understanding among all stakeholders of the issues that underlie sustainable development and of the types of policies and actions that are needed to bring it about.

Some of this recognition comes from direct observation of the negative impacts of development policies followed by countries of the sub-region over the past fifty years. It is reinforced by the widespread awareness created by the dozens of global conferences and extensive international negotiations that started with the United Nations Conference on the Human Environment held at Stockholm in 1972 and included the Earth Summit at Rio de Janeiro in 1992. It is particularly important to note that the primary stakeholders— the people of the sub-region—have begun to appreciate the opportunities and limits offered by a more sustainable pattern of development. The secondary stakeholders— their leaders and decision-makers—are beginning to define clearer priorities for making such development happen. A great deal, however, remains to be done before the economies of South Asia become genuinely sustainable.

Although the global concern for making development processes more sustainable originated with the Stockholm Conference and centered largely on questions of environmental degradation, it has subsequently evolved to encompass a much broader range of issues. Perhaps more than in any other region of the world, experience over the past thirty years has helped South Asian societies to appreciate the importance of striking an effective balance among the three major components of sustainability:

— Social
— Environmental
— Economic

Intellectual discourse, media coverage and occasional political statements testify to a widening appreciation of the need to pre-empt conflict among these different societal imperatives by designing development strategies that simultaneously try to optimize the combination of all three. Agenda 21, adopted at Rio, was the tangible confirmation of this need at the global level. This appreciation has, however, yet to be translated into policies and action that deal comprehensively with the problem. Within the global context, it is somewhat ironic that the debate appears to be coming back full circle to focus once again primarily on environmental issues. This factor is intensified by the low level of interest or involvement in the Decreasing Overseas Development Assistance (WSSD) process thus far by the ministries of finance at the country level or by some of the main international development actors. In the final analysis, sustainable development is simply a matter of achieving sustainable consumption patterns and sustainable production systems. Unfortunately, these goals are more easily stated than pursued, and few societies have in recent times come close to attaining them. Nevertheless, the cultures of South Asia, with their long histories and traditions of living in harmony with nature, rooted as much in the spirit as in matter, do have a head start and could provide a model of sustainable development that is applicable more widely.

Any successful effort to bring about sustainable development will necessarily require countries of the subregion to establish mechanisms for formulating policy and implementing it at the relevant levels:

— Local
— National
— Regional
— Global

At each level, it is now necessary to build capacity for understanding the basis of action for sustainable development, formulate policies and programmes to encourage such action, establish responsibilities, set up mechanisms for monitoring progress towards agreed goals and create mechanisms for accountability.

The results of past international negotiations, including the slow and inadequate implementation of international conventions such as those on climate change, biodiversity conservation and desertification, indicate the importance of accountability mechanisms. From a South Asian perspective, the primary function of the WSSD at Johannesburg, has to be to set up international regimes under which building such capacity is facilitated and to design systems of accountability that ensure the desired results. Unquestionably, implementing Agenda 21 and introducing policies, technologies and action that can make development more sustainable needs more money than is currently available for development programmes. This was clearly recognized at Rio but the international community has failed rather miserably on this front.

Concessional funding flows to the South Asian sub-region have been totally inadequate. In fact its share had declined from 17% in 1989 to 14% in 1996. But there is also a growing recognition that more money alone cannot solve the problems faced by nations in their efforts to modernize their economies. Fundamental changes are also needed in the global economy, as well as in the domestic economies of nations, if the benefits of increasing prosperity are to reach everyone, now and in the future.

If WSSD and future conferences at the global level are genuinely to address developing country issues, these countries must play a stronger role in setting the agenda of these conferences. Thirty years after the Club of Rome's "Limits to Growth" fueled global concerns on environmental degradation, it is now necessary to establish the "Limits to Poverty" to overcome the next constraint on sustainability of the present economic systems. Poverty eradication needs to be seen as part of the solution not just recognised as a problem. On these issues, South Asia has useful insights to contribute but these will only become visible when the developing world as a whole learns to set the agenda for international dialogue.

One major solution to all four priorities are:—eradication of poverty, arresting population growth, regeneration of the natural resource base and improved productivity of the economy—lies in the widespread creation of sustainable livelihoods. Sustainable livelihoods are jobs that require minimal capital investment; create incomes, meaning and dignity; and place least pressure on the environment. They produce goods and services that cater to the basic needs of the local people and simultaneously help them generate purchasing power to acquire these goods and services. The creation of sustainable livelihoods requires fundamental changes in the choice of technology, financing systems and the functioning of the marketplace. It also needs strengthening of the institutions of local governance, which must now be designed to create a sense of ownership by local people over the resources on which they depend for their livelihoods, and the decisions systems that guide their lives.

There is widespread consensus in South Asia, both at the official level and among civil society organizations that Social Mobilisation is the most effective instrument for creating both the supply of sustainable livelihoods and the demand for them. This is where the traditionally marginalised and vulnerable groups like women, indigenous people, youth and others play a critical role. The countries of South Asia have experimented with a broad range of social mobilisation options and are becoming increasingly familiar with the kinds of intervention needed. Successful social mobilization must be based on active participation by the stakeholders, transparency and access to information, technology, credit and markets. Certain institutional factors can accelerate the process of social mobilization. The most widely accepted ones include local self-government, clearly defined entry points and effective support systems.

Extensive field experience shows that local self-governance is one of the most effective catalysts for social mobilization. Unless communities have a sense of ownership over their resources, they tend to neglect them. Acquiring a sense of ownership is best made possible by real ownership, such as the right to tax and the right to decide how to use the resources. These issues are of profound implication for sustainable management of natural and other resources, but they must be resolved within the context of each country's constitutional framework and legal system. Effective social mobilization programmes often start with an entry point that is a priority for the local community, as identified by the people themselves: job creation, food security, literacy and primary education, health, shelter, credit or productive infrastructure. To get started and to keep going, social mobilization programmes also need support mechanisms that can supply essential inputs and services at the community level.

Experience suggests that community based organisations, micro credit facilities and social welfare agencies can best play this role. It is essential, however, that they carry out their specialized tasks within a broader understanding of the complexity of village life and help connect the community to other services that bring about education, enterprise and empowerment. In this manner, communities can build their capacity to make endogenous choices— their own decisions, reflecting their own realities, their aspirations and their knowledge of their resource endowment.

Governance of Sustainable Development

The primary responsibility of national governments in the sustainable development process is to empower and facilitate the functioning of local governance institutions. They need to ensure that governments at all levels are democratic, participative, transparent and accountable. Civil society, including community based organizations and non-governmental agencies are now growing rapidly in terms of their influence on people's lives. Such institutions need to be encouraged and nurtured, based on their track record particularly because they are usually better capable of delivering social mobilization services, and usually at a fraction of the cost. Because of their high levels of motivation and willingness to work within severely constrained circumstances, they are also effective innovators from whom many new solutions can be adopted on a larger scale.

The corporate sector is also beginning to realize the opportunities offered by the rural market in South Asian countries and can be a major potential partner in introducing sustainable development services to the poor. While corporate sector participation in the development process needs to be encouraged, governments and regulatory systems must ensure that profit motives do not deteriorate cultural values and traditional conservation practices. To encourage the corporate sector, infrastructure and other support services must be provided by government or it has to create an enabling environment for corporate sector to build the required infrastructure in rural areas on build-own-transfer (BOT) basis. Perhaps the most important responsibility that governments have is to set an example of efficient operations for agencies in the other sectors to follow. Some of the specific actions for better governance are outlined below :

— Facilitate meaningful involvement in policy formulation and implementation by representatives of the private sector, local authorities, NGOs, trade unions and other major groups.

— Respect indigenous peoples' intellectual and cultural property rights while recognising cultural diversity and ethnic plurality.

— Balance short-term economic benefits with medium and long term objectives, particularly in the social and environmental spheres

— Incorporate sustainable development principles in national Constitutions or legislation to accelerate the adoption of better development strategies

— Plan development activity on the basis of active public consultation as demonstrated by Bangladesh in evolving National Environment Management Action Plan

— Focus on design of legal and regulatory regimes that improve political and civil service accountability within the context of decentralized government.

Enhanced cooperation among South Asian countries will contribute significantly to addressing their common sustainable development priorities.

Food security in the sub-region can be considerably enhanced by strengthening the SAARC Food Security Board (SFSB) established in 1988 to advise governments on the food situation and prospects in the subregion including factors such as production, consumption, trade, prices, quality and stocks of food grains. With stronger research capability, the SFSB can play its full role in advising on the international trade issues to protect the social and economic rights of poor/marginal farmers. The SFSB may also consider the setting up of a South Asian Food Bank. Decentralised centres can be designated in different parts the sub-region to ensure that any deficits is a particular location, at any given time can be balanced with supplies from other centres.

Co-operation for disaster preparedness, protection against vulnerability and the management of disasters needs to be strengthened in the sub-region. These can be achieved through joint observation and monitoring, research and information sharing programmes for seismicity, storm surges, cyclones and weather prediction. Rapid action mechanisms can also be set up in the sub-region to respond as soon as disasters occur.

Trade and Economic Policies

Countries in South Asia need to pursue much more aggressively the potential and opportunities that unfold through strengthened sub-regional cooperation in trade and economic policies. Whatever be their political differences, countries need to recognise that their individual and collective macro-economic stability and bargaining power in the global market hinges on building a strong economic bloc.

Management of Natural Resources

South Asia is home to spectacular natural beauty and biological wealth. It harbours approximately 15 percent of the known global flora and fauna. Unfortunately the rich natural endowments, including the precious gene pool, are constantly under threat. On one end poachers and illegal traders exploit poor enforcement mechanisms. At the other end, inadequate environmental and social assistance of programmes like mining and dams cause enormous harm to environment and society. More recently, traditional knowledge and ownership rights of indigenous communities are also being threatened by global trade and patenting agreements. This is in spite of the ecological debt built up by industrialised economies over the years by systematically exploiting the natural endowments in developing regions. The loss of sub-regional biodiversity adversely affects the people of South Asia and also the global community. The South Asian biodiversity may hold the cure for some widespread diseases like AIDS and cancer. The sub-region as a whole needs to set up systems to manage this wealth judiciously. Some of the key priorities for action by the sub-region are outlined below:

— Assess, map and document the biodiversity wealth of the sub-region

— Demarcate and protect fragile habitats at all costs

— Revive traditional knowledge, especially among local communities, indigenous people and women, that promotes conservation practices and integrate conservation efforts in all sectors

— Facilitate the manufacture of high value added products from the resource base by industry in the subregion and curtail bio-piracy

— Use the rich biodiversity and products manufactured in the sub-region as a bargaining tool in the international market

— Formulate sub-regional policies and programmes, like the South Asian Regional Seas Programme and Biodiversity Action Plans, to address issues of biodiversity conservation and international trade

A broad range of opportunities exist for cooperation in energy aimed at environmental and supply security. Both renewable and fossil fuel based energy use can be substantially rationalised once the national policies are geared to the imperatives of sub-regional cooperation. Similarly the sub-region needs to develop a variety of cooperative mechanisms for sharing of water resources, data collection and analysis, and emergency response measures.

As evident from the experiences after Rio, South Asia is home to a diverse range of sustainable development initiatives at various levels. The more successful ones need to be scaled up and adopted by the sub-regional mechanisms like the Integrated Program for Action (IPA). Bhutan, has officially adopted the concept of Gross National Happiness as the index of the nation's progress. The important components of the index, beyond the usual economic constituents of GNP, include additional factors such as good governance, environmental quality and cultural promotion. Taking the cue from this pioneering policy initiative, it would be opportune for countries of the sub-region to explore setting up a composite South Asian Happiness Index. Such an index would provide a much-needed counterweight to the purely economic indices of progress that currently define and underlie economic and social development policies.

Responsible Global Systems

Commitments were made at Rio, but much more concerted efforts are required by the global community to fulfill them. More action and accountability is needed to promote sustainable consumption and production systems, strengthen global cooperation, and ensure fulfillment of government obligations and corporate social responsibility.

Sustainable development requires sustainable consumption patterns and sustainable production systems. Most industrial production systems today are not sustainable. They are too capital intensive, resource consuming, heavily subsidised and too wasteful. Yet, virtually every country today wishes to "become competitive in the global economy" by emulating the same technological strategies. This means that transforming production systems to meet the imperatives of sustainability will not be easy. Sustainable consumption is an even more ambitious objective, which aims at transforming the ways in which goods and services are used and disposed of so that the needs of all people are met and the environment is conserved.

Most of the action needed to make the lifestyles of people sustainable can take place only at the local or national levels. Nevertheless, the international community can influence the local and national decision making systems quite deeply, as for example in changing technologies for refrigeration as a result of the Montreal Protocol, or of changing energy policies as a result of the Kyoto Protocol. The instruments available to the global community range from international treaties to taxation and pricing systems. Consumption patterns and lifestyles are contentious issues at the international level: political leaderships find it difficult to commit the people of their nations to reducing their use of natural resources such as energy or water. Nevertheless, given the high level of disparity in the consumption of resources in different societies, and the limits set by certain environmental constraints such as the emission of greenhouse gases into the atmosphere, some degree of adjustment will have to take place.

Governments must now take some responsibility to help guide the driving forces that influence consumption patterns in any society. This means addressing issues such as market pressures (e.g. pricing, advertising, credit), the policy framework (e.g. perverse incentives), cultural expectations, technological innovation, infrastructure and land use as well as individuals purchasing decisions. This, in turn, entails tackling the institutionalised inertia in today's markets, policy and society, which currently prevents widespread action. Just as commercial advertising can deeply influence consumption patterns, new publicly funded methods must be evolved that communicate the advantages of more sustainable consumption.

UNCED called on the industrialised countries to take the lead in sustainable consumption and a number of governments, businesses and citizen organisations have now responded. Ironically, this has produced an agenda overly dominated by industrialised country concerns and solutions. This has also generated the false assumption that it is only an issue for the developed world, with only a single valid approach that is applicable to all countries and situations, and that developing countries have little to offer in terms of lifestyles for sustainability.

In this context, the words of the ECO-Asia initiative launched by the Government of Japan provide a salutary reminder of the value of cultural diversity: it called on countries in the region to "rediscover those elements in their traditional way of life suited to conserving the environment". Making consumption sustainable is a long-term task, which will require structural change in economies and lifestyles, tackling often entrenched expectations and vested interests. These issues cannot be addressed by policy alone, but will require political vision and determination to take tough choices where these are necessary, supported by a broad public movement for change.

Bringing about fundamental changes will need concerted effort on the part of international agencies, governments, corporations and civil society. They will need to establish innovative partnerships to support research and action globally and particularly in developing countries, on sustainable development and integration of economic, environmental and social issues:

— to eradicate global poverty

— to conserve the environmental resource base

— to ensure that the benefits of globalisation processes reach the poor and conserve the environment

— to ensure market access of the poor countries in the global market and global trade

— to create a financial institutional framework that ensures access to micro-credit and mini-credit.

— to ensure support for micro and mini enterprises and financial institutional capacity at local and community levels, particularly in poor countries

— to strengthen the capacity of developing countries to negotiate, access technology and ensure implementation of global conventions

— to develop global governance code of ethics on corruption and agree to eliminate corruption at all levels of public life.

The Earth Summit at Rio de Janeiro concluded with the signing of two conventions - on Climate Change and Biodiversity - and the adoption of Agenda 21. An integral part of Agenda 21 was the cost associated with implementing it, which was estimated at the time to be over $ 600 billion per year for ten years. Of this $125 billion was to be contributed by the international donor community and rest by recipient governments. The developed economies have failed to honor their commitments at Rio.

Though many international organisations are moving towards "poverty alleviation", one is hard pressed to see how their programmes have in any way changed to respond to this changed priority. Poverty now needs to be eradicated and the means for doing so exist. The Independent South Asia Poverty Commission strongly advocates that poverty eradication must be considered as the part of the solution and not just recognised as a problem. But the international system needs to put in extraordinary efforts and commitments to achieve this goal. Climate change and biodiversity loss are problems of grave importance to the countries of South Asia and the global community. These are the countries that will pay the highest costs resulting from these global catastrophes. It is the island and coastal nations in the tropics that are going to disappear under rising sea levels and floods. It is their agriculture that is going to need the genetic material of cultivars to stay ahead of pests and declining yields.

Judging from the performance of past Conferences, it would appear that the agreements made at UN Conferences such as the Earth Summit are not implemented in all its seriousness. The South Asian view is that a system should be put in place that ensures accountability and parties to agreements can be held responsible for implementing them. It is therefore of paramount importance to plan for enhancing the accountability with regard to international agreements made. Any international agreement must be accompanied by relevant and explicit mechanisms for ensuring compliance and accountability. To accelerate the process of sustainable development on a global scale, the international community should also:

— Seek new financial mechanisms to support sustainable development objectives, e.g. tradeable permits, taxes on financial transactions (Tobin tax), and taxes on fuel used in all international aviation, including military.

— Eliminate duplication of programs and activities among international secretariats for sustainable development global accords.

— Expand and strengthen the role of UNEP to promote the coherent implementation and monitoring of the environmental dimension of sustainable development within the UN system and reassess the roles of UNEP and UNDP in environmental technology and capacity building.

— Expand the mandates of UN financial institutions and others to support indigenous programms on sustainable development, indigenous rights, spiritual knowledge, lands and resources.

— Strengthen implementation, monitoring of global conventions

— Support research in developing countries on sustainable development and integration of economic, environmental and social factors.

The corporate sector responded positively to the processes at Rio. Subsequently several initiatives were taken either by corporates themselves or in conjunction with governments or international development agencies. As a consequence large corporations have started to act on their environmental and social activities. However a vast majority of the small and medium enterprises do not still find it viable to act on environmental and social concerns. The global community needs to focus on mechanisms that make it meaningful for corporations to act on the triple bottom line—financial, environmental and social. In this context the efforts like the Global Reporting Initiative (GRI) need to be encouraged. Attempts are being made to evolve more comprehensive monitoring mechanisms with the participation of a broader set of stakeholders.

The Global Compact initiated by the United Nations Secretary General also aims to involve the corporate sector much more in sustainable development efforts. South Asia today stands at a crossroad. A decade after Rio, it is still ridden with poverty and natural resources degradation. On the other hand, immense latent potential exists within the member countries. There is a broad consensus on the thematic priorities of poverty eradication, managing population growth, conserving natural resources and building macro-economic stability. However, the challenge is for more action and accountability at various levels. Besides housekeeping within the countries, the sustainable development processes initiated at the local and national levels need to be multiplied exponentially. This is possible only through much stronger Subregional cooperation, keeping aside socio-political differences. South Asia today has immense potential in all the three key inter-related components of sustainable development.

On the social front are the unique diversity of traditional values, arts, crafts and cultural practices, besides modern industrial products, services and pool of contemporary brainpower. On the environment front the subregion is endowed with approximately 15% of the known biological wealth of the world. Finally on the economic front, besides being the second fastest growing region in the world, the sub-region also has the largest consumer base. The initiatives required are fairly well known. The political will for cooperation supported by a robust operational mechanism can transform the sub-region into a strong and sustainable entity within the global community.

6

Environmental Sustainability: Future Trends

In many developing countries, productivity is low, growth is stagnant, and unemployment is high. The number of people living on less than $1 a day is dropping but it is still a challenge, and more people are living on fragile lands. Income inequality is rising. Many of the poorest countries are wrecked by civil conflict, with animosities deep and prolonged. Stress on the environment is increasing. Science and technology are will not be sufficient without complementary changes in institutions. The world community, in confronting some of the challenges, is grappling with new strategies and goals. Development agencies are shifting to more participatory and holistic approaches with a medium-term perspective, through the Comprehensive Development Framework (CDF) and focused poverty reduction strategies, backed by actions on the ground through partnerships, broader inclusion in the preparation of assistance strategies, and some shifts in lending and grant aid. The private sector is more committed to sustainable development, with greater use of triple-bottom-line accounting by firms and greater use of environmental and social criteria by investors. Governments and civil society are supporting the Convention on Biodiversity, the Convention to Combat Desertification, the Convention on Climate Change, and the Millennium Development Goals. And civil society is demanding more public and private accountability. Although encouraging, these advances are small relative to the many challenges of sustainable development. Sustainability requires thinking long term, but acting now-it also requires coordination.

Technologies and preferences will change, and resource allocation and distribution issues cannot be neatly separated. Managing risk is important. Not all risks are insurable. Not all irreversible changes are bad, but some are. For the assets most at risk-the natural and social-markets cannot provide the basic coordinating functions of sensing problems, balancing interests, and executing policies and solutions. These types of assets have impacts, good and bad, that extend beyond individual transactions and thus require coordination to promote good spillovers and minimize the bad. The rising income can facilitate but not guarantee better environmental and social outcomes by permitting countries to simply "grow out of " pollution or civil conflict. Problems with impacts and risks that are diffuse and long term (such as climate change and biodiversity loss) are less readily perceived and appreciated than those immediately felt and measured (i.e., some forms of local air and water pollution and deforestation).

Assets that are public goods or common property goods-such as clean air, forests, fisheries, and water-are a challenge to manage sustainably. The reason is that private property rights are difficult to assign or enforce, or if improperly designed they fragment and undermine the underlying joint functions of an asset-say, an interconnected ecosystem. In addition, the concerns of the poor and powerless are less likely to attract the attention of society's many institutions than those of strong and vested interest groups. That is why greater equality in access to assets and voice makes a difference in the kinds of environmental and social concerns that society addresses. When the poor lack voice and a stake in society, social assets (such as trust) and environmental assets (on which the poor depend) are eroded, stability is undermined, and the ability to solve economic, social, and environmental problems dissipates.

At the very least, inequality and the lack of hope for the poorest countries will inhibit attempts at solving global problems-not just the current preoccupations with cross-border spillovers of conflict and terrorism, but also the currently unimagined problems that will require global cooperation 20 or 50 years hence. That is why ending global poverty is much more than a moral imperative-it is the cornerstone of a sustainable world. In the future, we will also witness completion of the urban transition in most countries. The demographic transition will permit greater savings if the working age population has jobs and investment opportunities. The urban transition will facilitate income generation, but over the next 50 years it will also require massive investments. Many of these investments are likely to be long-lived-so getting them right by incorporating environmental and social concerns in their design now is critical. Even the next 15 years could bring a record period of economic growth in developing countries.

Driven by growth in China and India, income in the low- and middle-income countries will almost double-accounting for more than a third of the 60 percent increase in world output. This period offers the opportunity to lay the foundation for inclusive growth-which will require confronting barriers to change. Institutions that can manage the social and economic transitions, by partially compensating losing interests, are much easier to create in rapidly growing economies than in economies where inclusion requires a battle over stagnant shares. For many countries whether the opportunities generated by new growth are inclusive, or whether they lock in vested interests and exclusive institutions, will depend on decisions taken in the next few years.

Sustainable development requires action across many sectors and disciplines, including water, energy, health, agriculture, biodiversity, and others. In a companion document, the World Bank sets forth some recommendations and action plans to advance sectoral goals. Achieving all the broad sectoral goals will involve problem diagnosis, decisions with distributional consequences, and coordinated and sustained commitments to action. These functional capabilities require general improvement in coordinating institutions within and across countries. Making progress on the sectoral issues, for example, requires first a better understanding of local conditions and a better ability to diagnose local problems. Domestic and international institutions will be required to fund and implement R&D where local capacities are deficient. Health and water services often deteriorate after costly initial investments for lack of routine funding and maintenance. This speaks to the challenge of organizing beneficiaries for sustained commitments.

The same is true for environmental is-sues-the status of biodiversity, air pollution, lead in gasoline, or the drawdown of acquifers in arid regions. There is a need for significant investment in information and indicators at global and local levels, where this information would find users and audiences. The initiative must go well beyond current attempts to devise indicators of sustainable development, including summary indexes that try to capture sustainable development in a single headline number. If society is to sustain development, it needs good indicators, but it also needs individuals and groups who demand and use detailed, and quality information to solve problems, and others who produce information to meet that demand.

Environmental and social problems are easy to misdiagnose when there is a lack of reliable, current, and geographically disaggregated information. For many important aspects of the environment, global conditions or trends are worrisome, but society lacks the detailed data to monitor, diagnose, and manage the problems at local, national, and global levels. For most countries, reliable, up-to-date, spatially desegregated information is lacking on poverty and many other social concerns (health, education, crime). These data gaps inhibit understanding of-and consensus on-the impacts of policy reforms, national and international, on poverty in the developing world. They also impede the formulation and execution of strategies to combat desertification, other forms of ecosystem degradation, and biodiversity loss. And they muddy the discussion of the nature and impacts of global inequality. Fortunately, rapid changes in communication and information technology make it more feasible to gather this information through a combination of surveys, reports from ground observers, and information from satellites and other sensors. As information costs continue to plummet, the scope for expanding the collection of this kind of information is immense.

Innovative information systems can track and deter industrial polluters and illegal deforestation and forest fires. Although information provision can sometimes be a catalyst for change, the most effective systems are those that create constituencies for information. The constituencies may be public agencies that use the information to plan and assess strategies for pollution control, crime prevention, or public health delivery. Or they may be civil society organizations that use information to mobilize dispersed interests. It is demand by users that stimulates and maintains the production of relevant, reliable information. To equitably and efficiently balance interests within a society, two elements are necessary: first, getting everyone fairly represented at the bargaining table; second, facilitating negotiation once everyone is there. For many problems at the level of the community or nation-especially those relating to environmental and social issues-the responsibility lies with the government.

But governments vary in their capacity to undertake these tasks. An expanding set of institutional tools can assist or complement governments in balancing interests, and they can assist citizens in ensuring that their governments are fair and responsive in doing so. These tools become even more important at the international level, where they must substitute for government. It is fundamentally difficult to balance interests in heterogeneous societies. But taken together, in a context of increasingly democratic institutions and decreasing costs of information and communication, these tools give some hope. Providing this kind of information helps level the playing field for negotiation, since less powerful interests will typically have poorer access to information. Performance reporting can also help governments, companies, and other organizations understand the effectiveness and impacts of their own actions, for instance National reporting-transparency in fiscal affairs, reliability of legal institutions, and adequacy of environmental impact reviews-can all provide the information and incentives necessary to improve governance and the balancing of interests.

Basic principles for balancing interests therefore include minimizing the losses, compensating losers, or providing incentives that reconcile private and social objectives. One way to do this in the environmental sphere is through market-based permits. Where actors have different costs of complying with social objectives, trading rights or obligations can substantially reduce compliance costs for individuals and for society as a whole. Assignment of valuable permit rights is also a means of compensating potential losers and ensuring participation in a reformed system. Certification systems are another means of aligning private and social incentives. Certification of firms helps investors identify companies with better environmental and social performance, thus promoting incentives for more socially responsible behaviour.

Certification of financial institutions can promote standards for assessing the environmental and social impacts of investment projects. Certification of products (wood, coffee, fish, beach resorts, garments) can allow consumers and investors to reward firms that employ environmentally and socially sustainable production processes. Certification of diamonds and other lootable commodities can be part of a strategy to avert civil conflict over point-source wealth. Even governments may find it advantageous to participate in voluntary certification schemes. For instance, the Alaska state government applied for, and received, certification by the Marine Stewardship Council for management of its salmon fishery.

The success of these efforts depends on how they influence producer, consumer, and investor behaviour. And that depends on the costs of certification, the proportion of the industry that is sensitive to certification, and the legitimacy, integrity, and reliability of the certification criteria and process. To become more widespread and effective, certification systems require coordinated international attention on several grounds. First, there are important links to the world trade system and a need for coordination with WTO activities-to ensure that standards are not used to disguise protectionism. Second, careful attention is needed to monitor the possibility that complying with certification procedures may be too burdensome for small firms. Third, and probably most important, there is a need to ensure the integrity of the evolving certification systems. For these systems to work on a large scale, they will probably require a massive expansion of "markets for honesty." These are the networks of private auditors and certifiers, and their accreditation agencies, that provide ISO certification, shipping certification, and audits of corporate earnings. Implementing and executing policies and programs requires appropriate institutional capacity.

Mention of capacity-building evokes respect and approval-but not always excitement or enthusiasm. It has usually been seen as an add-on to projects and programs with other, more important purposes. It is often identified with failed technical assistance projects that relied heavily on the ephemeral input of foreign consultants. The same is true of monitoring and evaluation, another project add-on that often fails to be executed with rigor or to provide much insight. Promoting capacity-building and problem-solving in the developing world. Yet, despite technical cooperation grants of $201.3 billion over 1990-2001, 6 progress in institution-building in developing countries has been disappointing. Most of those funds, to be sure, have been devoted to project preparation. Such investments may have been effective in achieving project goals through reliance on expatriate inputs, but at the cost of forgone opportunities to bolster local capacity. There are failures, too, in the demand for institution-building. Often, lack of ownership, lack of government interest in bolstering capacity, and pressures for rent-seeking have kept competent institutions from taking root.

Several new approaches could help place learning and institutional development at the core of sustainable development efforts-that is, projects and programs designed around institutional development, rather than vice versa. These approaches recognize that capacity-building is not accomplished in a few years and thus is not well suited to lending for individual projects or adjustment programs. These approaches also recognize that capacity has a strong social capital component, involving not just people but enduring networks that link policymakers, experts, civil society, and the private sector. And these approaches generate virtuous circles when information and indicators are made available to groups that demand and act on that information.

The new approaches use a variety of new types of learning organizations to stimulate both the demand for and supply of institutional skills; they include: Scientific research organizations, based in the developing world, that combine local and global expertise and help to nurture "policy entrepreneurs" at home in both scientific and policy worlds. Learning networks for sharing knowledge, such as the Union of Capital Cities of Ibero-America-real-time, demand-driven learning networks run by national and international associations of mayors, local government officials, and city practitioners share experiences among their members and other cities through the Internet and workshops.

These groups that independently monitor and report on government and corporate expenditures and activities have proliferated recently. They can help improve government and corporate accountability, create incentives for monitoring and evaluation within government and corporations, and mobilize pubic demand for institutional improvements. Donors and multilateral development banks can support the evolution of this intellectual ecosystem of organizations that learn-and apply that learning to improving policies and projects. Donors can support these organizations, through direct funding and twinning arrangements on a large scale. These are long-term efforts that bear fruit over a decade or two as the institutions train people, enhance the prestige of necessary but neglected professions, such as policy analysis, and build dense networks of trust and knowledge.

Funding must be committed over periods much longer than traditional projects, and funders must accept that the impacts of these investments, though potentially enormous, will be deferred and difficult to quantify. Donors can also design projects with learning as a central output, providing hands-on monitoring, evaluation, and implementation experience to learning organizations. At the transnational and global level, assessment institutions such as the IPCC have shown their value in forging consensus on the problems and the options for addressing them. More institutions like the IPCC are needed to address the new global problems that continue to emerge all the time.

Trade policy is an area where more systematic analysis of options might help in forging agreements. Deepening scientific knowledge exposes overlooked transnational environmental processes. For instance, there is increasing attention to the global nitrogen cycle and its effect on marine ecosystems. Technical change, too, brings new problems and risks as well as opportunities. Balancing the environmental risks and benefits of genetically modified organisms is a clear example. And social changes require ongoing and forward-looking attention. For instance, intensifying pressures for international migration have far-reaching ramifications.

In all of these areas, there is a strong argument for concerted international attention-and for achieving some consensus on the relevant issues. Ensuring greater inclusion Increased voice and major increases in substantive democratization. Inclusiveness can be expanded through significant changes in governance that increase representation and accountability, such as empowering local government through well-designed decentralization reforms; electing rather than appointing mayors; replacing military with elected regimes, or empowering groups excluded from decisionmaking-women, indigenous people, and other disadvantaged groups, who may be in the majority.

Better distribution of access to assets. Dynamic growth and development processes create more assets and new types of assets. It will be much easier to increase inclusiveness by ensuring that the poor and disenfranchised, as well as the middle class, have greater access to these newly created assets. By increasing access to education, which build human capital; by expanding market-based rural land reforms to increase smallholders' access to agricultural land and complementary assets (water, roads, and know-how); by expanding the provision of secure tenure (protection from arbitrary eviction) in urban slums or other informal urban settlements; by increasing access to knowledge (the new asset frontier). To overcome the barriers to solving collective problems more rapidly and systematically requires mutual commitments by developing and developed countries to a bold global vision and accord. This vision requires a massive and steady effort to eliminate poverty and to protect and manage a broader portfolio of assets that will ensure the well-being of future generations.

A self-enforcing global accord may be required to get the commitment to finance such a scaled-up effort, to build capacity to use the funds wisely, and to take on difficult reforms in developing as well as industrial countries. There is growing recognition of the need for mutual commitments and for accelerated improvements in key development indicators. Support for the Millennium Development Goals, which propose to cut the proportion of people in extreme poverty by half by 2015 is now widespread. The goals set ambitious quantitative targets for reducing hunger, increasing primary schooling, improving health, promoting gender equity, and ensuring environmental sustainability. One calculation puts the cost of meeting just the nonenvironmental targets at $40 to $70 billion a year above the current $50 billion in development assistance. The International Conference on Financing for Development in Monterrey also confirmed the need for more aid, trade, and debt forgiveness by industrial countries, in tandem with domestic reforms in developing countries to increase domestic resource mobilization and facilitate foreign direct investment.

Many of these long-horizon initiatives will yield benefits in the medium term in support of the Millennium Development Goals. But because many future problems cannot be foreseen, it is important that institutional foundations be strong and that a process and a framework be developed that are robust in picking up new signals, balancing a broader range of interests, and maintaining commitments to the global vision. Most of the physical capital required for the economy 50 years hence has not yet been created. This provides an opportunity to incorporate inclusiveness and sustainability criteria in new investments now. The potential is there to shift development paths, provided institutions that adapt and implement better policies can be put in place.

Investments in global poverty reduction and in greater inclusiveness will help ensure the representation of all interests in the design of the new and improved institutions. There is no understating the difficulty of these challenges. Social inertia is great, and institutional change can take decades. Overcoming the inertia to tackle these difficult problems-the fears and risks of unilateral action-requires coordination. Providing the necessary funding. Capital markets can cover much of the funding required to shift to a more sustainable path if appropriate policies are in place.

The estimated funding requirements for the Millennium Development Goals, would not be enough to support a broader and deeper agenda of institution-building. A development strategy that emphasizes inclusiveness, shared growth, and better governance places large demands on leaders in developing countries. They must commit to better economic, social, and environmental management-and thus to better governance. Schooling, health care, and provision of environmental assets that protect health, market-based rural land reform, and regularization of urban tenure all promote asset generation for the poor. An open and verifiable flow of information is important to tighten accountability in government and the private sector through such steps as opening procedures for bidding, strengthening meritocracy in the civil service, and making sure that public and corporate budgeting and resource management are governed by law, open to the public, and under proper oversight institutions.

The success of the reforms would be long term; they would secure opportunities and voice for families and their children so they can save, invest, and engage in their communities. But good policies, to be sustained, will require committed support and the legacy of reversals and stalemates is stunning. Research on aid and policy shows that aid is not worth much without good policies and institutions; in fact, it can even be harmful. Research also shows that good policies and institutions are essential to growth and development. Funds and assistance will not be available without the conviction that there is capacity to use them effectively. But capacity-building requires patient investment to remove critical barriers because its pay-offs are large but take time to be realized. Fundamental reforms require better institutions, which evolve slowly. These requirements are interlinked. So developing country leaders need to know that they will have long-term, reliable support from the larger development community. Without such support-and the quid *pro quo* on reform to support it-many developing countries will remain in cycles of promise and disappointment. With support, these cycles can be broken.

Enabling developing countries to develop more rapidly through increased aid, trade, migration, and access to knowledge and technology will place big demands on leaders and voters in developed countries. Developed countries should strengthen the ability of developing countries to pursue sustainable development by providing development assistance that supports public goods and attracts private investment. Developed country trade barriers impede exports from developing countries and undermine the livelihoods of the poor. Unrestricted access to developed country markets in textiles and clothing could yield $9 billion a year, and access to agricultural markets $11.6 billion a year. Improve developing country access to technology and knowledge. Implement incentives to promote the transfer and dissemination of technologies to developing countries-including those for climate mitigation, disease prevention, and agricultural development. Together the developed and developing countries must address the most urgent problems facing humanity.

Their joint responsibility is to establish a global partnership to set the rules for making rules and the modalities of burden sharing. As the world becomes more interconnected-environmentally, economically, socially-new institutions and rules must be agreed on and implemented. These will include rules for international trade; rules to avert conflict; rules on migration; rules governing the use of the biosphere; and rules affecting property rights in ideas, technological processes, and genetic information. The consequences will be enduring. Governments of developing, transition, and developed nations; provinces, cities, and local communities; civil society organizations; private firms; individuals. All governments can improve the accountability of public agencies and the provision of information about social and environmental conditions-to improve the ability of the general public and civic groups to identify problems, balance interests fairly, and come up with solutions.

Civil society organizations can help to aggregate the voices of dispersed interests and provide independent verification of public, private, and non-governmental performance. The private sector can advance economic, social and environmental objectives by helping to construct a framework that provides appropriate incentives for firms to be accountable in all three dimensions. If the global community sees merit in such an accord, the accord's elements will need more careful work over the next few years to develop an implementable program that can adjust to contingencies without undermining the promise of the accord. One interpretation of overconsumption is that it refers to the environmental externalities associated with consumption at higher levels of per capita income.

Carbon dioxide emissions, and their contribution to climate change, are highly correlated with consumption of electricity, home heating, transport services, and energy-intensive manufactured goods-all of which tend to increase strongly with income. In these cases, the over prefix is justified, since the externalities are by definition inefficient and usually inequitable. But the overall level of consumption is not the source of the problem. It is the combination of the specific consumption mix and the production processes that generates the externality. Another interpretation of overconsumption, much more difficult to document, has to do with social externalities. People judge the adequacy of their consumption-clothing, automobiles, housing-in part against norms set by others. If this is true, consumption takes on some of the aspects of an arms race. Mutual restraint is needed to shift resources from competitive individual consumption to consumption of public goods. But these externalities need to be much better understood before there can be any agreement on the actions to address them. Despite great promise for improving the agriculture of the poor, biotechnology in general and transgenics research in particular have barely begun to address the problems of the poor.

Comfort with the new technology is determined in large measure by societies' comfort with their scientific and food safety institutions and their feelings about emerging concentrations of economic power in multinational "life-sciences" corporations. Solutions to these complex issues are all playing out against a backdrop of globalization-related uncertainty, which has left many people unsettled over their capacity to control their lives and their environment. It is the rural poor in developing countries who most need access to these new agricultural technologies.

Strategies for a Sustained Future

Sustainable development requires altering social relations and recognizing the intensely political nature of environmental change and poverty. It transcends economics because economics has failed to recognize the fundamental processes of nature, the commodification of nature, social struggles to claim rights over nature, externalities arising from the exploitation of nature and labour, and the depreciation of nature by such exploitation. Sustainable agriculture does not require merely curbing the more egregious excesses of high-input industrial agriculture controlled by marketing and input-supply cartels. It also requires scrapping the system itself and moving in a revolutionary direction toward a holistic or systems approach to agriculture. Systems thinking revolves around social relations and nature. It seeks to affirm the power of a mobilized society and to establish a new, healthier balance among State, market, and society.

Sustainable agriculture implies new ways of approaching rural development. It is not so much a criticism of past approaches as a recognition of the shortcomings of narrowly focused technocratic solutions.

The people's organizations must share interests but not be predicated on the assumption of a homogeneous "community" of shared interests. They are bound to clash with local elites over access to and use of local resources. They must therefore pay careful attention to dispute resolution that recognizes asymmetries of power and strives for equity and justice in outcomes. Water-users' groups, forest-users' groups, production and service cooperatives, micro-credit borrowing groups, landless water sellers, and equipment and work-sharing groups, among others, are already active in many countries' attempts to mobilize farmers for livelihood improvement. They have encountered many difficulties, perhaps the most serious of which has been their takeover by the elite and powerful who use them to obtain subsidized inputs, retain control over resources such as irrigation water or timber, maintain coercive social relations, or head off organizing by the poor.

Fortunately, many groups have managed to remain cohesive, operate efficiently and effectively, and build the power of the poor, women, and other socially excluded groups. Sometimes organizations benefit the communities as a whole, especially those that are more homogeneous, less faction ridden, less stratified, under less pressure from outside market or State forces, and have rural classes with common interests. The catalytic organizations' goal is to create many loci of action throughout rural areas. They will sometimes oppose and sometimes support State interventions, but they will always seek to mobilize local creative energies expressed as ideas, traditional knowledge, labour, savings, locally available resources, and aesthetic sensibilities. Their efforts are motivated by the belief that it is necessary to wean people from the idea that the State can and will solve problems of poverty, environmental destruction, social dislocation, and social exclusion.

Catalytic institutions such as people's organizations, user groups, NGOs, and co-operatives flourish in the fertile and sustaining soil of democracy, which respects human and political rights, has high standards of government accountability and transparency, and listens to and responds to the pleas of the powerless. Decentralization does not mean divesting higher levels of government of responsibilities that are rightfully theirs, but rather devolving responsibilities and powers to the appropriate level for efficiency and effectiveness. Environmental regulations, for example, will remain the responsibility of nonlocal authorities, but monitoring and sometimes enforcement can be delegated to accountable local authorities. Reducing Poverty-Findings and Implications reveals that decentralization of authorities and resources to the local level, which weakened governance, has increased poverty. Therefore, such decentralization must be accompanied or, preferably, preceded by establishment of good governance and capacity building.

Agricultural knowledge, for example, has too often been assumed to be the exclusive realm of the outside expert. More and more, however, it is recognized that sustainable agriculture requires a process of mutual learning between the farmer and the expert and that both can contribute to finding new and better ways to attain sustainability. Barriers to equal access to land, credit, extension, education, and health care need to be removed. At a more profound level, however, is the recognition that women's exclusion from resource access stems from inherent structural and institutional discrimination. Change at this level requires mobilization, organization, collective action, and increased political representation of women or other socially excluded groups. Legal rights enable such positive change to happen.

Price distortions are caused by implicit or explicit subsidies on fertilizer, fuel, electricity (including that used for irrigation pumping), pesticide, and credit. Carefully targeted subsidy elements-such as grants to institutional development and group organizing of rural financial institutions-can be non-distorting and non-crowding to competition if correctly designed.

Incorporate in prices additions that reflect the external costs of use of the commodity. The needs of environmental sustainability, women, the poor, and the socially excluded through agricultural extension, agricultural research and development (R&D), primary-school education, adult literacy training, other nonformal education, user-group formation, local government strengthening, infrastructure investments, and rural development projects in general.

Land and other properties have been lost to agricultural traders and chemical input dealers, to financiers and moneylenders. Unable to pay for their production input credits, farmers were forced to mortgage their lands and household appliances. To combat the cycle of debt and poison, many NGOs and people's organizations in the Philippines have turned to one form or another of sustainable agriculture, emphasizing diversification and little or no use of chemical inputs. There are many stories like theirs as biodynamic agriculture spreads in their municipality and beyond. Everywhere in the region, austerity is meant only for the less powerful. Cuts in public services must therefore be restored, although mere restoration and increase in public service budgets are by themselves insufficient to increase services relevant to sustainable agriculture.

Some countries, mostly those in South Asia, must be committed to providing primary education for all, which requires improvement in quality and not only financial increases. Better quality requires more government accountability, guaranteed rights for women, a citizenry willing and able to challenge poor school performance, and access by all to education. Countries such as India,

Philippines, and Pakistan, which have refused to acknowledge the importance of landholding patterns on both equity and productivity, have failed to reduce rural poverty. All countries, however, need to continuously re-examine their land distribution patterns, land markets, tenancy relations, gender rights and restrictions to land use and ownership, guarantee of indigenous systems of land stewardship, and the allocation of land among State, community, and private ownership, to assess how allocation can be improved.

They require a local approach-one sophisticated enough to distinguish among land management and ownership rights, tree and other product rights, and water rights. While democratic community user groups should exercise most of the control, they may co-manage resources with the State. Water is essential to promote health and agriculture. Water management and allocation have strong equity dimensions. Priority must therefore be given to radically improving the efficiency of water use. Ninth Aspect Providing financial services to residents on marginal lands, the poor, women, and fishers. Such services are essential to promoting environmentally sound resource conservation and management and to improving the livelihoods and capabilities of powerless groups. People need credit, secure savings, and insurance- crop insurance, disaster insurance, and burial and marriage funds-which can greatly help households face risk and broaden their agricultural production possibilities.

Rural areas are characterized by imperfect markets for inputs and outputs. The resultant fixed transaction costs are negatively biased against small farmers. If they must purchase and sell alone, they are forced to buy dear and sell cheap. Some technologies may be out of their reach altogether. Agricultural production and service cooperatives are a primary means to overcome these market biases and empower small farmers or other groups of rural disadvantaged. Cooperatives have faced many difficulties in Asia over the years, but the successes such as the dairy and oilseed cooperatives of Gujarat, India, show the importance of cooperatives in a strategy that fosters smallholder agriculture. Cooperatives offer the possibility of capturing scale economies in production or processing of agricultural commodities. Capital-intensive technologies become available to small farmers. Marketing power and competitiveness increase for cooperatives that can buy in bulk, negotiate with powerful outside buyers and sellers, improve access to credit, and save substantially on transaction costs. Cooperatives offer the possibility of improved access to technologies, markets, and knowledge about marketing and production opportunities.

Cooperatives reduce the risk for individuals and thus open up many opportunities currently the exclusive domain of rich farmers. Giving up on cooperatives dramatically tilts the playing field in favour of the already advantaged. In the future, smallholder agriculture depends upon co-operative formation and that cooperatives are one way to foster competitive, efficient markets in many agricultural services. Otherwise, the pressures that lead to oligopoly and monopoly and small farmers' limited access to information will lead inevitably to concentrated market power.

The many different types of cooperatives should be investigated for their utility, not only in production but also in input supply, marketing, and information dissemination. Research and development are the key to sustainable agriculture. If agriculture is to move toward holistic resource management, sophisticated mimicry of natural processes, reduction in expensive external inputs based on cheap energy, and long-term maintenance of soil and water qualities, then agricultural R&D must focus on these needs and on the knowledge and requirements of the small farmer. There have been successes and it is important to build on them. Agricultural R&D needs to abandon the silver-bullet approach that seeks a one-size-fits-all solution to agricultural production. This approach yielded dramatic results on favoured land and for favoured farmers in the green revolution.

Sustainable agriculture, however, demands an approach tailored to specific conditions, less-favoured areas, and less-powerful people. The nuances of how technology dovetails with social relations, agro-ecological conditions, and cultural norms need to be a part of R&D based on local knowledge and conditions. Agricultural market institutions intersect with social relations to segment markets in numerous ways, including by excluding women. Women, are often restricted to localized, small-scale, lower-risk, and less-remunerative forms of trade than men. In the year between 1995-1997, the first set of 50 people's biodiversity registers and covering 50 village clusters, distributed over seven states in India. They were prepared by college students and teachers, NGO workers, or forestry officials after extensive discussions and field visits with local people. They involve mapping the landscape and delineating the different user groups in terms of their relationship to the natural resources.

The processes are followed by systematic group as well as individual interviews and field visits involving representatives of different user groups and individuals particularly knowledgeable about living resources. Particular attention is paid to the reconstruction of the recent ecological history focusing on changes in the landscape as well as in populations of plant and animal species. Of particular relevance are patterns of access to and harvests of wild as well as cultivated living resources, and the appropriation of the benefits of their utilization by different segments of local society and by outsiders. Continuance, erosion, or emergence of practices of sustainable use and conservation of biodiversity, local as well as State sponsored, are carefully assessed and related to cooperation and conflicts among locals, as well as with outsiders, in the context of use of natural resources.

State policy, legal systems, harassment of women by officials, social norms about what is appropriate activity and behaviour for women-all play a role in excluding women. Markets themselves, however, are hardly gender blind as their organization in most rural settings restricts access of many groups to contracts and information through shared systems of trust but also of exclusion. Deregulation may or may not open up markets to the excluded, but experience has shown that liberalization often intensifies exclusion. Policy attention to information, R&D results, extension, storage facilities, among other things, is essential to truly make markets effective and equitable allocative arenas. R&D thus needs to be situated in a real and existing social and economic system. It needs to look well beyond production technologies alone although the opportunities there are truly staggering as suggested by experience with agroforestry, horticultural tree crops, alley cropping and other hedgerow methods, living fences, and a wide range of water-harvesting and soil-contouring techniques.

Agricultural R&D financed and directed by the private sector, propelled by the profit motive, fuelled by market power, and constrained by an agenda set by interests outside the region, cannot deliver the goods. Their methodology is deficient, being based upon reductionist science, which breaks down the components of a complex world into discrete parts, analyses them separately, and then makes predictions about the world based on interpretations of these parts. Their motives are suspect, being driven by the capitalist imperative to grow and concentrate power, and their environmental and social sensibilities are primitive and laggard. The state must be deeply involved in agricultural R&D and in regional approaches to developing an alternative agriculture. Providing employment guarantee schemes that function not only as social safety nets but also as work programs to provide rural infrastructure for environmental improvement.

Employment generation schemes must be integral to rural development and emphasize developing skills and infrastructure as well as providing wages in times of need. Effective agents of change cannot pick and choose their favourite items from the above list. They must take an integrated approach to agricultural transformation. For example in Maharashtra has had a highly successful employment guarantee scheme since 1975. It has provided an average of 132 million work days on productive projects in soil and water conservation, small-scale irrigation, reforestation, and local roads. About half of employment guarantee scheme employment has gone to women.

The employment guarantee scheme has been successful because (i) the right to employment is enshrined in state law, (ii) courts have upheld the right, (iii) funds are provided through earmarked taxes (mainly on professionals) and state government contributions, (iv) relative transparency governs the schemes operation, and (v) employment guarantee scheme job seekers are mobilized to demand their rights. Sustainable agriculture conserves resources increases the ecological efficiency of farming to get more out of fewer resources while creating fewer negative side effects. It does so through greater resource productivity and through use of closed-loop systems of production that mimic natural processes.

The creation of new local institutions that increase the market strength of small farmers, and the presence of State policies that level the playing field permit the powerless to compete and make sustainable agriculture economically feasible. Ultimately, sustainable agriculture will lead to a new kind cf agriculture that eschews waste and external inputs entirely and is based on cooperation rather than competition with nature.

In the last quarter of the 20th century, the reality of poverty and environmental degradation, however, can no longer be so blithely dismissed, and the subject of land and its role in sustainable development is once again on the policy agenda in Asia and the Pacific. A number of reasons to be concerned about land and land reform have to do with efficiency, equity, empowerment, and environmental sustainability. They have strong poverty, gender, social-exclusion, and quality-of-life dimensions. Many of the issues are relevant to urban as well as rural areas. Simple solutions do not exist, and facile generalizations are nearly always wrong, except for one: land will continue to be one of the most urgent issues in rural Asia in the early 21st century. Because, first, the importance of land reform to economies having impressive growth is undeniable. Second, there are strong efficiency arguments for focusing on land use in agriculture.

Economy of scale is rarely, if at all, possible in agricultural production as long as somewhat competitive markets for inputs and outputs exist, including rental markets for farm draft animals and machinery. Small farmers are at a disadvantage because of their greater transactions costs in imperfect markets and lack of access to financial and extension services. The goal of government policy should therefore be to increase competition and access. However, the large farms need to supervise hired labour, which is difficult. A negative relationship between farm size and productivity exists in many countries and farming situations.

Efficiency and equity work hand in hand as long as small farmers are also ensured access to inputs and services. The history of land reform is littered with failures due to farmers' lack of access to financial services, appropriate extension services, and marketing opportunities. In the Philippines, farmers have often been forced to sell the land allotted to them back to large landowners because they could not pay for the necessary inputs. As poverty is concentrated among the landless and near-landless, land redistribution can have a significant impact on the incidence and severity of poverty. Farmers who own land not only have a productive resource, but also access to other resources that increase agricultural productivity. Lack of collateral prevents individuals from making investments that can be financed only with credit, including quality schooling, bullocks, wells, or perennial crops. Gender equity is strongly influenced by landholding patterns.

One related issue concerns intra-household effects of giving women more access to economic resources, as would be the case if they had control over land. Another issue relates specifically to land and how its control affects women. As far as the first issue is concerned, more economic resources in the hands of women-in their direct control and not mediated through the husband-translates into better nutrition, schooling, and health care for girls. It usually also translates into better household nutrition in general as women are more likely than men to convert economic resources into food. Poor women normally spend all of their earnings on the household while men nearly always spend a large part of their earnings on themselves. Yet another important issue is what women do with land under their control.

Given general and widespread discrimination against women, any woman-directed land reform has to be accompanied by reforms in complementary sectors such as agricultural extension, marketing, and financial services. Women may very well crop land in ways different from men's, which is likely to have a positive effect on the environment. While men normally prefer cash crops if given a choice, women, whose primary interest is the family, may well opt for a diversified mix of cash crops, food crops, vegetables, fish, and small animals, the sum of which will improve household nutrition and reduce vulnerability to unexpected changes in weather or markets. Nutritional welfare and ability to survive periods of stress, even famines, is very much affected by access to land. Access to land is considerably more important than redistribution of income equivalent to the output value of the land because land is a substitute for insurance and an efficient source of self-employment.

Communal tenure systems in many parts of the region periodically redistribute land precisely because the insurance benefit is so high. Women's right to land can have profound effects on women's rights in general. Land is a potent symbol of power, and studies in a number of countries have shown that where women have the right to land, they are less subject to violence from their husbands or other family members. Men and women who have the right to land enjoy the respect of general society-whether represented by a local political leader, a government civil servant, a banker, or a nongovernment organization worker. The more evenly rights to land are distributed, the more even the playing field for economic development.

One of the most important land reforms in the region is to identify forestlands that have been used for agriculture for many generations and to regularize their ownership. Most forest-land statistics in Asia are a fiction, as large tracts of land have no forest cover at all. By refusing to allow the tillers secure tenure over these lands, however, there is an understandable lack of willingness to invest in sustainable agricultural improvements, such as terracing, small dams, or soil erosion control structures. The land redistribution empowers the community, as it can only happen through collective organizing. The process of successful organizing, whether by groups of women, socially excluded castes, indigenous groups, or underprivileged classes, can bolster individuals' and groups' confidence in their abilities and worth. It can be the catalyst that may lead to freedom from poverty and social exclusion. In the absence of social revolution, mode of land reform must adopt an experimental attitude and a pilot-project approach.

Financing is an obvious key, and the role of donors is clear and vital. Few small farmers can purchase land and finance their mortgages out of the profits of the first few years. It is also crucial to finance the development of new and sustainable agricultural technology, financial institutions, and marketing systems. One approach is to reallocate the massive government subsidies now going to the better-off farmers to a grant program for poor farmers or farmer groups so they can purchase land on the market in an open and transparent manner. The beneficiaries, however, must be intimately and actively involved in the process, with the technical support of NGOs and/or government line agencies that can help them formulate farm plans and realistic farm investment proposals. Farmer groups would also be advocates for rights of their members and conduits for providing extension and marketing information. These process of land reform can be part of a process of agricultural transformation toward the new green revolution. It can be based on (i) community land-use planning, (ii) integrated model-farm planning, (iii) provision of a package of inputs and services, and (iv) a holistic approach to agriculture that aims for both equity and environmental sustainability.

Communal tenure systems do not need dismemberment but support in (i) increasing accountability and effectiveness of cooperation, (ii) responding to external political and market pressures, and (iii) devising sustainable technologies. Communal tenure systems can break down, and when they do, it is the most vulnerable and least powerful that lose. The challenges are (i) to build security for households into communal systems and (ii) to encourage accountability of political leaders to the needs of the community.

Essential inputs to agricultural transformation are credit, savings, insurance, financial advice, and training. The need for credit arises from the seasonal nature of agriculture. Inputs are needed at the beginning of the crop season, while payment is received at harvest. Credit is required to finance input purchases and longer-term investments in perennial crops, draft animals or machinery, storage facilities, livestock, irrigation facilities, and soil and water conservation works.

Sustainable agriculture, based as it is on mimicry of natural processes, requires a great deal of investment in conserving soil, water, and fertility. Mobilization of local resources, so essential to sustainable development, implies mobilization of local savings. Reliance on the better-off and on resource extraction to fuel economic growth has had short-term success in terms of GDP growth. But the wreckage left behind as environmental destruction, social dislocation, cultural disempowerment, and poverty is now too foul to ignore. Only when the powerless cease to be so will the cycle be broken and poverty a memory of the past. Many studies show that it leads to increased incomes among credit recipients in the region.

The first loan issued by an International Fund for Agricultural Development (IFAD) project in Indonesia raised household incomes by 31 percent. The second and third loans increased the cumulative gain to 72 percent. An early assessment of a Bangladesh Grameen Bank program showed real household income gains of around 35 percent. While the attribution of all of these gains to credit alone may be questioned, it is undeniable that credit has had a significant impact on people's lives. Credit also has an important role to play in smoothing consumption and mitigating the impact of shocks to the household economy. Thus, credit plays an important insurance function. Credit also appears to alter the expenditure patterns of households-an effect that is especially significant when credit is advanced to women who tend to favour such expenditures as schooling and contraceptives.

Total household consumption also rises more when credit is advanced to a woman than to a man. Microcredit programs rarely reach only the poorest, but they do reach poor households and many of the most vulnerable in society. It is these households that face the most difficulties coping with income shocks. Credit has an important effect on the empowerment of women.

An IFAD review of Nepal's Production Credit for Rural Women Project found that female beneficiaries felt less housebound, more confident in interacting with the outside world, and more independent because they had their own cash incomes. They also had more access to extension services. Credit can also change power relations within the household, which can have both positive and negative impacts on women.

When women cannot obtain loans or have to wait too long for a loan, for example, male impatience can lead to violence. It needs to be emphasized, however, that the positive impacts of credit arise because other inputs are available. The literature is full of bickering over the significance of this or that regression analysis showing this or that impact of credit on various outcomes. Access to markets, a certain level of skill development, and information about opportunities are essential as well. It is also highly likely that, especially in the case of microcredit to women and to the poor in general, group-mobilizing efforts themselves are a major contributor to positive outcomes. Sustainability requires longer-term investments in soil and water conservation and soil fertility management. It also requires a diversified cropping structure that includes perennials. Credit is necessary not only for the investments themselves, but also for consumption needs during the transition period.

Grameen Bank in Bangladesh, has a savings program but does not aggressively reinvest the savings in rural development. When the State was the focus of development efforts, agricultural development banks were all the rage. They provided subsidized credit for farmers needing access to green revolution input packages. They made many attempts to target credit to the poor, which seemed doomed to failure until the invention of group-lending microcredit institutions. Rural credit open to individuals at subsidized rates was monopolized by the better-off, no matter what the targeting mechanism. When credit was not sufficiently subsidized, borrowers merely defaulted and faced no penalties for doing so because they belonged to the elite. Unfortunately, as microcredit has shown its success in actually reaching the poor, the better-off invoke sustainability criteria to show that it is nonviable and in conflict with market principles. The poor lose out once more, first to the State and now to the market.

Grameen Bank is also good at what it does, although it may need to make changes to improve its investment of group savings, modestly increase interest rates, and perhaps further improve efficiency. It seems wrong-headed to insist that it be financially sustainable given its excellent record in actually reaching the poor. But it does need to be emphasized that subsidies ought to be spent on institutional strengthening, expansion of operations, and social mobilization rather than on creating a dependence on cheap credit while crowding out private financial service initiatives.

If Grameen Bank were more selective in its targeting to better its financial performance, then it would not reach the poorest of the poor. If, however, Grameen Bank were to be more concerned with reaching the poorest, then it would inevitably be criticized for its financial unsustainability. The point is that Grameen Bank does reach the poor. Almost all of its clients are poor. That in and of itself is a remarkable accomplishment. Emphasis on financial sustainability and credit performance measured by high repayment rates has incentive effects on fieldworkers, which work to the disadvantage of the poorest households and even more profoundly to the detriment of women. As loans become larger with mature borrowers, men increase their control over loans although they may still be in the names of women.

For women to retain and increase their control over their own lives requires not just access to microcredit, however important that may be, but also improvements in women's productivity, mobility, access to markets, literacy, social status, and control of household decisions. These all take time and require (i) the building of women's institutions, (ii) the provision of technology and training support for women's investments, and (iii) women's consciousness raising.

In many instances, it may be that households want a secure savings scheme for consumption smoothing rather than credit per se. In other instances, the group support and input can make a big difference in outcomes to credit access. To the extent that financial management is one of the services offered, then it can often become as important as credit itself in helping move households out of poverty. Microfinance is not well suited to many types of agricultural investments and is, in fact, often used for rural nonfarm activities. But it can be successfully employed in intensifying low-input agriculture such as organic vegetable farming and marketing or low-input integrated livestock-crop-fish-fodder systems.

The reason is that credit alone, especially credit that is mostly nonagricultural in purpose, is marginal to the major earning opportunities operating in the rural economy: (i) agriculture; (ii) dynamic rural small industry; and (iii) trading in food grains, agricultural inputs, and commodities produced and consumed in the rural economy. Agricultural credit remains the domain of the traditional moneylender.

Rural productive opportunities remain tightly tied to landownership and control of productive assets. The landlord, the moneylender, and the merchant have the land, capital, skills, and access to State resources that are the truly determinant factors in rural poverty formation and maintenance. The growth elasticity of poverty varies widely across countries. Country comparisons imply that it is indispensable to pay close attention to the ability of poor and socially excluded households and individuals to participate positively in the growth process. "Participation" depends on access to resources, education and other social services, technology, and markets. The social relations and the resultant institutions that govern such access are of vital importance.

Common property resources have signal importance for the poor and women. Certain classes of common property resouıces are also among the most degraded lands in Asia. Thus, they highlight common causes of poverty and environmental deterioration. A useful simplification is to consider four broad types of landownership and use: (i) private; (ii) open access (where well-defined property rights are absent); (iii) State; and (iv) communal. All may involve some degree of common property rights. Even private property has historically and to this day been subject to rights of gleaning, with poor persons having "rights" to glean from private fields and orchards. Common property resources (forests or woodlots, pasturelands, coastal fisheries, inland waters, groundwater) are being degraded and closed to common access through privatization or takeover by the State. Both processes worsen access of the poor and of women.

There are many examples of traditional, local methods of management of common property resources. Institutional mechanisms have not only developed in many different circumstances, but also altered over time to adapt to changing conditions. However, they are obviously not impervious to shock if external conditions change drastically. Local resource control systems, social sanctions to protect the community's stake, and enforcement mechanisms worked effectively to protect the environment. The State saw the revenue and control possibilities in common property resources and often nationalized communal and private lands, sometimes for their own "protection." Market penetration, breakdown of cooperative values, land reform, and centralized uniform thinking led to privatization of communal and open-access lands. The process was led by and benefited the better-off and men.

In the end of the 20th century saw a proliferation of initiatives to restore some measure of environmental integrity to degraded forest and pasturelands and to improve management of irrigation systems. Similar efforts in coastal fishing communities are more recent, but high on the policy agenda. User groups have been advocated by development professionals, and many examples now exist of successful user-group formation and management of natural resources. Some user groups have built upon preexisting traditional community institutions, but many have been constructed from scratch. The good news is that user-group formation has achieved some impressive successes in halting environmental degradation and in managing water resources more efficiently.

Unfortunately, their successes have often (but not always) come at the cost of women and poor households, who are systematically excluded from access to common property resources, which have been vital to the livelihoods of large numbers of the poor. In India alone, common property resources add approximately $5 billion a year to the incomes of poor rural households. An average of 12 percent of poor rural households' income is from common property resources. In some areas, poor households derive considerably more of their total income from them. Fuel and fodder are the most important common property resources accessed by poor households, and women and children are responsible for their collection. All studies on India agree that common property resources are being degraded, reduced in area, and systematically closed to the poor.

In Nepal and India, many examples abound of green hillsides regenerating forests where a few years ago there was only brown scrub. "Wastelands" have been transformed across India. Nepal has not been completely deforested as some of the more hysterical international observers predicted a quarter century ago. A number of hill regions now have more forest cover and a higher quality of forest than they did 20 or even 40 years back. In many parts of Asia and the Pacific, incomes have increased, out-migration has eased, water has become more plentiful in streams and wells, and biodiversity has increased. They are remarkable accomplishments, but mixed blessings at best for women and poor households. Before discussing social forestry on common lands, it would be useful to point out that some private lands have also seen significant increases in tree cover and total biomass production.

Government financial shortages and donors' philosophical commitment to reducing the role of the State in developing countries have led to the creation of many programs devolving irrigation management responsibility to water-users' associations. It is generally asserted that the associations will increase water-user participation in decision making and that cost recovery, water-use efficiency, and agricultural productivity will increase as government subsidies to irrigation decline. A vast literature has sprung up on the subject of water-users' associations, mostly written by advocates of devolution. Strikingly few detailed, comprehensive, and quantitative studies are part of the literature, however, as authors rush to publish their breathless anecdotes of farmer management abilities.

Impacts on the environment, women, equity (inter-farm water allocations between head and tail of an irrigation system and access to water of the smallest farmers), farmer costs, water-use efficiency, and changes in cropping patterns and crop productivity are infrequently reported, and when they are, the accounts are usually qualitative. The push for devolution of irrigation services in the region has rarely arisen from either farmers themselves or from irrigation departments, but has been driven by donor pressure and government budgetary shortfalls.

The result has been hastily designed and implemented devolution programs often reflecting neither field realities nor a considered appreciation of the requirements of a successful devolution. Studies show that results have been both positive and negative. In Asia, impacts on women are found to be generally neutral to negative. Impacts on equity head-versus-tail are often not reported, and when they are, are done so anecdotally. Costs to government have decreased, although the only fairly comprehensive studies of this impact have been for the Philippines National Irrigation Administration where financial savings to Government were substantial in the early years. Head-versus- tail water deliveries, for example, have been generally positive, but negative in some Philippine schemes. Sri Lanka, Indonesia, and Nepal also saved money on turnovers of maintenance responsibilities to water-users' associations. Not surprisingly, costs to farmers have increased, often substantially, and, in some cases, the facilities have been abandoned as financially unenviable.

On the other hand, farmers have often cut operation and maintenance costs substantially and sometimes made pump use more effective, saving on pumping costs. The coastal zones of Asia and the Pacific are under pressure from unsustainable resource exploitation; municipal, marine, and industrial pollution; and increasing risks and impacts of natural hazards such as cyclones, typhoons, tsunami, and flooding. Traditional means of coastal zone management based on community management and sophisticated rules and sanctions have, for the most part, been rendered ineffective by powerful economic, institutional, technological, and political changes. Although consumption of fish and other marine and coastal products is declining among low-income households in many Asia-Pacific developing countries, worldwide market demand for fish, prawns, and other marine resources has surged.

Seafood has become a health and status food in industrialized counties. One consequence of this has been the dramatic depletion of fish stocks in the inland, coastal, and marine waters of the industrialized nations. Fishing fleets armed with new technologies for intensive fish harvest and driven by increasing market demand have thus combined with increases in the number of fishing vessels in developing countries to lead to overfishing of most species in most coastal waters. Industrial and municipal pollution, destruction of mangroves and corals, tourism and urban development, mining, erosion from deforested and cropped lands, and high demand for shells, coral, and aquarium fish all combine to exacerbate pressure on coastal resources caused by international market and technology changes.

Municipal fisheries are normally the most productive fisheries because of the presence of reef, mangrove, and seagrass ecosystems, but they are also especially vulnerable to pollution, land-based erosion, and mangrove and seagrass destruction. Municipal fishers face deteriorating ecosystems and the more efficient technologies of commercial trawl fishers in bays once reserved for them. For example, trawlers have fished out San Miguel Bay, Philippines, beyond the point of natural recovery. Coastal waters that were once a community asset have become open-access resources to anyone who can afford craft and gear. This is true from Kerala, India, to the South Pacific. Municipal fishers often resort to desperate measures, using dynamite, fine mesh nets, and sodium cyanide, all of which merely accelerate the decline of the fishing grounds. A related issue is hazard management. As unplanned and uncontrolled developments occur in coastal areas vulnerable to natural disasters, and as the role of the State in regulating development diminishes, institutional forms of hazard management and response become moribund and new institutional mechanisms are slow to meet the need.

In Viet Nam, for example, locally organized collective action for coastal defence and water management has been undermined by the dismantling of communal institutions such as agricultural cooperatives and the replacement of central and provincial planning and collective action with individual responsibility. As activities such as dike maintenance become increasingly monetized and professionalized, collective responsibility and local participation in a common task give way to uneven results. Some districts tax and spend the proceeds on dike maintenance; the poorer ones may not do so. Local autonomy and privatization have contributed to considerable loss of mangroves in coastal Viet Nam, further weakening coastal defences. Thus, in a very short period of time, a highly effective coastal management system has withered under economic reforms and is yet to be replaced by a suitable alternative.

Challenges Ahead

Environment and social issues, when not addressed, accumulate over time and have consequences that do not show up in the shorter time horizons typical of economic policymaking. Some study suggest that 2 billion people will be added to the world's population over the next 30 years and another billion in the following 20 years. Virtually all of this increase will be in developing countries, the bulk of it in urban areas. In these same countries, 2.5 billion to 3 billion people now live on less than $2 a day. The core challenge for development is to ensure productive work and a better quality of life for all these people. This will require substantial growth in productivity and incomes in developing countries. The challenge may seem daunting-and it is. But over the past 30 years world population also rose by 2 billion. And this growth was accompanied by considerable progress in improving human wellbeing, as measured by human development indicators.

Average income per capita in developing countries grew from $989 in 1980 to $1,354 in 2000. Infant mortality was cut in half, from 107 per 1,000 live births to 58, as was adult illiteracy, from 47 to 25 percent. Looking back to the 1950s and 1960s, it was feared at the time that the developing countries-particularly China, India, and Indonesia-would not be able to feed their rapidly growing populations. In the 1960s and 1970s the Club of Rome and many other groups forecast that the Earth would rapidly run out of key natural resources. So far, this has not happened, again because changes in technology and in preferences have allowed the substitution of new resources for existing ones-for example, fiber optics in place of copper.

Global action has also led to major strides in eliminating disease scourges (smallpox and river blindness), and in addressing new problems. But accompanying these achievements were some negative social and environmental patterns that must not be repeated in the next 50 years if development is to be sustained. Today, there has been a significant drop in the percentage of people living in extreme poverty. Even the absolute number of very poor people declined between 1980 and 1998 by at least 200 million, to almost 1.2 billion in 1998. The decrease was primarily due to the decline in the number of very poor people in China as a result of its strong growth from 1980 onward. Since 1993, there have also been encouraging signs of renewed poverty reduction in India.

Development strategies will need to do better in eliminating abject poverty. The estimated 1 billion very poor people is of the same order of magnitude as the independently generated figures on the number of people who are undernourished and underweight. The average income in the richest 20 countries is now 37 times that in the poorest 20. This ratio has doubled in the past 40 years, mainly because of lack of growth in the poorest countries. Similar increases in inequality are found within many (but not all) countries. In the 1990s, 46 countries were involved in conflict, primarily civil. This included more than half of the poorest countries. These conflicts have very high costs, destroying past development gains and leaving a legacy of damaged assets and mistrust that impedes future gains.

The increased scale and reach of human activity have also put great pressure on local and global common property resources (water, soil, and fisheries), as well as on local and global sinks (the ability of the biosphere to absorb waste and regulate climate). At the local level, hundreds of developing-country cities have unhealthy levels of air pollution. At the global level, the biosphere's capacity to absorb carbon dioxide without altering temperatures has been compromised because of heavy reliance on fossil fuels for energy. Global energy use traditionally has grown at the same rate as gross domestic product (GDP). Greenhouse gas (GHG) emissions will continue to grow unless a concerted effort is made to increase energy efficiency and move away from today's heavy reliance on fossil fuels.

In the past 50 years excess nitrogen-mainly from fertilizers, human sewage, and combustion of fossil fuels-has begun to overwhelm the global nitrogen cycle, giving rise to a variety of ill effects ranging from reduced soil fertility to excess nutrients in lakes, rivers, and coastal waters. On current trends, the amount of biologically available nitrogen will double in 25 years. Fresh water consumption is rising quickly, and the availability of water in some regions is likely to become one of the most pressing issues of the 21st century. One-third of the world's people live in countries that are already experiencing moderate to high water shortages. That proportion could rise to half or more in the next 30 years unless institutions change to ensure better conservation and allocation of water. More than a billion people in low- and middle-income countries-and 50 million people in high-income countries-lacked access to safe water for drinking, personal hygiene, and domestic use in 1995. Nearly 2 million hectares of land worldwide (23 percent of all cropland, pasture, forest, and woodland) have been degraded since the 1950s. About 39 percent of these lands are lightly degraded, 46 percent moderately degraded, and 16 percent so severely degraded that the change is too costly to reverse. Some areas face sharp losses in productivity. Grasslands do not fare much better: close to 54 percent show degradation, with 5 percent being strongly degraded. Deforestation is proceeding at a significant rate. One-fifth of all tropical forests have been cleared since 1960.

According to the Food and Agriculture Organization of the United Nations (FAO), deforestation has been concentrated in the developing world, which lost nearly 200 million hectares between 1980 and 1995. In the Brazilian Amazon annual deforestation rates varied between 11,000 and 29,000 square kilometres a year in the 1990s. Deforestation in developing countries has several causes, including the conversion of forests to large-scale ranching and plantations and the expansion of subsistence farming. At the same time, forest cover in industrial countries is stable or even increasing slightly, although the forest ecosystem has been somewhat altered. According to a 1997 World Resources Institute (WRI) assessment, just one-fifth of the Earth's original forest remains in large, relatively natural ecosystems. Through a series of local extinctions, the ranges of many plants and animals have been reduced from those at the beginning of the century.

In addition, many plants and animals are unique to certain areas. One-third of terrestrial biodiversity, accounting for 1.4 percent of the Earth's surface, is in vulnerable "hot spots" and is threatened with complete loss in the event of natural disasters or further human encroachment. Some statistics suggest that 20 percent of all endangered species are threatened by species, introduced by human activity, alien to the locality. The aquatic environment and its productivity are on the decline. About 58 percent of the world's coral reefs and

34 percent of all fish species are at risk from human activities. Seventy percent of the world's commercial fisheries are fully exploited or overexploited and experiencing declining yields. None of these social and environmental patterns is consistent with sustained growth in an interdependent world over the long term. Given the social and environmental stresses caused by past development strategies, the goal of raising human well-being worldwide must be pursued through a development process that "does better"-a poverty-eliminating growth path that integrates social and environmental concerns in pursuit of the goal of sustained improvements in well-being. The development process is about change and transformation.

Societies and cultures evolve at different speeds, creating stresses that need to be addressed and managed. Moreover, in an era of globalization, the growing scale and speed of change in human activity are in some cases outpacing the rate at which natural processes and life-support systems can adapt. Globalization and faster technological change are also altering the nature of social interaction and affecting the efficacy of existing institutions. Although globalization and technological change offer many benefits, they can have deleterious side effects if institutions at local, national, and international levels do not evolve fast enough to deal with the adverse spillovers.

The consequences of previous patterns of development are also beginning to bind, restricting certain growth paths or making them more costly. But these processes, if managed well, can create new opportunities. Of the many interrelated drivers of change and transformation, four stand out: scientific and technological innovation, income growth, population growth, and urbanization. The first two are likely to continue changing preferences and providing new opportunities to satisfy these preferences. The demographic and urban transitions, by contrast, are one-time changes, and the opportunities they offer are perhaps less well recognized.

The flow of information and ideas, boosted greatly by the Internet, can enable developing countries to learn more rapidly from each other and from industrial countries. It can also facilitate the emergence of networks to monitor a wider array of development impacts. Other technological changes can enable developing countries to leapfrog stages in the development process that rely on inefficient uses of natural resources. Science and technology can help address major socioeconomic problems. As noted, the green revolution was critical in enabling many developing countries to avoid widespread starvation. To benefit from these opportunities, institutions are needed that can stimulate and diffuse technological innovations and avoid or mitigate any deleterious consequences.

Increasing income growth may place a strain on the environmental and social fabric if there is too little attention to shifting consumption and production patterns. But this future economic growth will also require major investments in new human-made capital to expand capacity and to replace existing capacity as it ages. Making these investments more environmentally and socially responsible through appropriate investment criteria will go a long way toward putting development on a more sustainable path-an opportunity not to be missed. Today's industrial countries were themselves developing, their population densities and growth rates were much lower than those of developing countries today, and the pressure on their resources was consequently lower. They also had a more evenly distributed age structure and lower dependency rates, allowing social institutions to adapt gradually to the requirements of a changing population.

Populations in industrial countries as a group were fairly stable for most of the second half of the 20th century. As a result, the growth in world population in this period has been driven primarily by population growth in developing countries. The stresses and spillovers from this population growth are generally observed not, as was originally expected, at the aggregate level but, rather, in more insidious ways-in many smaller interactions between population, poverty, and resources. The outcomes are felt in greater pressures on fragile lands, in lower wages, and in persistent unemployment. It is now clear that a global demographic transition is well underway, even if it is not yet complete. This is a major historic opportunity. World population is expected to stabilize by the end of this century at 9 billion to 10 billion people, 20 to 30 percent lower than forecast in the 1960s and 1970s.

Many countries will have to deal sooner than expected with another problem-an aging population. This can have major consequences, especially for rural populations, for whom formal social safety nets are either nonexistent or not well developed. For example, one consequence of China's one-child policy-which dramatically and successfully lowered aggregate population-may be that by 2030 as much as one-third of the population will be over age 65. Influencing the demographic processes in many countries is the growing incidence of HIV/AIDS, malaria, and tuberculosis.

Eventually, dependency ratios rise again as these workers age, and the window of opportunity starts to close, as it will soon begin doing in East Asia and Eastern Europe. Some regions, notably East Asia, have benefited substantially from the drop in the ratio of dependents to workers. Investment in forming a skilled, healthy labour force, combined with policy and institutional settings conducive to using this labour force effectively, helped generate strong economic growth. Two keys to success were maintenance of an open economy and investment in sectors with high growth potential. Since most developing regions will continue to experience relatively low dependency ratios for some decades, careful preparation now can help make the most of their windows of opportunity. Until now, populations have been growing too rapidly for fiscally constrained governments to expand the provision of jobs, infrastructure, and public services enough to keep pace with people's needs. This task will become easier now that the global population is approaching stability. Governments in both urban and rural areas can move from catching up with the quantitative need for services, to upgrading their quality. Much of the social tension and frustration arising from unemployment and poor public services can then be attenuated.

Lower rates of population growth will reduce pressure on natural resources, but this will be offset by the increase in per capita consumption. The latter trend makes it essential to adopt the technologies and growth paths for production and consumption that will ensure the sustainable use of natural resources. To benefit from the opportunities a stabilizing population provides, it is critical to anticipate problems and identify development strategies for getting through the transition period without creating conditions that generate further conflict or resource degradation. As countries move from poverty to affluence, the required growth in productivity involves a shift from heavy dependence on agriculture as a primary source of employment and income to nonagricultural activities that do not make intensive use of land. This is generally accompanied by a major shift in population from rural to urban areas. Indeed, the most important socioeconomic and cultural transformation over the past 150 years has been the transformation of relatively closed, exclusive, custom-based rural societies into relatively open, inclusive, innovation-oriented urban societies.

Rural communities, especially in less accessible areas, have long adapted to their circumstances, developing vibrant, self-sufficient communities. As long as risks could be absorbed locally, these communities continued to learn and adapt. Dependence on local ecosystems, however, imposed limits on risk taking and innovation. This autonomous development path changes as rural areas become drawn into larger markets and strengthen their links with urban areas, making trade networks and distance from market centres more critical features of development opportunities and local resource pressures. Increasing densities in towns and cities, and the greater connectivity between cities, as well as between urban and rural areas, increases the catchment area of markets and the returns to economic endeavour. If managed well, this transformation enables the emergence of new activities and productive job opportunities. Towns, as market centres for a rural hinterland, start the process of creating economies of scale for nonagricultural activities. Urban society also permits the spreading of risks over larger numbers of people and activities. Knowledge flows more readily, through increased opportunities for face-to-face contacts among various actors. And the need to accommodate diverse views and meet rapidly changing challenges stimulates innovation and new applications of technology. As a result, larger cities become incubators of new values-among them, risk taking and innovation. Creativity, knowledge flow, the increasing scale of activities, and larger catchment areas are central to specialization and productivity growth. This is true not just for the production of goods but also for the provision of services.

A village or neighbourhood can support a primary school or basic clinic, and the local teacher or doctor can be a generalist. But providing higher, more sophisticated, and more differentiated education and health care requires more specialized skills. Because of the fixed costs of supporting these specialized skills, a larger catchment area is required. The higher population densities, lower transport costs, and lower communications costs in towns and cities make the more specialized operations possible. In moving further up the hierarchy of required specialization, the required catchment area also increases. So, the transition from villages to towns, and from cities to metropolitan areas, corresponds to the different functional capabilities of larger, higher-density conurbations. The potential benefits of higher densities and greater connectivity can be more easily realized if the investment climate is improved through better enabling rules and frameworks and better physical infrastructure.

Stimulating and attracting investments-in particular, by the small and medium-size enterprises that provide most of the jobs for growing urban populations-is the key to accommodating the expected growth in urban populations and ensuring their ability to pay for needed urban services and amenities. The most fundamental social and economic transformation-from traditional rural to modern urban-is manifested spatially. Except in the most populous countries, such as China and India, rural societies are relatively low in density and heavily dependent on agriculture as the primary source of employment and output. Modern urban societies are generally higher in density and dependent on activities that benefit from proximity and do not require a great deal of land, such as manufacturing and services. These activities and land use patterns generate different types of sociocultural and environmental problems. Most ecosystems, too, are defined spatially. Much flora and fauna is locally unique and adapts gradually to changes in local circumstances. Local problems and stresses appear earliest, whether in the form of local extinctions, the reduction of the ranges of many plants and animals, or soil, air, and water pollution. These changes, the result of local development pressures, do not show up at national and global levels until they accumulate, but they provide early warning of problematic consequences of current development patterns. The jurisdictions of many institutions that make or implement rules and laws (legislatures, constitutions, and government agencies) are also defined spatially.

Often, the spatial jurisdiction of institutions does not match the spatial nature of the social and environmental problems generated by economic activity-one reason for the persistence of these problems. People, where they live, and how they interact with each other and with nature, it is important to look at where people are now and where they are likely to be in the future. The world's population increased by more than 3.5 billion people in the past 50 years, and 85 percent of these added people were in developing and transition countries. The number of people living in fragile rural areas in developing countries doubled, in stark contrast to the declining numbers in this category in high-income countries. The number of cities with a population of more than 10 million people went from 0 to 15 in developing countries but only from 1 to 4 in high-income countries. In the next 30 to 50 years the 2 billion to 3 billion increase in the world's population will be almost exclusively in developing and transition countries, and virtually all of it will be in urban areas.

The growth of the urban population is driven by natural increase, rural-to-urban migration, and the incorporation of high-density rural areas on the urban fringe. The number of megacities in developing countries is likely to increase to 54, while it will stabilize at 5 in high-income countries. It is not yet clear whether the number of people living in fragile areas will continue to increase, but it probably will unless migration opportunities change. As many as 2 billion people will live in two areas that are difficult to manage: fragile rural areas and megacities. Dealing with these people's needs will be a major challenge, since there is not much experience in industrial countries that can be adapted to their needs.

Today, international migration is highly restricted, and while rural-to-urban migration is important for them, there are limited numbers of jobs at above-subsistence wages for unskilled workers, especially in the low-growth economies. As a result, as noted above, instead of declining sharply, the number of people living on fragile lands is estimated to have doubled in the past 50 years-despite some outmigration. The problem of feeding a growing and more urban population calls for better management of the interaction with nature, particularly with respect to land and water. Whether or not rural families have land, water, and education is critical to their current livelihood, as well as to their ability to move to cities in the future. More egalitarian access to these assets is also crucial for determining the quality of society's institutions.

A successful rural-urban transition requires the elimination of poverty for those who stay in the countryside and better preparation of those who move to the cities. It also demands protection of remaining natural ecosystems and habitats, given their central role in maintaining life-support systems and biodiversity. This latter requirement is one reason to intensify agricultural production in areas already under commercial crops and pasture. Intensification in such areas not only minimizes pressure on biodiversity and on marginal agricultural areas but also increases the food available to cities and leads to dynamic rural-urban linkages. Higher population density in these rural areas would also make investments in health and education more cost-effective and would increase the potential for off-farm employment and help farmers accept risk and innovate.

Today, cities of the developing world face a formidable undertaking, given the expected rapid rate of growth and sheer numbers of urban residents to be employed, housed, and serviced. The characteristics of periurban settlements, towns, cities, and megacities-higher density, large scale of settlement, and greater social diversity-facilitate the creation of productive employment opportunities, efficient provision of services, and access to ideas and learning. But having many people at close quarters also creates the potential for social problems-crime and social dislocation-and for environmental spillovers that pose health and safety hazards, especially for those living in neighbourhoods without sanitation or drainage and in potential disaster zones. The long life of urban physical capital stock can lock in certain development paths, making changes costly. If managed well, urban areas can be the future engines of growth.

The political, legal, and market domain for coordinating many activities is frequently the nation. Many externalities spill over beyond local communities and municipalities, and even across regional boundaries. The nation is thus often the level at which interests can be balanced, either directly or by facilitating negotiation among localities. National actors may be better placed to organize the provision of public goods and to take advantage of scale economies when the beneficiaries extend beyond subnational regions. Generating a strong investment climate, including sound macro-economic fundamentals, good governance, and basic infrastructure, requires a framework that is typically national in scope.

Dismantling perverse subsidies, husbanding forests and fisheries, and curbing water and air pollution in river basins and airsheds are major national challenges. Managing foreign aid and avoiding civil conflict are other key national concerns that determine whether development is sustainable. At the global level. Many economic, environmental, and social processes-knowledge, conflict, disease, pollution, migration, and finance-spill over national boundaries. A few of these processes generate problems that are purely global:

depletion of the stratospheric ozone layer is an example. But most global problems and opportunities are experienced at the local level as well. Automobiles that pollute local airsheds also generate greenhouse gases; wet-land destruction that disrupts local water resources also undermines biodiversity of global significance; new ideas that are generated in one place can benefit people in other places, near and far.

The public goods nature of many of these issues and the need to address the negative externalities requires co-ordination across boundaries. The distinctive challenge for global issues is to balance interests and commit to solutions in the absence of a global authority. Some problems of sustainability are already urgent and require immediate action; examples are local ecosystems where population is pressing on deeply degraded soils, and forests and water stocks that have been nearly depleted. In such cases productivity is already on the decline and opportunities for correction or mitigation may even have been lost; abandonment of existing practices and outmigration may be necessary. The urgency of some of these problems has been overlooked because the people most affected are physically remote from centers of power, or because their voices are not heard, or both. Some issues call for immediate action because there are good prospects for reversing the damage to the environment at relatively low cost, as in taking measures against air and water pollution. Even then, undoing some of the damage to the affected population may not be fully possible. But knowing the health impacts does create a moral imperative to protect those affected from further exposure, to compensate them to the extent possible, and to prevent others from becoming victims. Another category of issues unfolds over a longer time horizon.

The problems may not yet be urgent, but the direction of change is unmistakable. For these, it is essential to get ahead of the curve and prevent a worsening crisis before it is too costly.

Biodiversity loss and climate change are in this category: there is already a need to adapt to the consequences of past and current behaviour, but there is also still scope for mitigation, though not for complacency. Similarly, the need to anticipate urban growth by facilitating low-income settlements in safe areas and by setting aside major rights-of-way and spaces for public amenities makes it necessary to act now to avoid greater costs and regrets later. In looking back over past successes and failures in solving development problems, it is clear that there have been more successes where markets function well (for example, in providing food to people with effective demand), even where the problems that markets have to solve (such as transport and communications) are relatively complex.

The major problems that remain (inclusion, poverty reduction, deforestation, biodiversity, and global warming) are, however, generally not amenable to standard market solutions, although markets can help solve subsets of these problems. Sustainable development is often criticized as being anti-infrastructure, as if infrastructure necessarily implied centralized, large-scale, capital-intensive, supply-side, and monopolistic facilities. Infrastructure can also mean dispersed, small or medium-scale, competitive, labour-intensive, and demand-side investments. Some experience in industrialized countries has shown that it is not infrastructure *per se* that is needed but transport, communications, water, sanitation, and energy services that can be provided in a variety of ways, on a variety of scales, and in a wide range of levels of waste, efficiency, and environmental impacts.

During the year 1990s saw the spread of the relatively new demand-based or community-based water provision approach that mobilizes community knowledge, talents, and resources to plan, design, build, operate, and maintain water supply schemes. It differs from the supply-driven or target-based approach that had line agencies bring water supply to villages as a State-provided service. The traditional approach has long been criticized for its top-down and inflexible method and its inability to either mobilize community resources and knowledge to build better systems or to effectively maintain systems after the departure of the government agency. Tales of rural water supply schemes poorly designed, badly maintained, and inappropriately matched to community needs were transformed into calls for a new approach. The resulting demand-based approach is driven by community demonstration of interest in a water supply scheme. The government facilitates the project and provides technical assistance.

Participatory techniques determine community preferences regarding service options and design of the system. The community (i) contributes to investment costs, (ii) has significant control over how funds are managed, (iii) retains ownership of the facility, and (iv) is responsible for operation and maintenance. The approach (i) strengthens the community, (ii) lowers construction costs, (iii) reduces subsidies, (iv) delivers to households the level and type of service they are willing to pay for, (v) serves all in the community, (vi) listens to and heeds women, and (vii) keeps the facility running for its full life, with the members of the community having a strong sense of ownership. The shift of rural water supply schemes to such an approach has been uneven at best, but the process has involved considerable learning, and some successes have been achieved.

The most important key to success is user participation. It significantly increases (i) overall economic benefits, (ii) the fraction of target population actually reached, and (iii) the environmental benefits of rural water supply projects. In one study, participation was qualitatively evaluated to differentiate between situations where beneficiaries were merely provided information and where they had a decision-making role, and to identify whether beneficiaries had a role in design, construction, operation, and maintenance. In general, "in communities where household members made informed choices about whether to build a system, the type of system to be built, and the level of service to be provided, sustainability of water services was higher". Preexisting health education, community organization for cooperative ventures, mechanical skill development, accountability procedures for government line agency personnel, and experience in decision making with respect to community infrastructure can greatly increase the likelihood of success in a water supply project. Success in a water supply project can also lay the foundation for success in other community mobilization and cooperation ventures.

In Asia and the Pacific, municipal water monopolies whether public or private, struggle to keep up with the water demand of the industrial, commercial, and middle-class residential sectors. They generally have (i) large unaccounted-for water losses; (ii) tariffs far below economic (considering (a) the economies of long-run marginal cost of supply, (b) opportunity cost of water in alternative uses, and (c) externalities of water supply development); (iii) serious supply and distribution problems; and (iv) no independent government regulation. They have no formal and legal competition, and financial costs and risks are usually borne by the government. Experts advise privatization, which is no panacea. Privatization has been done in the absence of regulation, with governments bearing the financial risks, and in the absence of steps to increase competition in supply or distribution, with all attention to the supply side and none to demand-side management.

International water cartels have benefited and efficiency marginally improved in a few instances, but serious financial, coverage, and environmental problems remain. Many Asian cities have a flourishing water supply and sanitation private sector that serves the poor, unconnected areas of the city. It is composed of a large number of diverse actors, from households with connections selling water to suburban truckers with their own tube wells, NGOs organizing water sales at municipal water points or installing public latrines and bathhouses, night-soil carriers in India and the prc, and even a few private drinking water and wastewater treatment plants. The urban poor commonly purchase water from vendors and pay unit costs 20-100 times the meter tariff rate paid by the rich. This private sector, invisible to consultants and civil servants, must recover full cost or it is out of business. It has essentially no unaccounted- for water and receives no public subsidy. Only a few NGO schemes are not financially sustainable. Unlike water monopolies, small players are responsive to demand. They charge market prices that cover costs, and understand willingness to pay, assume all financial risks, reach the poor, maintain close customer relations, often provide varied related services, rapidly respond to changes in demand, try out and market-test new technologies, and disseminate new technologies quickly once they recognize market demand. They flourish under competition and in the absence of misdirected subsidies. Water provision by small players may be only an interim solution, but its replacement by cheap, high-quality piped water directly into every home is still a distant possibility.

Environmental damage is not caused by small-scale water entrepreneurs alone, but it is a generic issue in water resource management involving (i) allocation of water among sectors, (ii) environmental externalities of water supply and wastewater disposal, (iii) legal rights to water, and (iv) regulation of all phases of the water sector. Unserved areas in cities are disproportionately poor, and without the State's strong social or contractual commitment to serve them, attempts at cross subsidization through lifeline rates or rising block tariffs can discourage expansion by a profit-driven utility. Connection fees may be too expensive for poor households, and pro-poor policies should include modest subsidies of such fees or a system of several monthly payments. Financing of expansion costs should also be spread over all users of the service since most of them have paid little or nothing for expansion to their area. In-kind payments, primarily labour, can also be mobilized as a substitute for cash payments for connections. Community participation in planning and design of water supply and sanitation, including decision making regarding the level of service to be provided, can be a valuable way to reconcile costs with willingness to pay and affordability.

Bibliography

Ahmad, A., "The Narmada Water Resources Project, India: Implementing sustainable development." Ambio 28(5): 398-403, 1999

Albrecht, S.L., "Equity and Justice in Environmental Decision Making: A Proposed Research Agenda" Society & Natural Resources Vol. 8, No. 1: 67-72, 1995.

Arnold, C.A., "Planning Milagros: Environmental justice and land use regulation" Denver University Law Review Vol. 76, No. 1:1-153, 1998.

Barkham, J.P., "Environmental Needs and Social Justice" Biodiversity and Conservation Vol. 4, No. 8: 857-868, 1995.

Bowen, W.M. and K.E. Haynes, "Response to Downey: Environmental injustice: Is race or income a better predictor?" Social Science Quarterly Vol. 81, No. 3: 885-888, 2000.

Carlin, B.P. and H. Xia, "Assessing environmental justice using Bayesian hierarchical models: two case studies" *Journal of Exposure Analysis and Environmental Epidemiology* Vol. 9, No. 1: 66-78, 1999.

Cassidy, E.A., et al., "The distribution of environmental justice: A comment" Social Science Quarterly Vol. 81, No. 3 (2000): 877-878, 1999.

Durning, Alan B., Poverty and The Environment: Reversing The Downward Spiral, For Worldwatch Institute, Washington, DC, November, 1989.

Ellis, R.D., "Quantifying Distributive Justice - An Approach To Environmental and Risk-Related Public Policy" *Policy Sciences Vol.* 26, No. 2 (1993): 99-123.

Flanagan, M.A., "Environmental justice in the city - A theme for urban environmental history" Environmental History Vol. 5, No. 2: 159-164, 2000.

Geiger, S.L., "An alternative legal tool for pursuing environmental justice: The takings clause" Columbia Journal of Law and Social Problems Vol. 31, No. 2: 201-246, 1998.

Geisler, C. and E. Letsoalo, "Rethinking land reform in South Africa: An alternative approach to environmental justice" Sociological Research Online Vol. 5, No. 2: U3-U14, 2000.

Greenberg, D., "Reconstructing race and protest - Environmental justice in New York City" Environmental History Vol. 5, No. 2: 223-250, 2000.

Jodha, N. S., "Common Property Resources and Rural Poor in Dry Regions Of India" Economic and Political Weekly Vol. 21,1986.

Landrigan, P.J., et al., "Pesticides and inner-city children: Exposures, risks, and prevention" Environmental Health Perspectives Vol. 107: 431-437, 1999.

Ravallion, M., M. Heil, et al., "Carbon Emissions and Income inequality", 52(4): 651-69, 2000.

Index